Partial to Home

OTHER BOOKS BY BOB TIMBERLAKE

The Bob Timberlake Collection, 1977

The World of Bob Timberlake, 1979

Somewhere in Time, 1989

Roots and Reflections, 1997

Partial to Home

A Memoir of the Heart

Bob Timberlake

with

Jerry Bledsoe

Down Home Press, Asheboro, N.C.

ISBN 1-878086-81-2

Library of Congress
Catalog Card Number 99-074725

Printed in the United States of America

Book design by Beth Hennington

Cover design by Tim Rickard

Cover photo by Jeep Hunter

Down Home Press
P.O. Box 4126
Asheboro, N.C. 27204

For Kay, my children and grandchildren,
to the memory of Mom and Dad,
and for all my other family,
present, past and future

It is art that makes life, makes interest, makes importance...
and I know of no substitute whatever for the force and beauty of its process.
   —Henry James

Art must again touch our loves, our fears and cares. It must evoke our dreams and give hope to the darkness.

—Frederick Hart

The lot is fallen unto me in a fair ground: yea, I have a goodly heritage.

—The Prayer Book

Prologue

I don't know what's going on in my life, but the strangest things keep happening. I can't explain it. I don't understand it. I don't expect anybody else to either. I just know that something out of the ordinary is going on and has been from the day I was born—and maybe well before that.

At times, I feel almost as if my life is a play. The script is already written, but I haven't been allowed to read it. My lines and stage instructions are handed to me only when I'm supposed to speak them and act them out. The play is unfolding just as it is supposed to, but I have no idea what twists and turns the plot is going to take until they occur.

I don't even know what kind of play this is. It has many elements: comedy, drama, mystery. But more than anything else it seems to be a fantasy, an unbelievable but so far wonderfully happy fantasy.

I'm not sure what the point of this play is, although that may be becoming clearer. And obviously, I have no idea how it will end. I don't even know when it began, but I have a suspicion it was not in my own lifetime.

Could it have started on the murderous night of November 2, 1781, in what is now Davidson County, North Carolina, where I have spent my life?

That was just two weeks after General Charles Cornwallis surrendered to George Washington at Yorktown, Virginia, effectively ending the Revolutionary War. On that night, a band of Tories invaded two farm houses in my county.

They were on a mission of revenge, and they caught their victims off-guard. Wooldrich Fritz, who was fifty years old, was shot dead as he sat warming before his fireplace. Valentine Leonhardt, who was sixty-three, survived for sixteen days before his wounds claimed him.

The two men lived near each other and were close friends. They had been ardent revolutionists, and earlier that year they had formed a rag-tag army with another of their friends and neighbors, Colonel John Lopp, to fight against Cornwallis at the battle of Guilford Courthouse, just thirty miles away.

Both men were buried in the cemetery at Pilgrim Church, not far from their homes, laid side-by-side, eulogized as patriots and heroes who had lived together, worked together, fought together. Now their souls would be together as one, just as our nation would be one because of them and others like them.

Colonel Lopp vowed that their deaths would not go unavenged. He led a band of local men in pursuit of the assassins. It is told that he tracked them to South Carolina, captured them, brought them back across the state line and hanged them from the first sturdy tree.

What does this story have to do with me and the play I'm living?

Well, Valentine Leonhardt was my great-great-great-great-grandfather. Wooldrich Fritz was the great-great-great-great-grandfather of my wife, Kay. Our children and grandchildren are the joining of their blood.

I should point out that neither Kay nor I was aware of

this until long after we were married. Only recently did we learn that my lifelong best friend and next-door neighbor, John B. Lopp, called J.B., is the great-great-great-great-grandson of the man who is said to have avenged our fore-bears' deaths.

Coincidence?

I might be willing to think so if so many other such odd "coincidences" didn't keep crowding my life.

Surely, this story helps explain why family, home and heritage have such a strong hold on me, and why they have played such a major role in my life and work.

But what does it say about all the other unexplainable, and, dare I say, miraculous events of my life?

All of us have defining moments, but I know nobody who has had any so unusual as mine. Let me begin with one that was far from being the first, and perhaps not even the most important, but a major one—and wondrous for certain....

If you're going to be a flower, face the sun. If you're going to be a rock, be a diamond. If you're going to be a bird, be an eagle.

—Mao Zedong

Chapter 1

How many people can say that a magazine article changed their lives drastically and forever?

I can.

It happened in 1965. I was twenty-eight. I had come home tired from work, and after supper I sat down in the living room and picked up the *Life* magazine that had arrived in the mail that day. I wasn't really looking for something to read. I was just flipping through it. But on page ninety-two I was stopped cold by a stunning portrait of a proud old man from Maine named Ralph Cline, resplendent in World War I uniform. The portrait was called "The Patriot," and it had been painted by Andrew Wyeth.

I was vaguely aware of Wyeth, knew that his father had been a famous illustrator and painter, and that the son had followed in the father's footsteps to even greater success. But I really knew little about Wyeth and his work. Art wasn't part of my life then. I'd never been in an art gallery or museum. But this painting grabbed me and led me hungrily to others on the following pages—landscapes, more portraits, a painting of a young buck shot by a hunter and hoisted by its rear legs against a snowy backdrop, ready for rendering. I realized that I wasn't just looking at these paintings. I was *feeling* them. It was a powerful sensation.

An article in Wyeth's own words accompanied the paintings, and I was as deeply affected by it as I was by the visual images. He spoke of his excitement for painting, of that flash of recognition when a painting set itself in his mind. He spoke, too, of place and passion, subtlety and restraint, and I was swept up in his words. He talked of the profundity and emotion of landscape, especially of the areas of Pennsylvania and Maine that he knew so intimately, and I knew exactly what he meant, for I felt the same way about Davidson County, and about the barrier islands along my state's coast, and the mountains in its western end where I loved to prowl.

"When I'm alone in the woods across these fields, I forget all about myself," Wyeth said. "I don't exist."

I'd had that feeling.

"I can think of nothing more exciting than just sitting in a cornfield on a windy fall day listening to the rustle," he said.

I'd done that while bird hunting and had completely forgotten that I was supposed to be hunting.

There was one thing Wyeth said that I would never forget, and it would affect everything I did in the future. Art, he said, went only as far as the artist's love extended. I knew instinctively that that was true, and I still believe it with all my heart.

When I had finished that article I felt as if I not only knew Wyeth but that I was part of him. It was a really weird feeling, almost as if I had *been* him in a previous life, a kinship unlike any I'd ever experienced. I knew how he felt and why he painted, knew it at a place deeper in myself than I had ever probed before, and suddenly it was as if I had been Rip Van Winkle, awakening from a long and deep sleep. I had never known such excitement as overcame me while I was sitting on that couch holding that magazine.

15

I can do this, I told myself. *This is what I'm supposed to be doing.*

I'd never had a class in art, but I had drawn and painted relentlessly from the time I was a small child until I was about fourteen. After that, other interests had taken over, and I'd had little time for art. I'd been quite a copier as a child, and I'd gotten pretty good at it. I had copied western paintings, nature and hunting scenes, boats and sailing ships, almost anything that had a canoe in it. Not until years later would I come to understand just how valuable that had been to me. By copying, you learn the styles of other painters, open up the secrets and techniques of the masters, and as you move on to painting the things that you love, you begin to develop a style of your own. The more I copied, the better I got, and I had become quite proficient with watercolors, even at that early age. But I hadn't kept at painting, and I didn't even know if I still could do it half my life later.

After my encounter with the *Life* article, however, I went out and bought some brushes and watercolors and set up an easel in the basement. It didn't take long for me to realize that the instinct and love for painting had never left me. I descended those thirteen steps to the basement almost every night, and the techniques were quick in returning. About a month after I read the article, I went out into the front yard one night and picked up a cluster of oak leaves. I wanted to see if I could recreate it on paper exactly as it was.

My excitement grew with every stroke of the brush, and when I finished, I couldn't believe what I had accomplished. I was more than astonished, I was truly shocked. I had done this thing and had no idea how. It was almost as if somebody else had taken my hand and done it for me. I rushed upstairs with my painting, eager to show it to Kay, but she had already gone to bed. I woke her. I couldn't help myself. I had to show it to somebody.

She must have thought that something was wrong, because she jumped when I shook her.

"Look, look," I said, as she sat up, startled.

She looked all right. She gave me a look of total exasperation after she realized what I was showing her. Oak leaves. At two in the morning.

Later, she confessed that she really was impressed with this early effort. But I already knew what I needed to know about it. I could *feel* those leaves on that paper. I could *smell* them. I could *hear* their crinkle.

And I *knew* at that moment, as I had sensed when I finished that article in *Life*, that my own life would never be the same. I wasn't sure how it would change. I just knew that it would.

But not in a thousand lifetimes could I have conceived the fantastical journey on which I was setting myself.

Who could have dreamed that a guy with a wife and three children and a job at a gas company in a small town in North Carolina could read a magazine article that would cause him to take up an old hobby in his basement that would lead him to be honored by two presidents, to be summoned to Buckingham Palace to advise the future king of England, to come to know and love some of the most famous and powerful people of his time, to have his works exhibited in some of the world's most prestigious museums and galleries, to create the most successful line of furniture in history, to have his name literally become a household word, and to build a special world of his own in which even the unimaginable could be envisioned?

As I said, wondrous and unexplainable things just keep happening in my life.

The best thing we could all do for relatives we love who die is make certain there is some written record of who they were and what they did.

—Andy Rooney

Chapter 2

People I've just met—I don't like to think of them as strangers but as friends I'm just beginning to know—sometimes ask me why I still live in Lexington, my hometown. It's a strange question, almost as if they think that if you have gained some success and recognition you must automatically flee to a more cosmopolitan or exotic spot, as if everybody from a small and supposedly unexciting town or community has to consider home mundane.

If I answered truly, I'd have to launch into a soliloquy that surely would leave my questioners wondering why they'd bothered to ask, and maybe even thinking that I was more than a little daft. I'd have to try to explain, as Andrew Wyeth did in that *Life* article, how the simplest and most common things can be the most exciting. I'd have to describe how this is where my heart and most of my memories dwell, where I am completely secure and comfortable, the place where the people I most love reside, where I know almost everybody, whom to trust and not to trust, who will make you laugh, and who will bore you senseless, and who's apt to leave you depressed after even a brief encounter. I'd have to tell about Whitley's Barbecue, where so many incredible events take place, and the soda fountain at Lexington Drug when I was a boy, and the memorable milkshakes and Cherry Smashes I got there, the likes of which I've never found since. I'd have to go into detail about First Avenue and First Methodist Church, about my grand-mothers and my great aunts, about the three fat boys and all the rest of my family and friends—not to mention a few thousand wonderful experiences that come immediately to mind. I'd have to define love, heritage and devotion to the land on which you're born. And I'd have to spell out how this place and these people and my experiences with them are not only the wellspring of my art but of my very being. I'd have to bring up Wooldrich Fritz and Valentine Leonhardt and show how my roots are so deeply imbedded in Lexing-ton and Davidson County that I could not pull them free even if I tried—and how such a thought never would cross my mind in the first place.

Instead, I usually just smile and shrug and say, "Well, I guess I'm just partial to home."

When my grandfather, Edgar Anderson Timberlake, ar-rived in Lexington on May 1, 1903, he rode in on a magical mop. He was just twenty-seven days shy of being twenty-one years old, and he came to Lexington thinking that it would be the source of his fortune—and indeed it was, for it became his home, the place he loved. He had grown up on a farm in Person County, near the Virginia line, where Timberlakes were so abundant that the community in which he lived was named for them. His father had helped to es-tablish the post office there as well as the Methodist church.

My grandfather loved hunting, despite having had his brother die in his arms, the top of his head shot away in a hunting accident. He had worked as a hunting guide, and he especially loved bird hunting (it must be in the genes, for he passed on this love to his son, grandsons, great-grandson, and now great-great grandsons). I can't help but think that part of what attracted him to Lexington, the county seat of Davidson County, the center of North Carolina's piedmont plateau, was that this was a quail hunting mecca. In the early part of the century, rich northerners bought up huge tracts of the county as hunting preserves. They built lodges and kept managers and dog trainers on staff for their infrequent visits, arriving in luxurious, private rail cars. Some of these clubs were extravagently outfitted with bowling alleys and swimming pools.

But the more immediate—and practical—reason for my grandfather's arrival was the device he called "that floor-mopping whangdoodle," although never to his customers. To them it was an amazing labor-saving invention.

I never saw one, but as I heard it described, it was a stick with a broom on one end and a sort of mop and pan on the other. The idea was that you could sweep and scrub the floor with the broom end, then turn it around and mop and scoop up the water with the other end. The identity of the fellow in Roxboro who came up with this wondrous apparatus has understandably been lost to history, but he must have been quite an operator, for he induced several dozen young men into purchasing the rights to sell it in counties throughout the state. My grandfather ended up with the Davidson County franchise.

Of all those who bought into this scheme, my grandfather was said to be the only one who profited from it, proving what a natural-born salesman he was. These astounding whangdoodles sold for $1.75, no small amount at a time when forty cents was considered good pay for a day's work, and my grandfather was so effective at selling them that two months after being run off by a farmer who discovered him demonstrating one to the farmer's wife, the farmer wrote him a letter: "Send me one of those gosh damned things. There's no living in this house until I buy one."

My grandfather did so well with those gosh-darned things that a year after his arrival he returned to Person County, married his sweetheart, Dessie Arlene Fitzgerald, and brought her back to Lexington with four of her unmarried sisters and her mother.

Lexington was just a village of about 1,500 people then, with no paved streets or sidewalks, two cotton mills and a furniture factory that was rebuilding after having been burned down two years earlier. But the town sat at the junction of two railroads, and it was beginning a growth spurt that would see it nearly triple in population from 1900 to 1910 as the furniture industry established itself. It was a good place to build a career and to marry off country-born sisters-in-law.

The market for whangdoodles had been pretty much saturated by this time, and my grandfather went to work selling sewing machines door-to-door for a furniture store, riding about the county, and occasionally into adjoining counties, in a wagon pulled by a team of horses. He carried with him his old Trojan Parker side-by-side twelve-guage shotgun and hunted quail and other game as he went. I was told that he supplied the meat for many meals to his customers.

Tall and imposing, Grandfather Timberlake was a gregarious and dynamic fellow, and he sold sewing machines even better than whangdoodles. This work allowed him to get to know almost everybody in the county, and that would help him greatly later on.

In 1912, he and two partners took over a failing furniture store, but they were unable to turn it around and had to close it a year later. Broke but undaunted, the three partners managed to get a loan for $2,200 to start a new business on Main Street that they called Piedmont Furniture Co. This time they succeeded and by plowing their profits back into the store, they made the business burgeon. For the rest of his life my grandfather liked to tell people that he started in business without a nickel to his name.

Among the items my grandfather and his partners sold at the store were caskets that they assembled in the back room. That led them into the burial business. There was no funeral home in Lexington then and the town was growing rapidly. So they rented the building behind the furniture store and opened Piedmont Funeral Home. My grandfather went off to Cincinnati to study embalming. He later remembered that he buried only twelve people the first year. But business doubled every year for the first three years, after which a second funeral home opened in competition.

On July 5, 1929, my grandfather buried the first state highway patrolman to die in the line of duty in North Carolina. The trooper, George Ira Thompson, was killed when his motorcycle was struck by a T-Model Ford near Wadesboro. The State Highway Patrol had been launched only the day before with a ceremony in Raleigh attended by all the newly appointed troopers, and Thompson was on his way to his assigned post in Marion when he was killed.

All the troopers gathered again for his funeral at St. Luke's Lutheran Church in the community of Tyro, seven miles west of Lexington. Years later, when he was in his eighties and after having suffered a stroke, my father, who helped my grandfather with that funeral, could still remember every detail of it. More than 350 people attended, he said, and the temperature that day soared above 103 degrees.

My father was Casper Hill Timberlake, called Pappy by many in his later years. He was born on October 4, 1905, a year and a half after my grandparents' marriage. When he was two, my grandmother, pregnant again, tripped over a firewood box and injured herself so seriously in the fall that she lost the baby and couldn't have any more children. Dad spent his early years on East Center Street. Later, his dad bought a big house on First Avenue. He always spoke fondly of his childhood in Lexington. He never forgot how excited he was when "moving pictures" first came to town. A man named N.A. Beck began showing them on summer evenings on an outdoor screen on South Main Street. The first one Dad remembered seeing was *The Sinking of the Titanic* in 1912, not long after that mighty ship went down. He was not yet seven.

Even as a child, Dad spent a lot of time at the furniture store, and by the time he was in high school he was working there. He had his father's outgoing personality and eventually became an even better salesman. I think he always felt that he was in his father's shadow and that he had to be better than him to get his approval. I'm sure he never doubted that he was to someday take over the family businesses. But first he was to get a good education.

Dad had a lifelong love of sports. He was the catcher on a neighborhood baseball team and the center on the first football team at Lexington High School. After graduation he went off to Trinity College in Durham, a Methodist school, where he joined the Sigma Chi fraternity and played drums in a band. After two years, he won an appointment to the U.S. Naval Academy in Annapolis, Maryland. He loved the academy but after a training exercise on a steam-powered battleship the following summer, I think he had second thoughts about the Navy. "I shoveled coal all the way to France and all the way back," he used to tell us.

After his first year, he dropped out of the academy and returned to classes at Trinity College, which, after receiving a huge endowment from tobacco magnate James Buchanan "Buck" Duke, had become Duke University while he was in Annapolis.

Dad never said much about why he left the academy, but I'm certain the reason was to be closer to my mother, Ella Leonard Raper, whose roots in Davidson County went back more than 200 years. She was the great, great, great granddaughter of Valentine Leonhardt (the German family name was eventually Anglicized as Leonard). Dad and Mom had grown up across the street from each other and had been sweethearts since he was eleven and she was ten. He missed her desperately and just couldn't stand being away from her.

Mom was the eldest daughter of the eight children of Emery E. Raper and Lillie Leonard Raper. My grandfather Raper was one of the best known and most widely respected men in Davidson County, indeed in North Carolina. He was born in the Arcadia community of northern Davidson County in 1863 while his father was off fighting in the Civil War. He attended Yadkin College, which the Methodist Church had built on the Yadkin River not far from his home, and graduated valedictorian of his class. For four years he was headmaster of the school in the Bethany community, then studied under two lawyers in Greensboro and was admitted to the State Bar in March, 1885. He returned to Davidson County and went to work with Lexington's best known lawyer, Captain F.C. "Fitz" Robbins.

For the rest of his life my grandfather would tell the story of his first day at the law office.

A country fellow came in and asked, "Where's the captain?"

My grandfather said that he was out and asked if he could be of help.

"You a lawyer?" asked the man.

"Yessir," my grandfather replied confidently.

"You know the law?"

"I think I do."

"What is it?"

My grandfather said that he found himself unable to answer and would forevermore be pondering the meaning of that question.

That night he wrote an entry in his journal that expressed his uncertainty and self-doubt as he embarked on this new career.

"Success depends on my own efforts. I have but few friends to help me. I am unknown. O that I could see what is to come."

He might have been even more intimidated if he could have seen the future. By that fall, he was successfully arguing a case before the North Carolina Supreme Court, at twenty-two the youngest lawyer to do so before or since.

He went on to become a city commissioner, the county attorney, the county school superintendent, and a member of the state education commission. He was an organizer of Perpetual Savings and Loan Company and was very active in the First Methodist Church as well as in Democrat Party politics on both the local and state levels. He was an ardent advocate of women's rights, perhaps because he had so many bright daughters, and he wrote widely on the subject. He served as a delegate to his party's national convention in 1904, and North Carolina's popular statesman, the late Senator Sam Ervin, later told me that my grandfather had been one of his political mentors.

Although small and quiet-spoken, Grandfather Raper was nonetheless a man with strong convictions and an acerbic tongue. A witness he tore apart on the stand during one trial, a tall, burly man, confronted him on the street after court, and in a fit of anger picked him up and dunked him head-first into a horse watering trough. Although it left him soaked and sputtering, it did not extinguish his ardor.

In 1928, when Democrat Al Smith became the first Catholic presidential candidate, running against Herbert

Hoover, the minister at First Methodist Church made the mistake of launching into a tirade against Smith and Catholicism during a Sunday morning service. My grandparents and their children took up a whole pew near the front of the church, and when the minister's intent became apparent, my grandfather raised his hand. The minister was wound up and either didn't notice him or ignored him. He went right on raging about how the Pope would take over the country if Al Smith managed to get elected. That was when my grandfather stood up. This caught the minister's attention enough to disrupt his preaching.

"Mr. Raper, is something wrong?" he asked apprehensively.

"Yes, something is wrong," my grandfather said. "When you bring politics into my church, that's when I leave the church."

With that, he and my grandmother and all their children marched out—and most of the congregation followed.

The next Sunday, my grandfather and his family were back in their pew as if nothing had happened, and the minister never again mentioned politics from the pulpit.

Grandfather Raper suffered a heart attack while arguing a case in the courthouse on October 15, 1931, more than five years before I was born. The bailiff ran to my grandmother's house a few blocks away to tell her, but by the time she got to her husband he was dead on the courtroom floor at the age of sixty-eight.

When my father finished his courses at Duke and returned to Lexington, my mother was at her own mother's alma mater, Salem College in Winston-Salem, twenty miles from home, where she was not only a star student but a star athlete, lettering in five different sports. As expected, Dad went to work for his father, eventually looking after the furniture business while my grandfather concentrated on the funeral home. Mom left Salem and returned to Lexington to coach basketball—and to be nearer Dad.

They eloped on September 1, 1925, marrying at a Methodist parsonage in nearby Thomasville with two of their friends as witnesses. Both were nervous about telling their parents, and decided to do it separately. Dad waited on the street to see how it went with Mom before he went in to tell his own parents. The yelling that erupted from the Raper house indicated that Mom's dad didn't take the news particularly well—and that he had made the proper choice in not accompanying her inside.

It took Grandfather Raper a while to fully accept my dad—and forgive my mom. Yet there could not have been a better marriage on this earth, for my mother and father were devoted to one another for all the rest of their days.

Every child is an artist. The problem is how to remain an artist once he grows up.

—Pablo Picasso

Chapter 3

I was a tumor. At least that's what my mother's doctor said I had to be, because he had warned her that if she attempted to have another child she likely wouldn't survive.

My brother Tim—Casper Hill Jr.—had been born on November 29, 1932, more than seven years after my parents' elopement. My mother had a tough delivery, nearly died from internal hemorrhaging and was long in recovering. She was sickly for years afterward.

I don't know whether I was an accident or not, but I do know that my father hated being an only child and didn't want my brother to suffer the same fate. Maybe I was just the product of a moment of passion brought about by being in a different and more exciting place, for I was conceived in New York City where my father was enrolled in embalming school.

Anyway, nearly five years after my mother had been told that she could not have another child, she discovered that I was not a tumor after all—and that her doctor was none too happy about me. This had to have caused great anxiety for my mother—and perhaps even more for my father, who worshipped her and must have felt responsible for putting her in peril with this pregnancy. I know that he went out of his way to see that she had the best care available as my entrance into this world neared.

That's why I was born in the new hospital in Salisbury, in adjoining Rowan County (where my friend Liddy Hanford, who later added Dole to her name when she married a U.S. Senator from Kansas, also was born several months before my arrival). Surprisingly, I arrived without complications on January 22, 1937. I was named Roberts Edgar Timberlake, for my maternal great-grandfather Burl B. Roberts, and for my grandfather Edgar Anderson Timberlake. But from the beginning, and until I was grown, my family called me Bobby. Childhood chums called me lots of other things: "Stickriver," "Lumberpond," and almost anything else that had to do with wood and water. Since then, though, I have been Bob. Just Bob.

Soon after my parents' marriage, my father built a modest brick and frame house at 309 Hillcrest Drive just north of downtown Lexington. It was within walking distance of First Avenue, where my grandmothers and two of my great aunts lived, and it was even nearer to Grimes School, where I would endure my first years of education (I was never a great student, my imagination usually carrying me far from the classroom.)

On my first birthday, my mother wrote in my baby book: "You waked with a smile this morning and have been such a dear all day...(I clearly was born with this disposition, you see.) Sonny (Tim) gave you a rubber mouse that squeaks and a Humpty Dumpty. Jane Nelson (our next-door neighbor) brought you a ball, and Mother gave you some blocks and a rubber doll (All of which, collector that I am, I probably still have, if I could just remember where I put them.). You can hold up one finger to show how old you are (Beyond this, math has pretty much failed me.). You can't walk alone very well, but it won't be long...." (Maybe I couldn't walk so well because I was so chubby that I was thrown off balance. Looking at my early childhood photos, you might think I was an offspring of Buddha, if Buddha had had long blond curls and a perpetual smile.)

At two I became involved—at least peripherally—in international espionage. That was because the Goat Man came through our neighborhood. The Goat Man was of German heritage, as was I, and many of the people in our area. He had this huge, long-haired goat with great curved horns. The goat pulled a fancy cart, and the Goat Man went from town to town, house to house, letting children pose in the cart for his camera and selling the photos to their parents. I posed, of course, although I refused to get into that cart—something about it must not have set right with me, or maybe I just feared that the goat might take off and I'd be gone with the Goat Man. My friend Liddy Hanford in Salisbury also posed for the Goat Man soon after I did (she did get into the cart as I recall). Liddy, who as I write this is a candidate for President of the United States, probably never knew what I later was told about the Goat Man—and let's hope the press doesn't get onto this; I can only imagine what they might make of it.

I was standing in line at Lanier Hardware in Lexington one day a few years back when another customer told me he'd seen the photo of me with the goat cart in one of my books.

"Did you know the Goat Man was a Nazi spy?" he asked.

The goat cart was just a ruse to allow him to wander freely about the state taking photos of military bases, power plants, and other strategic targets to send back to Germany in anticipation of the coming World War, he said. But the Goat Man was caught during the war and sentenced to prison. Considering my refusal to get into the Goat Man's cart, I can only wonder now if I didn't suspect something at the time.

Another event when I was two had a profound effect on my family. My grandfather Timberlake died of a heart attack at age fifty-seven. I have no memory of him either. He had become a community leader, instrumental in building the Junior Order Home for Children south of town, the largest and most self-sufficient home for children east of the Mississippi, and in bringing minor league baseball—one of his great loves—to Lexington (my dad had gotten a semi-pro cotton-mill league going before that). Grandfather Timberlake—Pa-Pa, he was called in the family—was widely beloved, and his funeral was one of the biggest ever held in our town. Hundreds of people, black and white, passed by his bier at the funeral home he founded.

As expected, my father took over the funeral home and furniture store and worked long hours to keep them going and to provide for us. The Great Depression was not yet over and times were still hard, although Lexington had fared better than many places during the worst of it. None of our town's furniture plants or textile factories had been forced to close, but the workers had to take big cuts in pay and averaged only ten cents an hour for their labor.

My dad tried other businesses to keep going. He opened a record shop and started a bus line to haul mill workers to their jobs. The funeral home was taking more of his time as well, especially the hours that might otherwise have been spent with his wife and children. Family visitations for the deceased were held at night, and often my father wouldn't get home until after we were in bed. He frequently had funerals on weekends, and holidays, too. People didn't die to fit work schedules or children's wishes.

With my father away so much, my mother became the major influence of my early years, a total nurturer, always there for us.

Mom devoted herself to her family. She wanted us to be

content, happy and in harmony, and she worked hard to see that we were. She wanted us to believe that we could accomplish anything, and she convinced us that we could. I don't think I've ever known anybody with a more positive attitude, and she passed that on to Tim and me. Outside of her love, it probably was her greatest gift to us.

I'm sure it was largely because of Mom that I have only happy memories of childhood. She could even turn bad experiences into good.

When I was four or five (old enough, for sure, to remember a traumatic experience), I was out playing with my tricycle and happened across a nest of yellow jackets. They boiled out of the ground and stung me all over. I was screaming and leaping and slapping, and despite my pain and fear I remember being fascinated because I could smell those yellow jackets, a very distinctive, musty odor that emanated from their underground nest. I still smell it whenever I remember this, and anytime I'm near a jellow jackets' nest, I know it instantly.

Tim was playing nearby with some of his buddies, and he put me back on the tricycle and pushed me home as fast as he could run. Mom heard me screaming and ran out and snatched me up. By the time she got me inside, I thought my body was on fire, and I was becoming a mass of welts.

In those days, people put what we called "spit tobacco" on stings to draw out the pain and reduce the swelling. Spit tobacco was tobacco taken from cigarettes, plug tobacco, or snuff and mixed with the handiest liquid. In Mom's case that was tobacco from cigarettes she tore apart and mixed with water to make a paste. I was crying all the while she was dabbing me with spit tobacco. "Shhh, don't cry," she kept comforting me. "We'll go to Aunt Nona's. We'll go to Aunt Nona's."

That promise took my mind off my pain and turned my

attention to pleasure. I loved going to Great Aunt Nona Byerly's country house near Yadkin College. She was one of my grandmother Raper's sisters, and her big brick house was comforting even if you weren't in pain. She always had a pile of fluffy biscuits from the last meal, and I loved those cold biscuits spread with freshly churned butter from the ice box on the back porch, slathered with jam, jelly, or preserves from the many jars that lined her pantry shelves. One of those biscuits with that country butter and blackberry jam was enough to relieve almost any pain. It was almost worth getting stung all over.

Mom could just as well have taken me to Aunt Buff's to make me forget my misery. She was another of my great aunts whom I loved to visit, although we didn't get to go as frequently for she was farther away. We called Grandmother Timberlake "Gangy," and Aunt Buff was one of her sisters, all of whom my grandfather had managed to marry off well.

Aunt Buff was married to a very aristocratic man named Frank Butner, who seemed stiffly English to me, one of those people everybody always called Mister, even Aunt Buff. They lived in a 200-year-old house in Bethania, just north of Winston-Salem. Bethania was settled in the mid-eighteenth century by a religious sect called Moravians, who had fled persecution in Bohemia (later to become Czechoslovakia).

Aunt Buff's house was called the Cornwallis House, because General Cornwallis supposedly had commandeered it for a while on his way to the battle at Guilford Courthouse. To me, this was the most intriguing and mysterious house I'd ever entered. It was on several levels, and its walls were covered with scenic paintings as old as the house. An escape tunnel was said to be beneath it, although I never saw it. The house was crammed with rare and unique antiques. And Aunt Buff had a story about every item, some of them probably even true. I became completely caught up in her excitement about her antiques and her stories about them.

I'm sure that Aunt Buff was the earliest source of my lifelong love of antiques, and partly to blame, no doubt, for my obsession with collecting almost anything, not to mention my love of story-telling. I never went to her house when she didn't give me something—a marble, a Civil War button, or some other marvelous trinket that never failed to trigger my imagination. Every gift, of course, came with a tale.

She would give me a marble and tell me how a little boy had been down on his knees playing with that very marble when General Cornwallis came riding up. The general smiled and asked if he could play. The boy nodded in disbelief, and the general dismounted and got down in the dirt with his fine red uniform and shot marbles with the astonished boy. I still have marbles that General Cornwallis played with.

Once, because I asked for it, Aunt Buff gave me a ragged old quilt, handmade, of course, with a star pattern, orange and brown, that she was going to throw away. I'm sure she never dreamed that I would squirrel it away and that years later it would become the subject of several of my paintings, that ragged old quilt stirring fond memories for many people in many places far from Bethania, North Carolina.

World War II began just a month and a half before my fifth birthday and it played a big role in my imagination during my boyhood, as it did for most boys at that time. My friends and I had our own wars with rubber band guns and pretended we were shooting Nazi storm troopers and Japanese soldiers. I even had an army uniform, made by one of my great aunts.

My mother's brother, Uncle Emery Raper Jr., was a bombardier on a B-25 based in London, and he was my war hero. I was really excited when he came home briefly to get married, because I wanted him to tell me everything about the war. Uncle Emery married Mildred Ann Critcher. My great aunt Annie, another of Grandmother Timberlake's sisters who lived near her on First Avenue, had married Percy V. Critcher, who was one of Lexington's most prominent lawyers and was said to be related to Blackbeard, the pirate. Mildred Ann was their daughter. I was related to both bride and groom.

The wedding took place at Aunt Annie and Uncle Percy's house, and I'll never forget how dashing Uncle Emery looked standing ramrod straight in his officer's dress uniform at the foot of the staircase as my cousin Mildred descended in her wedding gown. I still can close my eyes see the scene as if it were a photograph. After the reception, Uncle Emery let me try on his uniform coat and hat and somebody snapped a photo of me, grinning proudly, the coat reaching all the way to my shoes, its sleeves continuing miles past my hands. I was something less than dashing, to say the least.

Before Uncle Emery left to return to the war, I told him to catch me a German army helmet when one came flying up by the plane during his bombing raids. He grinned and promised he'd try. For some reason, I never got that helmet, although Uncle Emery returned safely to Lexington.

It shouldn't come as a surprise, I guess, but another of my earliest memories is of painting—finger painting. My Dad's first cousin, Bobbie Green Holton, was an artist who sometimes taught painting classes. She was the daughter of another of my grandfather Timberlake's sisters-in-law, my great aunt Ruth, who had married Bob Green, the owner of a downtown clothing store and one of my favorite great uncles. They, too, lived on First Avenue. Starting when I was four or five, anytime I visited Aunt Ruth's house, Bobbie would give me paper and jars of bright paints and encourage me to make any kind of mess I wanted. I loved it. I was entranced by the colors, the way they blended, contrasted, and accentuated one another. I especially liked purple. It became my favorite. I was amazed at the designs I could create with those paints. I doubt that any of those finger paintings still exists, but to this day I can close my eyes and see many of them. I know people will think that's not possible, but it's true. Such was the effect they had on me.

Although I began as an abstract painter, I quickly turned to realism. All kids got crayons and coloring books, I suppose, and I was no different. But I never liked coloring pictures somebody else had drawn. I wanted to draw my own.

Well before I could read and write, I developed my own system of hieroglyphics. I drew pictures to communicate. If my brother Tim was going on a camping trip, I would make a list of all the equipment he needed to take—canteen, pup tent, pocket knife, mess kit, rope, hatchet, and all the rest—by drawing pictures of every item.

When I was alone, I usually filled my time drawing, and I was never bored. I drew almost everything I could see, including every piece of furniture in the house. If I wasn't drawing, I was forming figures out of modeling clay. When I became a Cub Scout, I learned to carve figures out of soap, and when I became a Boy Scout I moved up to wood. My first artistic award was second place for a lanyard slide I carved in Scouts. My buddy J.B. Lopp won first place, and he couldn't even draw a straight line, then or now. I still think he won only because he was older.

My drawings changed when I was about eight and finally decided for certain what I wanted to be in life: a cowboy.

And not just any cowboy. I wanted to be Tim McCoy. Tim McCoy was the best cowboy who ever lived. I know that because I saw all of his movies at the Granada Theater, which we called The Roach Palace, or the Rat Hole. It cost only nine cents to get into the Granada, and I went every Saturday with Tim and his buddy Angles "Ang" Lindsey to see the cowboy movies. Sometimes when we were short on money, they would sandwich me between them and slip me in without a ticket.

After I decided I wanted to be Tim McCoy, I switched to drawing only cowboys and western scenes, with an occasional Civil War battle thrown in.

Ironically, years later, I would become close friends with Iron Eyes Cody, the Cherokee/Cree actor who had traveled with Tim McCoy's Wild West Show and appeared in hundreds of western movies. Iron Eyes' father had been in the Buffalo Bill Show, which even more ironically had come to its end in Davidson County, just five miles south of Lexington, on October 29, 1901, when the train carrying the show's troupe was hit head-on by a freight train. Of the show's 200 highly trained horses, ninety-two were killed in the wreck and all but one of the rest were injured. That one was a big stallion named Duke, Buffalo Bill's favorite horse, found wandering unscathed in a nearby cornfield in the moonlight. Sixteen years later, Iron Eyes' father was one of five former members of his troupe who kept a vigil in a hallway outside Buffalo Bill's room as he lay dying.

Who could have imagined then that this boy who went to cowboy movies every Saturday and who sat for hours drawing cowboys and Indians would someday paint a portrait of Iron Eyes, the crying Indian who became the symbol of America's desecration of its landscape, and that that portrait would be seen by millions of people as the first national conservation stamp and poster, and that it might actually cause some of them to pause for a moment and think about what we are doing to ourselves and to the land on which we have to depend?

My mother, of course, encouraged my drawing, and she must have seen some early glimmer of talent, because when I was ten, she sent off to New York for a fourteen-color Colorcraft paint set and easel for my birthday. That was when I took to painting in earnest, copying illustrations from *Boy's Life*, *Outdoor Life*, and other magazines, eventually discovering the western paintings of Charles Russell and Frederic Remington and doing my best to reproduce them in exact detail.

If this is beginning to sound as if I were a lonely and isolated child who tried to fill his emptiness by drawing and painting, let me assure you that was not the case. I had a full and vigorous childhood, much of it due to my brother Tim. Tim had severe health problems in his early years, before I was born. He had rheumatic fever and a long-lasting lung infection that prevented him from engaging in physical activities, but he had regained robust health by the time I came along and was eager to take advantage of it.

Tim and I shared a pine-paneled upstairs room at the back of our house (the only upstairs room) from the time I was able to walk until the night before he got married and left home. He was a Boy Scout, as I also would be when I got old enough, but he went on to earn Eagle rank, something I would never achieve because I got too busy with too many other projects. Tim loved hunting, fishing, frog gigging, camping, hiking, and almost anything else that could be done outdoors. When I was too young to share these activities with him, I envied him and put myself there with him in my imagination and my drawings. But when I grew old enough to participate, he never excluded me, despite being more than five years older.

Among the many things Tim taught me was how to shoot. I started with my Daisy Red Ryder BB gun, and I learned to aim with both eyes open. I became quite a shot, if I do say so myself.

I got my first real gun, a Remington automatic .22 rifle when I was nine. I used it to hunt rabbits with a friend of my dad's, Fred Wilson, who ran a wholesale grocery. I'd started hunting with Mr. Wilson when I was seven, too young to use a gun. He had hearing problems and I was his ears, telling him where the dogs were running.

After I got my .22, I became as good a shot with it as I had been with my BB gun. Tim and I were floating down the Yadkin River in our old wooden row boat the summer after I got my rifle, and he bet me that I couldn't shoot a dragonfly out of the air. He lost. Twice.

I was twelve when I shot my first quail and first duck, hunting with Tim and Dad. Bird hunting was the kind of hunting that really appealed to me: doves, quail, grouse, pheasants, wild turkeys, ducks, geese. It was challenging, required skill, and the bounty was so good to eat. I'll never forget how excited I was on my 13th birthday when I got my first shotgun, a pump-action twenty-gauge. I knew it had to be that because of the shape and weight of the box, but opening the box and actually seeing the end of the barrel of that beautiful gun was one of the great thrills of my childhood.

By that time a new minister had come to First Methodist Church, where my family attended regularly. Howard Wilkinson was a warm and brilliant man who was loved by everybody in my family, as well as everybody at our church. He became a major influence in my life, and half a century later he remains a dear friend. But the thing that impressed me most about him then was that he loved fishing and bird hunting as much as I did, and we quickly became fast hunting buddies. When I was in the eighth and ninth grade, I'd get up well before dawn, go duck hunting with Rev. Wilkinson and arrive at school in wet clothes and muddied hip boots.

Of course, Tim and I hunted together all the time. I couldn't have imagined having a better brother. I idolized him. He wasn't just my big brother and best friend, he was my protector. Nobody dared bully me, because anybody who did knew that he would have to deal with Tim. He was my hero in more ways than I could ever say.

We both had our own friends, of course. Ours was a great neighborhood, filled with kids of all ages.

Early on, my buddies were Baxter "Punkin" Wallace, Lee "The Flea" Phillips, Johnny Wilson, Gordon Swaim, Samuel "Sambo" Hayes, Bob Grubb, who was a year older, all from my neighborhood. From First Avenue, where my grandmothers lived, were Joe Sink and Cloyd Philpott. Joe's daddy was the publisher of Lexington's newspaper, *The Dispatch*, Cloyd's would eventually become lieutenant governor and die only eight months after taking office.

All of us played at one another's houses and through our neighborhood and others, as well as on the grounds at Grimes School and in the graveyard behind it, where we chased ghosts on dark nights and later tried to scare neighborhood girls with tales of our exploits. We caught crawdads in the creek and garter snakes in the high grass. Punkin captured baby flying squirrels that the two of us once smuggled into school under our shirts.

None of us ever missed an opportunity to go camping, canoeing, fishing or frog-gigging at High Rock Lake south of town. We played baseball and football and all the old-time games that kids loved before TV and video-game shoot-outs came along. We built wagons and soapbox derby cars and raced them downhill, taking bad spills and crashing into telephone poles at top speed. We put on circuses and attempted to make performers out of neighborhood cats and dogs. Sometimes we put on our circuses in new houses under construction in the neighborhood. One of our clowns got trapped in the chimney in one of those houses, and the fire department had to come and get him out.

Several of us even started our own radio station in Johnny Wilson's garage with a transmitter Johnny built from a kit. I don't know how big an audience we had, but we were certain we were radio announcers as genuine as Edward R. Murrow, another North Carolina native whose wartime voice from the front in Europe was recognized by almost everybody.

Johnny was quite mechanical and was always coming up with new things for us to do. I'm sure he would have made a great engineer. Unbeknownst to our parents, we figured out how to make a zip gun, and we put one together in his garage using copper tubing. We even made our own lead balls to fire from it by melting toy soldiers and dropping little blobs of the hot lead from a second story window into a bucket of water on the ground. We got gun powder from firecrackers for the charge. But when we tried to fire the thing, it exploded, the copper splitting and curling back like a banana peel.

Looking back at some of the things we did, it's a wonder any of us survived, and indeed Johnny would not make it out of his teens. One of our friends, and I won't mention a name here, was chasing another friend up the steeple at First Presbyterian church. At the top, he made a leap for him. His friend ducked, and he sailed out of the steeple. We always said the only thing that saved him was that he landed on his head.

When I left Grimes School for Lexington High after the seventh grade, Joe Sink, Cloyd Philpott and I spent so much time together that people started referring to us as The Three Musketeers, but we called ourselves The Three Fat Boys. Every day after school, we'd head for First Avenue and go to the houses of my grandmothers and great aunts devouring whatever sweets they'd made for us. We set them against one another, competing for our "best dessert of the day" award, and they really outdid themselves making all kinds of pies, cakes, cobblers and every other kind of dessert to please us.

It may have been that every small town in the '40s and

'50s was a great place to grow up, but that was especially true of Lexington, which by my boyhood had grown to a population of about 12,000.

For one thing, Lexington smelled so much better than other towns. Just as the air over nearby Winston-Salem was distinguished by the pungent aroma of tobacco, Lexington's was immediately recognizable by the sweet fragrance of wood—oak, maple, cherry, pine, poplar, and cedar—above all the cedar, still one of my favorite fragrances. The scent rose from the huge lumber yards scattered around town, where the rough boards arrived from the sawmills; it came, too, from the kilns where the lumber was dried, and from the factories where it was sawed, and planed, and sanded to be made into furniture.

Another form of wood fragrance, the most wonderful of all, also made the air over Lexington distinctive. That was the tantalizing aroma of pork cooking slowly over hickory coals. Sid Weaver and Jess Swicegood were responsible for that. Back in the '20s they started cooking barbecue in pits they dug near the courthouse and sold it out of tents on court days. They went on to erect permanent buildings and brick pits.

By the time I came along, Weaver and Swicegood had sold out to Alton Beck and Warner Stamey, respectively. A whole school of barbecue grew out of those two places. People who worked for Beck and Stamey went on to start places of their own, spreading out through town and across the whole piedmont plateau. Lexington came to have more barbecue stands per capita than any other place in the country. Now the town's barbecue festival on the third Saturday of October draws more than 100,000 people each year and has been rated one of the top ten single-day festivals in the United States. I can think of few foods that can match a tray of Lexington barbecue, chopped, coarse-chopped, or sliced, with the traditional red slaw and hushpuppies.

The barbecue alone would have given anybody reason to be thankful to have grown up in Lexington, but the town had other attributes as well that made it a special place during my boyhood. Perhaps it was just as true elsewhere, but in Lexington people seemed to care more about one another. Families were closer. People took time to get to know others. Neighbors dropped in and out all the time, and they looked after each other. Hardly anybody ever locked a door, and kids could roam the entire town, as we all did, without fear or concern. On warm evenings, people gathered on front porches, chatted, greeted their neighbors, told stories, and created memories and unbreakable bonds.

Lexington remains a fine place to live, but much of that has changed. People seem to have more material things now but fewer rewarding associations and fewer happy memories. Who can say with confidence that such change was for the better?

The laws of Nature are the hand of God on the controls of the Universe.

—Archibald Rutledge

Chapter 4

World War II changed my family's life in an unexpected way. Many things were in short supply and rationed during the war. One was natural gas. The town of Lexington had supplied natural gas to residents, but when the supply dwindled during the war, the town went out of the gas business.

My dad had sold gas stoves and other appliances at his furniture store, and he felt obligated to his customers to see that they still could use them. When the war ended and production turned from war machines to consumer goods, pressurized gas tanks became available and Dad began getting them for his customers and supplying them with propane gas. Here, he realized, was the possibility of a whole new business. And he began to build toward it.

For three years after the war, he would load a gas cookstove, or waterheater, (along with the tank necessary to fuel it) onto the delivery truck when he closed the furniture store each evening. After supper he would set out to sell it, determined not to return home until he did. He always had a list of prospective customers to call on, and he always came home with an empty truck.

Without question, my dad was the best salesman I've

ever encountered. One particular story shows just how good he was. He once sold a water heater to a farmer in the county, and when he sent men out to install it, they discovered that the farmer not only had no running water in his house, he only had a hand-dug well with a bucket on a rope to retrieve the water. Dad went out and talked the farmer into putting a pump in the well and plumbing in the house so the water heater would be of some use to him.

Dad truly was one of those people who never met a stranger. He could read a person's mood and disposition and find an easy and friendly connection with anybody. Like my mother, he had an incredibly positive attitude and an uncanny ability to instill confidence in others. Not much ever threw him. Situations that would send others spiraling into dismay or depression only challenged him.

"When things seem to be going against you," he used to tell us, "they're really working for you."

By that he meant that seemingly bad situations were merely tests for finding new and better ways of dealing with problems and achieving goals. And if new ways didn't present themselves, he believed in patience and the confidence to wait things out. He knew that people's most desperate desires often were not necessarily the best for them because getting them might prevent better things from happening down the road.

I have found that to be especially true in my life. To me, problems and setbacks, as disconcerting and discouraging as they may seem at the time, have always been just temporary snags, detours on the way to something better.

I'm sure that this philosophy was a great help to my dad as a salesman. Salesmen are always getting rejections, and they have to be able to continue on, no matter how many times they are turned down. To Dad, selling was what a hobby might be to somebody else—something in which he found immense delight and deep satisfaction. He didn't think of it as work.

"The best salesmen," he always said, "are those who love what they are selling." A salesman, he said, had to believe in his product, be certain of its usefulness to his customers, and take joy in making it available to them. Dad truly believed in gas cookstoves (as does almost every great chef, I might add) and thought that everybody should have one. He could have sold a gas stove to the devil himself.

In 1947, Dad formed a new company called Piedmont Gas Service, but still operated it out of the furniture store. When he decided the two businesses needed to be separated, I went to Washington with him and Mom to get a small business loan so he could build a new facility for the gas company. He had to make a presentation and he was a little apprehensive, despite his usual optimism. Mom kept reassuring him that he would do fine, and he did, of course.

He came home with $100,000, bought an old house on the northeast corner of South Main Street and Fourth Avenue, tore it down and put the new gas building in its place. On the opposite corner across Fourth Avenue was another huge house into which he earlier had moved the funeral home. Now he had three businesses to run and was far busier than ever—and never happier. He would go on to build Piedmont Gas, which later would change its name to Carolane, into the biggest family-owned propane company in the Southeast, with branches in several cities. And that would not be the last business he would create.

How my dad managed to do all that he did was always an amazement to me, but the year after he started the gas company he also changed our lives in another—and to me, particularly satisfying—way. He built a vacation house in Myrtle Beach, South Carolina.

Like myself, Dad loved the coast and everything about

it. He took us to the beach for summer vacation every year. My first visit was when I was six months old, and I've never missed a year since. In the beginning we went to North Carolina beaches, first to Carolina, south of Wilmington, then to Wrightsville, closer by. Sometime in the early '40s, Dad discovered the Waterside Hotel in Myrtle Beach, and after that we never went anywhere else.

The Waterside was more like a home than a hotel. It was a rambling old house, painted white. It had maybe twelve or fifteen guest rooms and a huge wrap-around porch with a line of rocking chairs facing the ocean. It was run by a congenial lady that I never knew by any other name than Mrs. Farlow. She was like a mother to her guests, and she produced some of the best home-cooked meals I've ever tasted, served boarding-house-style in the dining room. The same people came to the Waterside at the same time every year, most staying for just a week, some, like us, for two, and we all became like family. Those were truly relaxing and fun-filled times.

It was on one of those vacations that Dad paid $1,200 for a 150-foot corner lot on North Ocean Boulevard, just across the street from the ocean front and only a mile and a half south of the biggest resort on the beach at the time, the distinctive, rambling old Ocean Forest Hotel, now, lamentably, long gone. The street wasn't even paved then.

Dad got a friend from Lexington, Cost Link, to build the house, a two-story colonial with eight rooms, a basement (unusual for the beach) and a big white-columned porch with an ocean view. He had the lumber for it sawed in Lexington. Cost and his crew finished the house in late spring, and we couldn't wait to move in. We spent our first night on the floor, because the trucks bearing the furniture had not yet arrived from Lexington.

Myrtle Beach in 1948 was nothing like the sprawling

metropolis that it would become. The huge, year-'round golf-ing and entertainment center that now attracts throngs from all over the country, indeed, the world, could not have been imagined then. It was just a small beach town with the busi-ness district wisely set back from the oceanfront. On the beach itself was a gaudy pavilion, a few carnival rides and an assortment of gift shops, hot dog stands, bingo parlors, a fishing pier, small inns and hotels that swarmed with people every summer and lay dormant and abandoned the rest of the year. The town had only about 2,000 permanent residents.

Professional fishermen still seined off the beach, row-ing through the surf to spread their wide nets during the semi-annual migration runs of mullet, spots and bluefish. Great expanses of forest separated Myrtle Beach from other nearby beach towns such as Windy Hill, Atlantic (South Carolina's black beach), Ocean Drive and Cherry Grove, all of which eventually became North Myrtle Beach. Need-less to say, those forests have long since disappeared. Now the Myrtle Beach oceanfront is mile after endless mile of high-rise hotels and condos. But when we started going there, it was mostly dunes and sea oats with scatterings of summer cottages.

As it turned out, fear would allow me to spend entire summers at Myrtle Beach for the next several years.

The great polio epidemic hit North Carolina hard in 1948 and grew steadily worse in the coming years. Polio struck children primarily (it originally was called infantile paraly-sis), although adults got it, too, the most prominent example being President Franklin Delano Roosevelt. Many of those who got it either died, or were crippled for life, or ended up living for years in huge, gasping, mechanical contrivances called iron lungs. A girl in our neighborhood came down with it and had to use braces. My friend Joe Sink and I carried her up and down the steps at Grimes School every day.

Hospitals exclusively for polio patients sprang up in Greensboro, thirty miles to the east of Lexington, and in Hickory, seventy miles to the west, and nobody with healthy children would even drive past them out of fear that something in the air might infect them. The patients confined inside were quarantined. Not even the youngest children could see their parents. Years later people who worked in those hospitals would say that some of their most searing memories of those days were the plaintive pleas of the youngest children crying for their mothers.

Polio struck in summer and nobody knew what caused it. The theories were many: flies, mosquitoes, water, close association with other children. As a result, swimming pools closed; movie theaters would not sell tickets to anybody under the age of sixteen; Sunday school classes were cancelled. Parents isolated their children to protect them, and mine were no different. I wasn't allowed to go anywhere that other children might be. I've never liked summer as much as the other seasons, and I suspect that all of this may have had something to do with that.

To make matters even worse, one North Carolina doctor theorized that polio was caused by too many sweets. Within hours, children all across the state were deprived of candy, cookies, ice cream, soft drinks, chocolate cake and banana pudding. Not a popular guy with children, this doctor.

For some reason, the disease was less prevalent along the coast. One reason Dad built the beach house, I think, was because of the polio epidemic. Mom and Dad decided that Tim and I should spend our summers at the house until the crisis passed. Myrtle Beach became my buffer against polio until I was in high school. I couldn't have been more pleased. We even were allowed sweets there.

By the time we moved into the beach house, Tim was

sixteen and had been driving for nearly a year (drivers could be licensed at fifteen in North Carolina then). He had a 1931 A-Model Ford roadster painted bright yellow, a pretty snazzy car, except for a couple of minor details. For one, it had a top speed of only about forty-five miles per hour. Tim had a sign on the back that said, "Don't Pass, Push." The other was that the car used more oil than gas. We'd pull into a service station and say, "Fill up the oil and check the gas." Wherever we went, we left a trail of smoke, like one of those sky-writing airplanes, announcing, "Here come the Timberlake boys."

Most teenage boys run with packs their age and don't want kid brothers tagging along. But Tim wasn't like that. He took me everywhere, and we did lots of things together.

After he started going out with Teenie Redwine, who was the daughter of our family doctor, and who later would become his wife, he even took me on some of their dates. I don't think Teen has forgiven me for that to this day. It must have been bad enough for her having to ride around in a slow-poking smoke machine without having to put up with me, too, but there I was. If they wanted to steal a little kiss, or whisper a sweet nothing, she'd just throw a blanket over my head. One time I had to ride most of the way to the beach with a blanket over my head.

Tim was always mature and responsible. Our parents trusted him completely and gave us free rein. Because of our mutual love of the outdoors, Tim and I had an especially good time at the beach. We swam and fished in the surf, gigged flounder in the shallows of the sounds, dug clams and gathered oysters (oh, the seafood dinners we had!). We hunted quail and doves in the farm fields west of town, and ducks along the nearby Intracoastal Waterway and in the abandoned rice fields behind Brookgreen Gardens, and even along the freshly built fairways of the now famous Dunes Golf Club.

Golf, too, was a part of our beach summers. Myrtle Beach truly is one of the world's great golfing centers, but when we first started going there only a single course existed, Pine Lakes, built in 1927, the birthplace, I believe, of *Sports Illustrated*.

Dad was an avid golfer, and he had played for many years. He had raised money to build the back nine holes of Lexington's Municipal Club course, and the pro there, Dugan Aycock, was one of his best friends. Dad used to take me to the golf course with him, and when I was six or seven, Dugan cut down an old set of clubs to my size and taught me to drive, chip and putt. I loved golf, partly because it made Dad proud of me and gave us something else we could do together.

I got to be good enough at it that when I was nine I played in a junior tournament in Greensboro. I was the only kid there who had two pros following him around. Dugan, who was vice president of the Professional Golfers Association, was my coach. And Skip Alexander was my caddy. Alexander was a tournament pro who was a friend of my father and Aycock. He holds the distinction of having played the finest round of golf ever in North Carolina, scoring fifty-eight in an exhibition match at Lexington Municipal Club against the great South African golfer Bobby Lock, whom Dugan discovered while serving in Italy in World War II and brought back to this country. Lock shot 68, not so bad at any other time. I won my flight that year and again the next. I still have the trophies.

I went on to play for my high school golf team, and I continued playing the game right up until I was about fifty when I quit because I just couldn't make time for it anymore.

The year we moved into our house at Myrtle Beach, a new golf course opened three miles away. It bordered the ocean, and to this day it is the only course that does at

Myrtle Beach. Dad became one of the original members of the Dunes Golf and Beach Club, and he and Tim and I played many happy and satisfying rounds there over the years. Before his death in 1996, Dad was the club's last surviving founding member.

One of Mom and Dad's good friends at the coast was Archibald Rutledge, who, like many of their friends, was a great sportsman. He and Dad hunted together. Rutledge was the poet laureate of South Carolina. He had published seventy books, only twenty-five of them volumes of poems. He had been the runner-up to Robert Frost for the Pulitzer Prize for poetry, had been nominated for the Nobel Prize for literature, and had won dozens of gold medals for his work.

Rutledge taught for thirty-three years in Pennsylvania before returning to his beloved South Carolina Low Country in 1937. He came to save his family plantation, Hampton, on the banks of the broad Santee River near Georgetown, about forty-five miles south of Myrtle Beach.

Like most coastal South Carolina plantations, Hampton had once used slaves to produce rice and indigo, but no crops had grown there for many years. The big house and the plantation's many other structures were disintegrating when Rutledge returned to his boyhood home. By the time I first visited Hampton, Rutledge had beautifully restored it to its former glory, and it was glorious indeed.

The big house was a four-story Georgian mansion with a slate roof and a portico upheld by eight tall white columns, each carved from the trunk of a single cypress tree. It sat amongst great live oaks draped with Spanish moss. It had been built in 1730, mostly of heart black cypress, heart yellow pine, handmade bricks and tabby cement. The great stairway that rose to all four floors inside was constructed of mahogany from logs that came as ballast on ships arriving at Charleston. Most of the furniture was mahogany as well.

The most impressive room was the ballroom, which took up the entire east wing of the house. It was forty-two feet long, with an arched ceiling twenty-eight feet high. The highly polished floor was of heart pine, imperious to termites. Those boards each reached the full length of the room and are thought to be the longest floorboards in any structure in America. The ballroom's walls were raised panels of cypress nearly seven-and-a-half-feet wide, each cut from a single log. Imagine the size of those trees, and imagine cutting them in the swamp and hauling them to the building site with horses and mules to saw those panels from them with hand tools. The huge marble fireplace in the ballroom was inset with scene-bearing tiles from thirteenth-century Italy, and could take logs seven feet wide.

George Washington had warmed himself by that fireplace, as had South Carolina's Revolutionary War hero Francis Marion, the renowned Swamp Fox, who used the house as headquarters for his guerrilla strikes on the British Army. On one of our visits Rutledge showed us a Chippendale arm chair made of ebony that had sat in the living room for 175 years with one arm missing. General Marion had fallen asleep in that chair in front of the fireplace after one of his swamp forays, Rutledge said. British Colonel Banastre Tarleton and a group of his men had surprised him there, and Marion had broken the chair arm in his attempt to get away. He escaped through a secret passage, leaped on his horse at the back of the house, raced to the river, swam across it and disappeared into the swamps where the British didn't dare tread.

His father, Rutledge said, had told him that the chair had never been repaired because it would be sacrilegious to replace something Francis Marion had broken. Rutledge apparently didn't consider the Swamp Fox to be a religious figure. He discovered the missing arm in a closet while restoring the house and fixed the chair.

Rutledge was in his late sixties when I first met him at thirteen or fourteen, and he was an impressive presence himself, instantly memorable, tall and lean, always well-dressed, even while hunting. He was courtly and erudite, yet open, warm and friendly, a true aristocratic country squire.

He was, of course, a great storyteller, and I could have listened to him for hours on end. As one of my grandfathers used to say, "The truth wasn't always in him." But that wasn't bad. It just meant that he wasn't above a tall tale now and then.

I'll never forget a story he told on one of our early visits. I wouldn't dare attempt to retell it with all of his embellishments, drama and eloquence, but here are the bare bones.

He was just a baby, he said, when his parents threw a big party in that grand ballroom. The guests had arrived in splendid carriages, the women begowned, the men spiffy in their finest. An orchestra was playing; everybody was dancing; the party was going great, when there suddenly came a scream and a great clatter and commotion at the back of the ballroom. More cries erupted and people began to flee.

Suddenly, a huge, graying stag stamped onto the dance floor, head down, snorting, his antlers swaying menacingly. Nobody ever had seen such a rack of antlers, and they were covered with gnarled growths and hung with Spanish moss, like the sprawling live oak trees nearby. The guests backed up against the ballroom walls, fear on their faces, the men jumping protectively in front of the women. But nobody dared challenge the massive buck.

He calmly surveyed the room, then started for his target: the cradle in a corner of the ballroom, where the infant Archibald Rutledge lay, attended by his mammy, as the black women who cared for the children of wealthy Southern planters were called at the time. The mammy fainted as the creature approached.

"I didn't know what was going on, of course," Rutledge said, "but I looked up and saw this gigantic beast looming over me, and for some reason I wasn't afraid at all. He lowered his big head to my cradle, and I reached up and grasped those great antlers and held on tight. He lifted me gently, whispered in my ear, tucked me back into my crib, then left as he had come, his mission accomplished."

I was entranced, hanging on every word, but Rutledge said nothing more. That was the end of the story.

"What did he whisper to you?" I blurted.

"The secrets of the forest," Rutledge said gravely, nodding solemnly as he puffed his pipe.

"What are the secrets of the forest?" I asked.

"Son," he replied, "nobody can tell you that. You have to wait for the great stag to seek you out."

If anybody knew the secrets of the forest, I'm sure it was Archibald Rutledge.

Hampton sat in the middle of a vast wilderness bountiful with game ranging from alligators to wild boar, and the big trophy room on the mansion's second floor was proof of it. When I was in my teens, Rutledge invited me to come and hunt at Hampton. I took my friend J.B. Lopp, but for a reason I can't recall, Rutledge wasn't able to go with us. It was a warm December day, and J.B. and I went out into the plantation's overgrown rice fields in quest of ducks. We didn't get any, but on the way back to the house, J.B., who was walking behind me, suddenly threw up his shotgun and fired a blast right past me. I hadn't even seen the monstrous cottonmouth moccasin that was coiled at the edge of the path, its tell-tale white mouth open wide, ready to strike as I passed.

We breathlessly told Rutledge about the close encounter when we got to the house. But our tale paled in the face of the snake stories he could tell. Hampton harbored not only cottonmouths but copperheads, timber rattlers, canebrake rattlers, and the greatest rattlers of all, the eastern diamondbacks. Rutledge once had shot a diamondback eight feet long that weighed twenty-two pounds and had sixteen rattles—and he still had the hide and rattles.

He told several frightening snake stories before inviting us to stay over and go turkey hunting with him the following day. For some reason, we had to get back to Lexington. A week or so later, I got a letter from Rutledge, which I still have, saying he had shot a twenty-one pound turkey the next day. And not many months after that I saw a story he had written and a photo of that turkey in *Outdoor Life*. I've kicked myself many times since for not staying another day. I had to wait another thirty-five years before I got my first turkey.

Myrtle Beach was primarily a vacation haven for the people of the Carolinas when Dad built our house there. By the time the '50s arrived, it had become a mecca for the young. A graduation trip to Myrtle Beach was almost a requisite for high school students in the Carolinas. Some got jobs and stayed for the whole summer. Others came as often as they could. And a whole new youth culture developed at Myrtle Beach and Ocean Drive that reverberates to this day.

These young people, all white and mostly middle and lower class, embraced the rhythm-and-blues music of the black honky tonks of the Carolinas. That evolved into a new entity called "beach music." This music was distinctively different from the later so-called beach music of California, as exemplified by the Beach Boys. It was get-down and earthy. And it spawned a new dance that would come to be called "shagging." Those who were truly creative at it, and their numbers were remarkably many, were a wonder to watch. I'll never forget the first time I saw couples doing the "dirty shag," which was a far more suggestive version of the same dance, at the Pad about 1955.

I was captivated by the music, and I loved to watch the dancing, but a distinct deficiency of rhythm combined with more than a little clumsiness kept me from becoming a shagger myself.

I was particularly taken by the fashion styles of that period, however. For girls it was remarkably dull and unsexy: calve-length skirts with bobby socks and saddle oxfords. But for boys it was much more dramatic and peacock-like. They wore their shirt collars turned up. Many greased their hair and combed it dramatically back into what we called "duck tails." They wore penny loafers, and their trousers were truly a marvel. They were called "pegged pants." These trousers were of the most wondrous colors, yellow, orange, violet and pink. They had welted seams and all the pockets, front and back, were scalloped. The leg openings were so tiny that it seemed impossible that some of the wearers could have wriggled such big feet through them. They surely must have had seamstresses standing by to tack them shut after they donned their pants.

By the time I was thirteen, I was wearing shirts with my collar turned up and pants that took me half a day to get in and out of, so gaudy that any light reflected from them surely would have served as a warning to ships far at sea. I thought I was the coolest cat at the beach. Thank goodness, no photos of me at that stage survive.

Although those fashions blessedly passed, the phenomenon of beach music and shagging has proven to be remarkably enduring. Half a century later, there are radio stations in the Carolinas that specialize in beach music and clubs that have shagging competitions. Regular—and huge—reunions of the old shaggers are still held at Myrtle Beach and Ocean Drive, usually called O.D. by the in-crowd. Albeit, the dancing is a little more arthritically creaky now and the odor of linament sometimes overwhelms the sour smell of the beer, but the oldtimers shag on, and may they ever.

I don't think Mom and Dad ever shagged, but they loved dancing as few others ever have. Theirs were the dances from the Roaring Twenties—the Charleston, the jitterbug, the Lindy hop, and others that followed in the Big Band Era. During my childhood, they attended the Saturday night dances at the Lexington Municipal Club for many years but they rarely got to dance. That was because Dad was the drummer in the band. On the front of the big bass drum, he'd had painted, "Shimmy and Shake with Timberlake."

Many years later, after my mother had suffered five heart attacks and could no longer climb even a few steps, Mom and Dad went with Kay and me to New York for the opening of one of my shows, as they always did (this would be the last show my mother ever would attend). On the night of the opening, my parents returned to the hotel early. It was late when I got back, and I went by their room to check on them. Nobody was there.

Concerned, I went looking for them. I found them on the dance floor in the hotel ballroom staring lovingly into one another's eyes, and without disturbing them, I left them to dance the night away.

The reward of a thing well done, is to have done it.
—Ralph Waldo Emerson

Chapter 5

It's a wonder I ever got through high school. When I look back at all the things I was doing then, I can't imagine how I even found time to attend classes. My primary focus, I'm sure, wasn't all that different from many other boys my age at that time: cars, football, and girls, or in my case, one particular girl. But those were far from being my only interests. I worked. I remained in the Scouts until I was a junior. I was involved with Sunday School and Youth Fellowship at my church. I prowled with my buddies. I still spent a lot of time hunting and fishing. And I don't think I was ever without a major project demanding seemingly unending hours of my time.

Dad instilled his work ethic in Tim and me. He expected us to work, and we always wanted to. When I was just a little kid, maybe four or so, I remember standing in a chair in the office at the furniture store punching the old adding machine, cranking the handle and thinking I was making money. When I was six, Dad had me and Tim selling used clothes and seconds from the sewing plants on Saturdays in front of an abandoned gas station on Main Street. He always had something for us to do. We were expected to earn our own way and we did.

All through high school I worked some at the furniture

store or the gas company after school or on Saturdays. I even worked at the funeral home, although I never cared much for that business. When I was eight, I was taking a shortcut through the funeral home and unexpectedly came upon a corpse that had just been brought in, the first I'd ever seen. It scared the hound out of me, and I think I even wet my pants. I wouldn't even go back into the building for a long time. In those days, funeral homes operated ambulance services, and I occasionally drove an ambulance in high school, but only to take people back and forth from the hospital, never on emergency runs. When I spent the summer at the beach, I got part-time jobs there. One summer, my buddy Hal "Skeets" Bellamy and I worked at the Myrtle Beach Pavilion. I rented umbrellas and pulled duty in the bathhouse. The next summer I was a lifeguard.

Dad always encouraged Tim and me to take initiative and do things on our own. We loved High Rock Lake and spent a lot of time there. Dad had land on the lake and we'd tried to get him to build a place there. When he tore down the house on South Main to put up the gas company office, he loaded all the salvageable material from the house onto the furniture delivery truck, hauled it to the lake and dumped it there (a frugal man, Dad; he never wasted anything).

"If you want a lake cabin," he told Tim and me, "build it."

And we did, with help from Ang Lindsey and some of Tim's other buddies. I don't remember the cabin's exact dimensions. It must've been ten or twelve feet by fourteen or so, big enough for two iron, double-decker, army surplus bunks, a table and straight-back chairs. It was a little primitive, I guess. Well, more than a little. We had no running water, but we did dig a pit and build a little outhouse over it. We bathed and washed dishes in the lake.

We put in two windows overlooking the water, and we

got some leftover linoleum from the furniture store for the floor. We flattened cardboard boxes and nailed layers of them to the inside walls to keep out the wind. We had a little Dixie woodstove for heat and ran a flue through a piece of tin out the back wall. A small round oven was built into the flue of the stove. We baked some of the best biscuits in that thing I've ever tasted.

Tim and I, and some of our friends, spent a lot of winter nights at the cabin so we could be duck hunting at dawn. We'd fill up that stove with so much wood that it would be glowing red when we went to bed, but when it came time to get up, the fire would be out and our breath would be freezing in little clouds above our sleeping bags. We'd lie there arguing about whose turn it was to get up and start the fire. Seems to me I lost a lot of those arguments. After all, I was the youngest, and it was supposed to be a privilege for me to be there.

My bare foot would hit that cold linoleum and actually stick to it. I would be hopping around like a frog, certain that I was leaving little patches of skin wherever I landed. Our neighbor across the lake, Lonnie Davis, still tells me that whenever we stayed at the cabin in cold weather, he'd get up several times during the night to look across the water and make sure the cabin wasn't on fire. He was afraid we were going to burn it down with that little heater. He was always concerned that something might happen to some of us on the lake, and he would have a role in it when it finally did happen.

We spent time in that cabin year-round (I sometimes tell people that I've fallen into High Rock Lake in every month of the year), and boy, did we have fun. We ran trot lines for catfish. We seined and set out fish baskets for bream, crappie and bass. We trapped turtles (lots of people in our area ate them; cooters, they called them, and they'd make cooter stew with onions, tomatoes, corn and butterbeans). We gigged frogs and fried up big batches of frog legs (I can taste them still). We hunted ducks and geese. We canoed, boated, water skied, put logs in the water, climbed onto them and rolled them with our bare feet. We built big fires outside and sat around roasting weenies and marshmallows and telling tales. Sometimes Lonnie Davis would come over and tell ghost stories. He could send shivers up your spine telling about the ghost of High Rock Mountain.

A couple of years after we built the cabin, when I was thirteen, Tim went off to the University of North Carolina. After that, the cabin became a hideout for me and my buddies. J.B. Lopp, Punkin Wallace, and Lee Phillips were there often. Johnny Wilson didn't get to come. His mother was afraid for him to be around water. She thought the lake might rise in the night and claim him. It would prove to be premonition.

On January 3, 1954, halfway through my junior year, I drove to Anson County to meet Tim for a goose hunt. I returned home in a windy, misty rain, crossing the Highway 8 bridge at High Rock Lake about 6 p.m. Not until the next morning would I learn that as I was passing over the lake, three of my friends were out there in the icy water, and two of them, Johnny Wilson and Tommy Lopp would not survive. They had been duck hunting with Scott Craven in a boat too small with a motor too large. On their way back to the cabin from which they'd set out, the wind kicked up, the water got rough. The boat swamped and capsized.

My friends were wearing thick hunting clothes, heavy boots, and had knives strapped to their belts. They were far from shore without life jackets. Although overturned, the boat didn't sink and the three clung to it, their only hope for survival. They realized that unless help came soon, hypothermia would kill them. And darkness was descending, making it unlikely that anybody would spot them. Scott decided to try to make it to shore and go for help. He put his arms through a seat cushion that had been thrown free and set out, but darkness and cold water overcame him.

When the three boys didn't show up at home as expected, families became worried and went in search. Lonnie Davis was Tommy's uncle, and he and Tommy's first cousin, J.B. Lopp, my close friend, set out by boat, probing the darkness with spotlights. They saw no sign of the boys' boat but found Scott still alive. He'd managed to reach shore and crawl up on the bank but had gotten no farther. He had stuck his hands in the mud, trying to warm his numb fingers.

Lonnie and J.B. summoned the rescue squad. Scott was taken to the hospital, and many more grim searchers descended on the lake. They came upon the overturned boat later that night. It had drifted almost to the dam. But Johnny and Tommy were not to be found.

I went to the lake with Dad the next morning when we learned what had happened. We took propane tanks to fuel heaters and cooking devices for the searchers. Dad had been one of three founders of the rescue squad. A base camp had been set up, and many volunteers had come to aid in the search. A tent city was springing up at the site while men on the water threw grappling hooks, hoping to snag the bodies.

Drownings were not uncommon at High Rock Lake, and I had seen several, but they usually occurred in warm weather when boaters, swimmers and fishermen were out in force, and the bodies usually were found quickly. I had seen many other searches for drowning victims, both at the lake and the beach, but it was a different and far more sobering experience when the victims were close friends. Not until March when their bodies surfaced were Johnny and Tommy finally found.

Dad had always stressed to Tim and me that we had to respect the water, and he had drilled us in safety procedures. But losing my friends this way made me even more aware of the danger, and even more cautious. To this day,

I never get in a boat without thinking of Johnny and Tommy. Scott, incidentally, recovered quickly from hypothermia. He eventually became a physician, now retired and living in North Carolina's mountains.

When I entered the ninth grade at fourteen, I had to take an industrial arts class, shop, for short. Shop was big in Lexington, a training ground for the town's furniture factories. A lot of boys took it every year and intended to go to work in the factories straight from high school. I had no such intentions, but I did have an interest in woodworking, because it was one of Dad's hobbies. He had a lot of woodworking tools set up in the basement, and whenever he could find any free time, he would be down there making things. Whatnots, he called them. He once made a big batch of bullgrinders—little wooden crank devices that went in circles, accomplishing nothing—and sent one to every member of the South Carolina Legislature. I don't recall what they had done to inspire such largess.

Dad had taught me a little about his tools, enough to use them without cutting off an arm, but the height of my woodworking accomplishment before shop class was using a bandsaw to cut out a rubber band gun to which I attached a clothespin with a small nail. I wanted to learn more.

A young man named A.B. Hardee was the shop teacher. He knew that I drew and painted and enjoyed working with wood and tools, and he took a special interest in me from the beginning.

Every student in shop had to have a project for the year. Some made small cedar chests, or bookcases. I was more ambitious. At the urging of Mr. Hardee, I chose to try to replicate an eighteenth-century Pennsylvania Dutch dowry chest that I had seen in a color photo in a magazine. The chest recently had been purchased for $28,000 and was on display in the Abby Aldrich Rockefeller Folk Center in

Williamsburg, Virginia. I'm not sure what attracted me to it, but it was a real work of art, thirty inches high and five feet long, with colorful panels inset in its black lacquer finish.

Mr. Hardee wasn't just encouraging about this grandiose project, he was enthusiastic. At that time, the Ford Motor Company sponsored a national contest for high school industrial arts students. The year before, one of Mr. Hardee's students, Jimmy Shoaf, who now works at my gallery, had won a regional award in it. If I built this thing, he said, I would win the national contest. He was certain of it.

I believed him. Never before had I worked so hard on anything. Hour after hour I labored, not only during class but after school as well. Yet it never seemed like work; I was having too much fun. Older and more experienced guys in shop helped me with it, and I completed construction of the chest in a matter of weeks. The exterior was maple, the interior lined with cedar. There were two drawers in the bottom, separated from the main part by molding. The construction, though, was the simple part. It was the finish that was the challenge.

Five arched and intricately detailed decorative panels had to be set in the chest's black lacquer exterior, two on top and three on the front. I made templates for these before applying coat after coat of lacquer to the chest. More coats of white lacquer set the panels in place. Then I put the designs on stencils and traced them onto the panels. I painted the designs from tiny vials of model airplane paint—dope, we called it, although I never knew why; in actuality it was lacquer, too. I used twenty-four different colors, including gold, but heaven only knows how many tiny vials I went through. Not until years later would I wonder why I didn't try to find out if model airplane dope came in bigger containers. I painted birds and flowers, unicorns and swashbuckling oriental figures on horseback flashing swords. When the panels were done, I had to paint more designs on the black lacquer around them, as well as on the drawers and sides.

When I finally finished the next spring, Mr. Hardee got permission to take the chest to one of the United Furniture Company plants where we sprayed it with coat after coat of sealer, highly polishing and buffing each coat. At the end, you could have looked into that lacquer and combed your hair.

Everybody who saw that chest was impressed with it, and I'll have to say that I was proud of it. Never before had I felt such a genuine sense of accomplishment. The furniture factory helped us crate it so it wouldn't be damaged and we shipped it off to Michigan. After it was gone I tallied the number of hours I'd worked on it: 342.

I don't recall any anxiety about awaiting the results of the contest. I trusted Mr. Hardee and never doubted that I would win. I was at the beach when he called in early July to tell me that indeed I had. He was all excited. I was the first Southerner ever to win a first place national Ford Industrial Arts Award, he said. And we both would get a free trip to Detroit in September for the presentation of the certificate and the hundred dollar prize. On July 12, my picture appeared in the *Lexington Dispatch* for the very first time along with a story about the award.

Mr. Hardee and I flew to Detroit on a Piedmont Airlines DC-3 in late September, the first time I'd ever been in an airplane. After I saw what some of the other winners had accomplished, I began to wonder what I was doing there. I'd just made a chest. My roommate, who was from Ohio, had built a half-scale Mercury automobile engine out of clear plastic—and it ran.

But that wasn't what impressed me most about the trip. That could be found in a postcard I sent to my parents from the Dearborn Inn.

Dear Mom & Dad,

We're having a great time.... It's the finest hotel up here. All we have to do is write a check when we eat no matter how much it is, boy am I eating, steaks three times a day.... We're going out to eat tonight at a big hotel in Detroit and as usual it is on "Henry." The ball is tomorrow night. We will be home Sunday afternoon, so I'll see you then.

Love, Bob

I didn't actually eat steak every meal. In Detroit, I made acquaintance with my first smorgasbord. Never had I seen such a grand, beautiful and tantalizing display of food. I think I had some of everything, even the stuff I didn't recognize. "Henry" was still paying. To this day, a lot of my trips are marked in my mind by the food I ate, especially if it was remarkably good—and if somebody else was paying.

By the time Mr. Hardee and I had gone to Michigan to tour car plants and eat free steaks, I had my own car (I'd started driving at fourteen, which was legal in South Carolina). Appropriately, it was a Ford. I had inherited Tim's old "Don't Pass, Push" Model A. The time and energy that I had devoted to my prize-winning chest the year before I now directed to keeping this smoke bomb mobile. I worked on the engine in the hope of cutting the oil costs and making my whereabouts a little less conspicuous but succeeded only in accomplishing the release of intermittent clouds of smoke instead of a steady stream, something resembling the signals that Indians once sent with campfires and blankets in those old cowboy movies. I could picture people all over town saying, "There goes Bobby Timberlake. What's he trying to say now?" Reconfiguring the gears did allow me to spread the smoke a little faster, but I think it only caused confusion to anybody trying to decipher what message I might be sending.

I was always having to do something to that car, and even when I didn't have to do something to it, I was doing something anyway. Lots of boys in the South at this time were afflicted with this particular car-tinkering disease. Anyway, I worked on that Model A a lot more than I drove it. No matter what I did to it, though, the battery or ignition failed with frustrating regularity and I'd have to push the car to get it started. I used to say that if I hadn't lived on a hill I never would have gotten anywhere. When I did get the engine going, people in the neighborhood complained that it interfered with their TV reception. I don't see how that was possible. It may just have been the noise that bothered them. I did stir a bit of a racket wherever I went.

As fond as I was of that car, about the time I finally got it running good and looking right, I began lavishing my attentions on another.

Any other person probably wouldn't have been attracted to this particular vehicle, probably wouldn't even have noticed it. But I was drawn to it the moment I spotted it. It was a 1931 Plymouth roadster, and it was sitting in the edge of the woods near High Rock Lake, clearly abandoned for many years, long unloved. Weeds and briars grew around it and honeysuckle vines twined through it. It was wrecked and rusted, the front end smashed, the motor and front wheels missing, the windshield shattered, the interior a decaying shambles. Mice, chipmunks and blacksnakes nested inside, along with mud daubers, spiders and various other critters. It was practically a little, self-contained eco-system. But I knew it had potential. It cried out to me. Another project.

The fellow who owned the car couldn't believe his good fortune when I stopped to inquire about it. I think he would have let me have it just for hauling it away, but I paid him thirty dollars.

My friend "Fat Cat" Jack Copley went with me to get it. We backed a boat trailer up to the car, lifted the front end onto the trailer and chained it down. And as critters scattered in every direction, we set out to my house and parked this magnificent find in the driveway, wilting vines still hanging from several parts.

I'll never forget my dad's face when he came home from work and saw what his younger son had dragged in.

"What on earth is that?" he asked.

"It's a car," I said. "Most of one anyway."

"What are you planning to do with it?"

"I'm going to fix it up."

"I hope you don't think that you're going to be doing that in this driveway," he said.

Actually, I hadn't given thought to much more than getting the car home at that point, and I suddenly realized that I should have planned a bit more ahead. Dad suggested that I call Lonnie Smalley. He had known Lonnie a long time. Lonnie's son, Roy, worked at the furniture store. Roy was a big, strapping, friendly guy, extraordinarily strong. He could pick up a heavy sofa as if it were a kitchen stool. Soon after Roy came to work at the store, Dad discovered that he didn't have a driver's license, although he'd tried several times to get one. Being turned down happened often to black folks, Roy explained. Dad would not tolerate that. He took Roy straight to the motor vehicles office, and when they returned, Roy had his license. Ever since, he had been the furniture store's delivery man.

Lonnie lived in a small, country house about a mile off Highway 52, north of the city limits, not far from the facility Dad had built for the gas company's storage tanks. Lonnie must have been about sixty then, a hardworking man, well respected in the community. He had a sort of garage and blacksmith shop in a cluttered, dirt-floored, tin-roofed, unpainted outbuilding beside his house. There he worked on tractors, farm equipment, old trucks and almost anything else mechanical. I had met Lonnie but didn't know him well at the time. That was about to change.

"Sure," Lonnie said, when I called to ask if I might work on the car at his place, "bring it on over."

I don't think he was expecting the sight that presented itself when Fat Cat Jack and I pulled up with that wreck on the back of a boat trailer. He must have had grave doubts about whether I had the skills and perseverance ever to get this pile of junk running again, but if he did he didn't express them.

He just smiled bemusedly at the rusting heap and made a single observation: "Looks like you've got a right smart of work ahead of you."

Indeed I did. And I wouldn't have accomplished it if not for Lonnie. He was a wonderfully tolerant and patient man, smart and amazingly inventive. No matter what problem I ran into, Lonnie could figure it out and guide me through it. He was always willing to help, no matter what else he had to do. He taught me more about metal and mechanics than I ever dreamed I would know. But more than that, he taught me patience. In that, he was my greatest teacher. Over the next seventeen months, I not only came to respect Lonnie immensely but to love him deeply. And when I finally finished that car, Lonnie had as much pride in it—and in me—as I did.

But before I got very deep into that project, my buddies Punkin Wallace, R.B. Smith, Jack White, Stein Smith and I had our final big experience as Boy Scouts. In July 1953, before my junior year in high school, we went off for three weeks to the national jamboree in California. It turned out to be the wildest excursion of our lives. More than twenty Scouts from Lexington attended the jamboree with several scoutmasters as chaperones. We took a train to Atlanta where we boarded another train, a special, that carried 450 southeastern Scouts across the country. A second train carried another 450. I'd read Jack London and I felt like an adventurer heading off on the rails into the great unknown.

That trip proved to be an adventure for certain. I still feel sorry for the scoutmasters who were supposed to try to maintain some semblance of order on that train. They quickly realized the hopelessness of it and just did what they could to make sure the train kept moving and and we didn't end up in jail, or hurt too seriously. But two Scouts would die in falls from these trains, going and coming.

Four hundred and fifty adolescent boys on a train for days on end with nothing to entertain them but their energy and imaginations is a force to be reckoned with, and the result was not exactly one becoming to the Boy Scout image. Punkin and I taught some of the younger boys to play poker and ended up with more than a little of their travel money. We hung out of windows throwing rocks at signs. We created all kinds of bizarre games. We declared war on other cars, sent out spies and guerrilla teams and took captives. There was a lot of yelling and running from car to car. Anytime the train stopped, we made mad dashes to nearby stores for candy and cookies and soft drinks, and sometimes we were racing to get back as the train was pulling away. I can only imagine the relief the scoutmasters must have felt when we finally reached our destination.

Fifty thousand Scouts attended that jamboree on Irvine Ranch at Newport Harbor. Once there, our activities were organized and strictly supervised, but we still had a great time. The Blue Angels, the Navy's precision flying team, put on a show for us. And one of the celebrities who made an appearance was Iron Eyes Cody, who danced around chanting and beating on a drum. I was eager to see him not only because he'd been in so many cowboy movies but because of my childhood interest in all things western. I was high on the bank and far away from the earthen amphitheater stage where he appeared, and he was just a tiny figure in buckskins. But even from that distance, I remember being impressed by his great dignity. In my wildest dreams I couldn't have imagined that one day he and I would be the dearest of friends.

More than forty years later, on a business trip, I would return to the very site of this jamboree, which by then was occupied by a huge shopping mall where furniture and other products bearing my name were being marketed, and where I was to make an appearance. The people who had come to the airport to pick me up asked if I'd ever been in the area. Oh, yes, I said, and told them about the jamboree long ago.

"In fact," I went on, "they put up a bronze plaque somewhere there to commemorate my visit."

I was just joking, of course. But when we reached the mall, we got on an escalator and at the top was a plaque with an image of a Boy Scout on it noting that this had been the site of the jamboree that I had attended.

"See," I said, "there I am."

I don't know who was more flabbergasted, them or me.

That jamboree did provide a lot of adventure for innocent boys from North Carolina. We went sailing off Balboa Island. On the way out we stopped in Colorado and climbed Pike's Peak. And after the jamboree we went to San Francisco and on to Seattle before taking the northern route back.

In San Francisco we rode the trolleys and toured

Chinatown, the most exotic place I'd ever been. We ate fried rice, sweet and sour pork, chop suey, chow mein and other foods I'd never even heard of. Chinese restaurants would be a long time arriving in Lexington.

I had an experience in Chinatown that I thought was highly unusual at the time. Not until much later would I come to consider it quite normal. Punkin and I were strolling down the street, feeling as if we were on another planet, when I heard a voice behind me saying, "Bobby, what in the world are you doing here?"

I turned around to find my distant cousin, "Red" Raper, grinning at me. I was so startled that I never even asked what he was doing there.

I had to make many more trips before I realized that no matter where I went I inevitably would run into some relative, friend, or acquaintance from home. I'm sure that if I ever climbed Mt. Everest, I would claw my way to the top, gasping for oxygen, only to find somebody from Lexington enjoying a picnic on the summit. Most likely barbecue from home.

When I returned from the jamboree, I went immediately back to work on that hapless, thirty-dollar, '31 Plymouth. In the beginning, I'd had no idea even where to start. A close examination soon told me that I wouldn't be fixing up this car so much as building a new one from the bottom up. One thing had been obvious. I had to have a motor. The running gear, too, turned out to be missing. And the frame proved to be so gravely damaged that it was useless.

At Myrtle Beach, I found a wrecked '51 Ford, got the motor and running gear at a steal and hauled it back to Lexington. I found the front end of a Model A frame at one junkyard, the rear part of a '28 Chevy frame at another, and Lonnie assured me that I could fuse them into one with a "little" work.

Neither Lonnie nor I had welding equipment or fancy tools. I cut rivets with a cold chisel, and Lonnie taught me to use the forge to make steel pliable and pound it into place. To this day, I'm amazed that I still have full use of my thumbs and all my fingers, so many times did I cut and whack and burn them. I still have the scars.

Hour after hour, day after day, week after week, month after month, I was at Lonnie's garage after school, at nights and on weekends, and gradually the car began to take form. I finally reached a point where I had a frame with a motor, four wheels and running gear. I had replaced all the wood framing in the body, using Dad's tools in the basement, and I was ready to put the body, minus front fenders, on the frame. It was an exciting moment. Lonnie's son Roy helped me set it in place.

There was just one problem. It didn't fit.

Not by a long shot. I'd mismeasured the frame by a foot.

I wasn't just disappointed and frustrated, I was fit-pitching, door-kicking, crying mad.

"What in the world's wrong with you, boy?" I heard a deep voice suddenly say behind me.

It was Lonnie.

"Look," I yelled, "all this work and the dadgum thing won't fit." I didn't cuss even in high school, and still don't.

"I'm through with it," I told him. "I'm quittin'. I don't ever want to see this piece of junk again."

"Why won't it fit?" Lonnie asked calmly.

"The frame's too blasted long!"

"What would a person need to do if the frame's too long?"

"You'd have to shorten it."

"Well," he said, and handed me a hacksaw, "cut a foot out of it."

With Roy and Lonnie helping, within a few hours we'd cut a foot out of each side of the frame and fused it back together. This time the body fit perfectly.

Like the chest I'd built the year before, assembling the basic car was just the beginning. The glory was in the finish.

I have no idea how many hours I spent pounding, sanding, and melting sticks of lead into the body of that car to eliminate every dent and flaw, but not one was visible when I was done.

My friend Lonnie Davis, J.B.'s uncle, was owner of the Chevrolet place, and he allowed me to paint the car in the body shop after work hours. That was no small job itself. I put thirteen coats of white lacquer on it, polishing every one, just as I'd done with the chest.

I installed a wrap-around windshield that I'd taken from an old boat and put motorcycle fenders over the front wheels. I got some oversized, white-walled ambulance tires from Dad that really looked good with that gleaming white paint job. Then I went to work on the interior, upholstering the two side-by-side seats in red, and covering the entire interior with plush red carpet left over from carpeting our new church.

Anybody who saw that car after I finished knew that it wasn't just special, it was unique. Not until years later would I realize that I had created a work of sculpture in that car, just as I had with the chest earlier, but unlike the chest, which was a copy, the car was an original. Not another like it was to be found anywhere, before or since. It was a genuine hot rod.

By the time I started my senior year, I was driving my new car, and it attracted attention wherever I went—without blowing any smoke at all.

Racing was getting to be a big thing in our part of the country then. Red-clay stock-car racing tracks had sprung up all over, and lots of boys my age tried to emulate the daring race drivers on city streets as well as back roads, sometimes with deadly results. My car looked fast—and it was. It didn't weigh much and it had a lot of power. I could hardly pull up to a stoplight without some would-be Lee Petty or Curtis Turner pulling alongside to challenge me to race. I didn't have anything to prove. The car said it all, and I didn't want to risk damaging it after all the work I'd put into it. I'd just smile and wave them off, no matter what they called me.

Drag racing was also seeping into the area. A track had opened near Burlington about fifty miles to the northeast. One weekend some of my friends talked me into going over there. My buddy Lee Phillips had turned a '32 B Model Ford roadster into a drag car, and he was going to race it. He hauled it to the track on a trailer, and everybody expected him to win. Instead, he had to drop out because somebody sabotaged his carburetor after we got there, leaving him no time to repair it before the race.

Only three other roadsters were running, and my friends began telling me that I had to enter, I guess to uphold Lexington's honor. I had no intention of doing it, but they finally talked me into it. Next thing I knew, I was sitting on the starting line, revving my engine ominously, but it was completely drowned out by the car I was matched against. I don't recall what kind of car it was, I just remember that it had big V-8 heads sticking about a foot out of the side of the hood.

The green flag dropped. I popped the clutch, stomped the accelerator and the front of that little car sat up as if it were about to leap into space. Black smoke was pouring out the back, and for a moment I thought I wasn't going anywhere at all. Suddenly, I jumped way out in front. I couldn't believe it. Was I going to win this thing? What I didn't realize until later was that I had more torque in first gear than my far more experienced opponent. When he hit second, the power created by those big heads sent him roaring past me in such a blur that I thought his wake was going to spin me around. I could hardly see him as he disappeared down the track.

It wasn't until I got back to the staging area that I discovered what had caused all that black smoke at the back of my car. The rear fenders barely cleared those oversized ambulance tires, and when the back of the car sat down at the start, the fenders came in contact with the tires, burning off almost all the rubber. It was a wonder the tires didn't catch fire. They got so hot that they bubbled those thirteen layers of polished white lacquer on the fenders. I not only had to get new tires, I had to remove those fenders and sand and paint them all over again. That gave me my fill of racing.

I couldn't have been happier with my life during my senior year of high school. Not only was I driving the most distinctive car in town, I was dating the cutest girl at Lexington High, and I also was co-captain of the football team. What more could a boy ask?

Kay Musgrave was a year younger. I first took notice of her when I was about twelve or thirteen. She was wearing a kilt and dancing in some kind of program at the Junior Order Home. I didn't get to know her, though, until much later.

Kay had an older sister and a younger brother. Her family lived on Highway 8, south of town (I drove past her house every time I went to High Rock Lake and I was always craning my neck in the hope of catching a glimpse of her). Her father, Clyde, was in charge of maintenance for all the plants of Dixie Furniture Company.

I didn't ask Kay out until the first half of my junior year. We went to a movie. Our second date was at First Methodist Church, where she helped me paint scenery for the Christmas pageant.

By then, of course, I was deep into working on my car and didn't have a lot of time for dating. I did take her to the junior-senior prom that year, but I didn't truly realize just how special she was until I called and asked if she'd like to come to the Chevrolet place one night while I painted my car—and she said yes.

Of course, she came to all the football games during my senior year, and that turned out to be quite a season for Lexington High. I had first gone out for the junior varsity team in the eighth grade but ended up a reserve. I suited up for junior varsity games in the ninth grade but spent most of my time on the bench. The same was true when I went out for the varsity team the next year. But I got to play quite a bit in my junior year.

During my first two years on the varsity team, it was coached by three great coaches, Harold and Carroll Bowen, who were twins, and Vernon Price, called V.G., son of Lexington's police chief. Not long before I joined the team it had made national news because in addition to having twins as coaches, its two best players, Hoyle and Foyle Wagner ("Big Wag" and "Little Wag," they were called) were not only twins but high school All-America players. Twins also were co-captains of the cheerleading squad that year.

After my junior season, the Bowen twins decided to return to teaching, and we got a new coach for my final year on the team.

Preston Mull, whom everybody called Pres, would become one of Lexington's best and most beloved coaches. He wasn't just a great coach, he was a great man, genuinely concerned about his players and their futures. Coach Mull was one of those congenial people who never raised his voice. He called us "gentlemen" and spoke to us as if we were. He believed in hard work, perseverance and never quitting, and he drummed that into us. Most of all, he was patient and fair, and we all respected him immensely. He was a great influence on all of us, and I still feel honored to have played for him and to call him friend. Only recently, a group of his former players gathered to hold a tribute dinner for Coach Mull, and some of the town's most outstanding citizens came forth to tell how he had touched and changed their lives.

That first year, Coach Mull was busy changing the way we played football. We'd run single wing before, but he took us to the split T. We didn't have but about four main plays, but we became one heck of a running team. Our star runner was Scott "Crazy Legs" Craven, who had survived the hunting accident at High Rock Lake that had drowned two of our friends. He danced all over the field and hardly anybody could stop him. We were a big team, in sheer bulk probably the biggest ever at Lexington. We had two huge tackles, the biggest being my buddy Fat Cat Jack Copley, who stood six-three and weighed about 280. My childhood friend Joe Sink played center. He, too, was six-three and about 220. Our fullback, Bob Stafford, who was co-captain with me, was a veritable stump, short and chunky, 210 pounds. Mickey Byrd, the left tackle, stood about six-two and was as strong as an ox. We also had a six-foot-five end, a six-foot-three quarterback and two running backs from the Junior Order Home who would run full speed into a telephone pole if the coach told them to do it, bounce off and keep hitting it until either it, or they, went down. The team must've averaged about 220. I played left guard, and I was one of the runts at five-eleven and 185 pounds. Jack White, my counterpart on the other side of Joe, also was about my size.

We lost only one game that season, to Albemarle, our arch-rivals, and that by a single point. But we got another crack at them in the playoffs for the conference championship at Catawba College in Salisbury at the end of the season. They had a twenty-nine game winning streak, but we broke it. What a moment! We all went wild, the team, the cheerleaders, the band and everybody from Lexington in the stands. I'd never known such exultation.

Without doubt, that was one of the milestones of my life.

The remainder of my senior year was sort of anticlimactic. I'd always known that I'd be going to college, and from the moment I first set foot on the campus of the University of North Carolina in Chapel Hill to visit Tim, I'd fallen in love with the place and knew that was where I'd go, too. Tim had graduated with a degree in business the year before and was off in the Army. But during his four years at Carolina I had gone there often for ball games and to meet Tim and his friends for fishing and hunting trips. Tim and his roommate, Ernie Shore from Winston-Salem, even kept a bird dog in their room for part of the year. I'd sleep on the floor with the dog.

Despite my feelings for Carolina, in the spring, as I was awaiting acceptance, I briefly flirted with the idea of studying architecture at North Carolina State University in Raleigh. I genuinely loved drawing houses and house plans, and I had become enamored with the idea of building when I helped Tim and his buddies build our cabin at High Rock. But Dad's gas company was growing dramatically, and he'd started yet another business, a finance company. As soon as Tim got out of the Army, he was coming home to work for Dad. I knew that I was expected to do the same, and I, too, chose the school of business, majoring in industrial relations.

I knew this might be the last chance I'd ever get to spend the whole summer at the beach and that was where I headed. I saw Kay whenever I could get home, and when I left for Carolina that fall, we made no commitments. She still had a year of high school to go, and I would be away at Chapel Hill, too much strain for a serious relationship. Still, this I knew: As much as I loved Lexington, my family and friends, when I came home it would be mainly to see Kay.

*To get the full value of joy, you must have some-
one to divide it with.*

—Mark Twain

Chapter 6

I learned by example from my family about the importance of the vital connection between picking the right mate
and finding happiness in life. The rule was apparent from
their lives and it was a simple one. Choose well—and only
once. My parents and grandparents had chosen well, and
they had been blessed.

For some, the choice is instinctive, and it seemed that
way in my case. Deep down, I somehow knew from the
first time I saw Kay Musgrave dancing in her little kilt that
she was the one for me. Joining hearts with her certainly
was the right decision, for only she makes me whole. With
her, I feel as if I can accomplish anything. Without her, I'd
be of little use.

But during my first two years at Carolina, circumstances
kept us mostly apart. After graduating from high school,
Kay decided to work for a year to save money for college
and took a job at Lexington State Bank. The following year,
she enrolled at Woman's College in Greensboro. I took her
there at the beginning of the fall semester. We hauled all
her stuff to her dorm room, and after she was settled, we
said goodbye, and I left to start my junior year in Chapel
Hill, fifty miles to the east.

I hadn't gone two blocks before I was seized by an overwhelming sense of loneliness. It was almost as if in leaving Kay there, we were setting ourselves on different paths. It would be four years before she finished college. What if something caused her to change her mind about me? What if she met somebody else?

I thought about it all the way to Chapel Hill, and I knew that I wanted this sweet, smart, adorable girl more than I had ever wanted anything in my life. And I wanted her now. I didn't want to wait four years. I didn't want to wait four *hours*. I couldn't risk the chance of having something come between us. By the time I got to Chapel Hill, I had made a firm decision. I was going to ask Kay to marry me as soon as possible—beg her, if necessary—and pray that she would have me.

One of the first things I did was to call Dad and ask if he could sell my beloved '31 Plymouth roadster (I had another old car that I drove to campus, one with a top on it.).

"I guess so," he said, "but why?"

"I've just outgrown it," I told him. "It's time to sell it."

I didn't want him, or anybody, to know my real plan: to get money to buy an engagement ring.

It didn't take Dad long to sell the car. He got $800 for it. I didn't want to be there to see it go. (Remarkably, after passing through several hands over more than four decades, the car is now owned by a friend of mine, Louis McMillan, who bought it at a car show in Charlotte. We often have breakfast together.)

Tony Schiffman was my friend and fraternity brother, and his father owned a jewelry store in Greensboro. I drove there to buy the ring. I chose a beauty, an oval diamond, but I wanted it in a different setting. When the ring finally was ready, I called Kay and arranged for her to come to Chapel Hill for a football weekend.

I had pledged to Sigma Chi fraternity during my freshman year, and as a sophomore I had been inducted into the Order of the Gimghoul, a secret society that was sort of a fraternity of fraternities. The Gimghouls had a huge stone castle on a hilltop at the edge of the campus. We had parties there in the great hall after football games and often had well-known singers and musicians to perform for them.

Don't ask me who Carolina was playing that Saturday, or who won, for my mind was on only one thing that day, and it wasn't football. I used a ruse to get Kay away from the game early. I told her that I had to raise the flag over the castle turret before the party. I just wanted to get her on the turret before anybody else got there. I knew it would be a memorable place for what I had planned. Surely few people other than princesses get marriage proposals on castle turrets, and Kay was my princess. I slipped the ring from my pocket as we stepped out onto the turret to take in the view.

"I've got something to show you," I said.

She turned and saw the ring—I clearly had surprised her—and before she could say anything, I said, "I also have a question. Would you please marry me?"

To my immense and everlasting relief and gratification, she looked up at me with tears in her eyes and said yes. It was a magnificent moment, surpassed only by the moment we spoke our vows at First Methodist Church in Lexington only weeks later on December 20, 1957, the day after classes ended for the semester. My long-time minister and hunting companion Howard Wilkinson had left our church a few years earlier to be the chaplain at Duke University (he later would become president of Greensboro College), but he came back to perform our service, just as eventually he would return to marry all of our children.

Kay and I went to my parents' house at Myrtle Beach for a short honeymoon and returned home to be with our families for Christmas. Both of us treasured those traditions. What a Christmas!

Kay decided not to return to college. We got a two-bedroom apartment on the second floor of a new, eight-unit cinderblock building on Davey Circle in Chapel Hill that soon would fill with young married students, most of them our friends. Tony Schiffman and his wife, Madelyn, moved in beneath us. Kay got a job in the admissions office at the university to help pay the bills. I had been working part-time for my dad while I'd been in Chapel Hill. He'd opened a branch of the gas company in nearby Durham and another in Roxboro in Person County, where all of our Timberlake ancestors had come from, and I had worked out of both. Because I now needed more money, I had to increase my work load.

I was in Navy R.O.T.C. and had been getting a check for $30 a month for that. My commander had been Dad's roommate at the naval academy. I soon discovered that married men were not allowed to remain in R.O.T.C., and I had to resign. That cut our income slightly but gave me more time to work and increase our earnings.

Despite all the time I had to devote to work and study, we still had great fun in Chapel Hill. Maybe it just seemed that way because we were young and so happy to be together. But we made friends who would remain our friends for life. We got together often and went to the beach on weekends. We had the best of times.

I went to summer school full-time after my junior year so that I could graduate earlier. The fall brought wonderful news. Kay was pregnant. We were overjoyed, as were our parents, but my joy was somewhat dampened by concern about my studies.

I was taking a course in statistics, and I hated it. I had to have at least a C in the class to graduate, however. And as the end of the semester neared, I realized that my chances for a C were questionable. Before the final exams, I went to see the professor and bared my soul. I told him that my wife was pregnant, that I would be leaving Carolina for good at the end of the semester, and that only a C in the course would grant me my degree, which would mean so much to me, because if I didn't get it, my family would be devastated.

I wasn't attempting to make him feel guilty, you understand, only trying to get him to see the situation. Nonetheless, it was with great trepidation that I went by his office after the grades were finally posted. When I saw that C by my name I not only could have danced out of the building but all the way to Davidson County.

Neither Kay nor I ever questioned that we would return to Lexington. We didn't even discuss it. Kay wanted to be near her family and Dad was counting on me, just as he had with Tim. I was eager to get back, get started at work and move on with life. And that was what we did.

We rented a little, two-bedroom, white house on Beckner Street and moved into it in January. I went to work for Dad immediately.

One thing that Dad had made clear to Tim and me was that he did not want us involved with the funeral home. Although it was a highly successful and lucrative business, it simply was too demanding, he said, requiring too much time away from family and important events. This, we realized, was his way of telling us that he regretted not spending more time with us when we were younger. We both knew, though, that that had been a different era, and he had done what he had to do to provide for us then and bring us to this point. But some things are just understood and never spoken. He knew that we never doubted his love, nor did he ever doubt ours for him.

Tim had returned home from the Army two years earlier and had been running the gas company's biggest branch in Winston-Salem. As my first job, I was given the sad task of closing out Piedmont Furniture. As Dad had gotten more involved with his other businesses, the furniture store had begun to decline, demanding more and more of his time and producing less and less return. Seeing it closed was especially hard for my grandmother Timberlake, Gangy. It had been our family's financial base, and my grandfather had taken such pride in it. But before I could complete this unhappy assignment, our family had new reason for joy.

On May 14, 1959, Kay gave birth to our first child at Lexington Memorial Hospital, a daughter we would name Robin Kelly. She was delivered by Dan Redwine, our doctor. who'd always seemed like family and now truly was as Tim's father-in-law. In those days, unlike the custom now, fathers weren't allowed in the delivery room. But Kay underwent twenty-three hours of labor and I was with her until they took her to delivery. I endured my anxiety in her room until Dr. Dan came to tell me that we had a beautiful daughter. I was allowed my first glimpse of her through the nursery window.

The nursery was presided over by a big, jovial black woman with a tremendous sense of humor and a resounding laugh. She was named Smith and was known to almost everybody in town as Smitty. Everybody loved her. She'd talked my dad into donating rocking chairs to the nursery. She loved the babies, and she'd rocked and sung lullabies to almost all the children in Lexington. She saw me waving at the window after I got the news and went immediately to fetch a baby from its crib. She cradled it in one massive arm, then stopped at a second crib and got another. *What is this?* I thought. Nobody had said anything about twins. She backed up to the window and grinning broadly pulled back the blankets to reveal one black baby and another alarmingly red little girl.

"Which one?" she mouthed into the glass.

"I'll take both," I mouthed back, and she erupted in uproarious laughter.

Mom started crying as soon as I called to tell her that we had a little girl and that she was stunningly beautiful, even if she was a trifle red for the time being. Tim had already given my parents a grandson and two granddaughters, and Mom greeted each with tears of joy.

I finished closing down the furniture store that summer, and early in the fall I replaced Tim in the Winston-Salem office. He returned to Lexington to work in the main office. I commuted the thirty miles back and forth every day in one of the company trucks. Kay and I never considered living in Winston-Salem. We were already planning our own house in Lexington. I designed it, and Kay's grandfather, Dan Musgrave, agreed to build it for us on a lot on Rosewood Drive that Gangy gave us.

The house was built from 200-year-old brick that I salvaged from Old Salem, the Moravian settlement that predated the adjoining town of Winston. Every day after work I drove by Old Salem, loaded 500 bricks onto the company truck and hauled them to our lot.

We moved into our new home in May of 1960. It was a ranch-style house with a broad front porch and three bedrooms. I had to take out a mortgage for $24,000, and I wondered if I'd ever be able to pay it off. I was making less than $11,000 a year at the time.

Kay wasn't working. She was taking care of Kelly, and she was pregnant again. Our son, Ed, Roberts Edgar Timberlake Jr., was born on January 18, 1961, delivered by Dr. Redwine. Our second son, Dan, Daniel Lee Timberlake, also issued into this world by Dr. Redwine and named for him and Kay's grandfather, Daniel Christopher Musgrave, followed his brother by two years, two months and two days. My grandmother Timberlake took special joy in Dan's birth. She was suffering from colon cancer, and she was determined to live to hold Dan in her arms, as she had held all her other grandchildren. She died three months after Dan's birth. Grandmother Raper was then an invalid, confined to bed. She would live another eight years, until April 5, 1971, and her death would be followed two days later by the death of her son Bill. We would hold a double funeral for them.

In just over five years, I had gone from being a more or less carefree college student to being a family man with three children, a mortgage and a responsible job. And I couldn't have been happier. I loved my wife, I loved my children, I loved my new house, and I loved my job.

I was settled in my life, perfectly content. I wanted it to go on just as it was, and I couldn't foresee it changing barring some unexpected disaster. I just hadn't counted on a magazine article that would set me on a whole new path.

The drop of rain maketh a hole in the stone, not by violence, but by oft falling.

—Hugh Latimer

Chapter 7

Although I knew in my very bones that nothing would be the same after the *Life* magazine article on Andrew Wyeth caused me to take up painting again, I still had no idea how my life was going to be different, how long the change might take to show itself, or what I should be doing, if anything, to bring it about. I just felt compelled to keep painting.

At that time, many North Carolina farmers were switching from the traditional way of curing tobacco in log barns with wood fires and turning to gas burners, and I was extraordinarily busy at work. I would spend the day tramping around the countryside, installing curing units and propane tanks, and come home dead tired, but I still couldn't wait to get down to the basement with my watercolors and easel.

I painted dolls for Kelly, cute little scenes for the boys' room, almost anything else that caught my eye. I even started copying other painters again, although I never had the nerve to take on Wyeth. I didn't realize it then, but I was simply reviving techniques I'd picked up as a child and trying to enhance them.

In effect, I was teaching myself to paint without any true knowledge of how it should be done, or why I was doing it. I didn't have a goal. I was just having fun. But I was learning more every day, and not only from my painting. I was reading articles about painters and the art world and checking art books out of the library. I started going to all the nearby art exhibits that I heard about, most of them showing the work of amateurs and hobbyists.

One of Lexington's best known amateur painters was A.S. "Stuffer" Myers. I'd known Stuffer all of my life. He was in his sixties and he ran an auto parts store. I'd bought many parts from him when I was working on that '31 Plymouth. He decorated his store with his own paintings. He was primarily a watercolorist (later he would organize the North Carolina Watercolor Society, of which I would be a founding director) and he painted local scenes, flowers and butterflies. He sold art supplies with the auto parts. He loved to talk about painting, and he was a great teacher. I'd go by to pick up a few supplies and we'd have long conversations about art. Now and then I'd take a painting to show him and get his advice. He was always excited and encouraging about whatever I was doing.

Stuffer arranged for a professional artist from Charlotte, John Brady, to hold a series of lectures at the YMCA, and I signed up for it.

Brady was adept in many fields of art. One week he'd talk about painting with oils and demonstrate techniques. Next week it might be watercolors, or pastels, or glazes, or gilding. We would bring our own efforts for critiques, and whenever I brought in a painting, he got excited about it and singled it out for praise.

He took a distinct interest in what I was doing, and his appraisals gave me confidence. Whenever I'd shown my paintings to family or friends, they always were complimentary. They'd say things like, "Why, that looks real," or, "Bob, that's really good, you should try to do something with those." I expected them to say such things. But this was a guy who knew enough about painting to lecture on it. His opinion carried weight.

Davidson County had an art guild, made up mostly of people from Lexington, and it occasionally held exhibits at furniture showrooms, Belk's Department Store, and other places. I entered a couple of paintings, and when I learned that people actually wanted to buy them and were willing to pay as much as $35 for one, I was immensely pleased and impressed.

It embarrassed me to put a price on paintings, and more often than not, I gave them away. If some friend or family member said that he or she liked one, I'd say, "Here, take it." Or, "Just pay me for the frame."

People would say, "How can you part with that after all the work you put into it?" But I wanted to share it. I was doing it so people could enjoy it.

The restored Moravian village of Old Salem attracts a lot of tourists to Winston-Salem. I love the place. My parents took me there often as a child. Salem College, which my grandmother, mother and daughter attended, is there. So is the wonderful, wood-fired Moravian bakery with its magnetic aromas. I often prowled in Old Salem when I was working in Winston-Salem.

After I took up painting again with a fervor, I discovered an art gallery in the old bank building in Old Salem. Ironically for such a historic spot, it was called the Gallery of Contemporary Art. It must have been early in 1967 when I first dropped in. I was thirty, and it was the first time I'd ever set foot in an art gallery.

I started going by frequently after that, and emboldened by the reaction I was getting to my work in Lexington, I asked one of the volunteers, Lucy Wilson, how a person might go about getting a painting displayed there.

"We have juried shows," she told me. "Anybody can enter."

In fact, the deadline for one was coming up. I got some paintings together for it but got there one day too late. Sorry, Lucy told me, but rules are rules. I'd have to wait a year for the next show.

Later, Lucy and I became good friends, and we often talked about how things might have been different if I'd gotten those paintings there on time. My work wasn't very well developed then. What if I'd been rejected? How would that have affected me?

As it was, my work was far better by the time the next show came around. Not only were my paintings accepted but they sold quickly.

By then, I'd made the acquaintance of Ted Potter, who had just become the gallery's first paid director. I often stopped by to chat with him, and I learned a lot about the art business from him. We began to talk about holding a realist show, and I, of course, encouraged it vigorously because it would be another show in which I could get my paintings exhibited.

Another event in 1968, one of sheerest happenstance, or so it seemed at the time, turned out to be crucial to my future. Somewhere Mom read a brief article about an upcoming event to raise money for an art museum in an old grist mill on the Brandywine River in Chadds Ford, Pennsylvania. The Brandywine River country had been the home of many famous artists, prominent among them the great illustrator Howard Pyle, his student Newell C. Wyeth, and, of course, Wyeth's son, Andrew, who lived at Chadds Ford. The event was to feature an exhibit of Andrew Wyeth's paintings. Mom knew that I admired Wyeth, and she mentioned to Kay that maybe we ought to go up to see the show.

I couldn't have agreed any quicker when Kay told me about Mom's suggestion. I'd never seen a Wyeth original, of course, and I got more and more excited as the date for the trip grew nearer.

Work was just beginning on restoring the old mill. It still was in rough shape. Not for three more years would the museum officially open. But an area had been fixed up for the show.

I was absolutely overwhelmed when I walked into that building and saw those paintings for the first time. They literally took my breath away. At one point, I got emotional and had to go outside. I was wandering around the parking lot, trying to get hold of myself and understand how those paintings could have set off such feelings in me, when I noticed a fellow in a chauffeur's uniform standing beside a big Cadillac. I don't know why I went up to him, but I did. We started chatting, just passing time. It was calming for me.

It turned out he was the chauffeur for Henry T. du Pont, who had come for the show. I told him I was from North Carolina, and he said that he passed through a couple of times a year, driving the du Ponts back and forth to Florida. We got to talking about good places to eat in North Carolina, and one thing and another. Our conversation was interrupted when a stately woman approached to greet the chauffeur, an acquaintance of hers. I recognized her immediately. I'd just seen her portrait inside. Her name was Margaret Handy. She was a pediatrician, and she had been the doctor to the Wyeth children. She was eighty-one, still practicing, and was legendary in the area.

I introduced myself and told her what a terrific painting Wyeth had done of her. It was called "The Children's Doctor," and it showed her in a heavy coat on a wintry night, arriving to treat a sick child, no doubt one of Wyeth's sons, Nicky or Jamie, and then again as she was leaving. I had stood before it for the longest time, studying the textures. You could actually see the veins beneath her skin.

"Thank you," she said, "but that was twenty years ago."

"But it's great," I said.

I went on and on about it, just gushing.

"He wants to paint me again," she told me.

"That's wonderful."

"Oh, it would just be a lot of trouble," she replied dismissively. "You have to sit there for hours, and he talks all the time."

"But you've got to," I told her. "It'll make you immortal."

"I don't think so."

"I can't believe you're saying that," I said, getting the feeling that she was quickly tiring of me and my enthusiasm.

"Well, I'm still thinking about it," she said. "He wants to paint me in the nude."

That shut me up in a second.

By then, Kay and my parents had missed me and come in search. I introduced them to Dr. Handy and to the chauffeur. Kay and Mom started talking with Dr. Handy while Dad and I chatted with the chauffeur, and they must have told her that I was an aspiring painter, because she soon turned to me and said, "You know, I have a lot better paintings at home than that portrait of me. Why don't you come on up to the house and I'll let you see them."

She lived not half a mile away in a reproduction of an old Pennsylvania stone house that sat just a couple of hundred feet behind Andrew Wyeth's studio, the small house where he and his wife Betsy had lived earlier in their marriage. She'd been away in Maine for the summer and had stopped by the museum before going home. I helped her disconnect the alarm system before she could unlock the door. The house was dark, dusty and musty, but she started flicking on lights, pulling covers off furniture. She apologized that she couldn't even offer us a drink, but what she could offer was a treasure. Her house was a virtual art museum. She owned some very famous paintings, not only by Andrew Wyeth, but by his father, his son, Jamie, and by Howard Pyle and other artists from the region.

She kept pulling original paintings out of closets and from behind her desk. She brought out a watercolor board on which Andrew Wyeth had painted studies of a premature baby she had delivered and treated, and I will never forget how much the baby's eye looked like a chicken's.

By the time we left Dr. Handy's house that day, I felt as if I'd known her all my life, and I knew that we had begun a lasting friendship.

The trip to Chadds Ford affected me even more powerfully than the *Life* article nearly three years earlier. Seeing Wyeth's originals was the most energizing event of my life. I had examined each painting closely, hoping to absorb Wyeth's techniques, scrutinizing each for perspective as well. Why did he choose this subject? Why did he paint it from this angle? Why with this light? What gave it such depth of feeling?

I couldn't wait to get back home to my paints and brushes, and when I did I flung myself into painting with an intensity that verged on compulsion. The problem was that I had almost no time to give to it.

I was busier than ever at the gas company, where in addition to dealing with a steady increase in business I was attempting to do some innovative things and had several projects underway. I was experimenting with gas air conditioning for the Whirlpool folks. I was converting forklifts to run on propane, and I was doing the same to a 1968 Buick I bought. I had gotten to know some local artisans and was working with them. I set up a gas kiln for my friend Clyde Gobble, an insurance agent who decided he wanted become a potter (and is now a very successful one). I set up a gas furnace for John Nygren in Walnut Cove, who is now one of the most respected glass blowers in the country.

Beyond that, I was a vice president of the gas company and the funeral home, and Tim and I had started three new businesses of our own. We were buying and selling real estate through The Land Company. Through another company we were constructing rental properties and building and selling cottages of my own design at High Rock Lake. A third company financed appliances. It seemed that I was always running hither and yon just trying to keep up with what had to be done at the moment.

All of that left me with little time even to fulfill my family responsibilities, much less to indulge a hobby that was overwhelming my senses. I had come home from Chadds Ford with a whole new vision, all fired up to paint, and the only way I could do it was to rob time from something else.

Still I did it. Sometimes I would paint until well after midnight and be resentful that I had to stop so I could get a few hours of sleep before I had to get up and go to work again. The result was fatigue, frustration, and tension unlike any I'd ever known. Yet I couldn't stop painting. I began to wonder what was more important to me, my work or my painting. And the answer that kept presenting itself was more than a little disconcerting. My work was just that. Painting was a passion.

More and more I realized that what I really wanted to do was paint. Yet I had never known anybody who actually made a living as an artist. I knew that it was possible for a few exceptionally gifted people such as Wyeth. But I was far from being in his league. I had sold only a handful of paintings, and the most that any had brought was $200. I wasn't even sure if I had a genuine talent.

Dreams don't die easily, though, no matter the realities. What I had to recognize was that the dream of being a professional painter was not only imbedded in my mind, it was growing daily. A quote I'd heard in Sunday school kept repeating itself to me: "A dream unexpressed is only an illusion." When I finally began to acknowledge my dream, I had to face the realities. I had a wife and three children that I loved above all else, and they came first, no matter my desires. I had to support them. I had obligations to Dad and to Tim. I couldn't let them down. I couldn't just drop everything and start painting and hope that it all worked out.

The pressure from this conflict grew daily until it was almost explosive. It kept eating away at me, and for the first time in my life, I didn't know what to do, or where to turn.

Then came a night when I suddenly realized that I couldn't go on like this. I was in real trouble, and I had to do something about it.

That was early in February, 1969, and on that night I had slipped down to my basement garret after supper, hoping to paint. I soon heard my son, Dan, tramping down the steps, calling for me. He was only five. I don't know what he wanted. Maybe to play. Maybe just to get a little attention from his daddy. But before I even knew what I was doing, I had snapped at him in frustration.

"Can't I have just one hour to myself? Leave me alone!"

I'll never forget the look on his face. The surprise. The hurt. He didn't say a word. He just turned around and walked back up the steps. That hit me like a blow from a sledgehammer. I sat there asking myself, "What have you done? What is happening to you?"

This thing that had been growing like a tumor had bothered only me until that point, but now it was affecting my family. I could not allow that. I knew that I had to do something. But what?

I wrestled with that question through a fretful night. And it worried me through the following day at work.

Talking with someone about what was going on within me was not an option. I'd always believed that you solve your own problems; you don't burden others with them. Besides, I didn't know who to talk to.

Although Kay had to have suspected that something was bothering me, I especially didn't want to drag her into my turmoil. We had a comfortable, settled life. A happy life until this point. We were living out our dream. I couldn't selfishly allow my personal yearning to threaten that. What would I say to her? *"Hey, I've decided I want to be an artist. I'm going to quit work and start painting. We'll just have to get by the best we can."* I was afraid she'd think that I'd gone crazy.

And I certainly couldn't talk to Dad. He had worked so hard to build a future for Tim and me, and now that we had it how could I tell him that I wanted to walk away from it? Even my mother, who'd always encouraged me in anything I'd undertaken, hadn't seen art as more than an avocation for me, something to fill my idle hours and keep me content, as she always wanted her family to be.

Maybe she was right. Maybe a hobby was all that painting ever could be for me. I had no idea what level of talent I had, if any. What if I couldn't live up to this dream that was nearly devouring me? What if I attempted it and failed?

All of this was going over and over in my mind as I drove home from work that day, and it was making me nearly distraught, almost physically ill. That was when it hit me. What do you do when you're sick? You call a doctor. And I knew only one doctor who might actually be able to help me, only one who knew anything at all about art. Dr. Handy in Chadds Ford.

When I got home, Tim's mother-in-law, Hazel Redwine, was visiting. She and Kay were talking and laughing with the kids in the kitchen. I came in the back door and walked right past them without saying a word. I went into the bedroom, closed the door, found Dr. Handy's number and dialed it.

I had written to thank Dr. Handy after our visit in August, had spoken to her once by phone since. Surely, she must have been surprised hearing from me now. I apologized for bothering her and explained that I was having a real crisis and that she was the only person I could think to turn to. I poured out my heart, all my uncertainties and worries, everything that was disturbing me and causing so much distress.

"I just don't know what to do," I told her. "I guess what I want is for somebody to tell me if I've got any real talent or not. I know I've got to do something."

She was silent for a moment. "Well," she said, "why don't you call Andy? He would be a bigger help than I can be."

Andy. It sounded so casual, so open and friendly. But she meant *Andrew Wyeth*.

Such a thought never would have crossed my mind. I wouldn't have dared think it. I never could have summoned the audacity to intrude on a man who was such a majestic figure to me. You don't just ring up the king and ask favors.

"They're at home," she was saying. "I was just talking to Betsy. Let me give you their number."

Only naivete and my deep need for resolution to this situation could have caused me to dial that number without even hanging up the receiver after talking with Dr. Handy, but that was what I did.

A man answered, and I suddenly was so nervous that I could barely speak.

"Is this Mr. Wyeth?" I asked uncertainly.

"It is."

From that point, I can't be sure what I said. I know that I introduced myself, told him where I was from and that I admired his work. And I must have told him that I was having this dilemma about painting, and that Dr. Handy had suggested that I call. I don't know if I asked if he would consider meeting with me, or looking at my paintings, or what, but I do remember him saying, "When can you come up?"

"I could come anytime," I blurted, but I wanted to pin him down as quickly as possible. "How about next week? I think I could drive up Tuesday."

"That's fine. Just call when you get here."

And that was that. I suddenly was standing in my bedroom in stunned disbelief, the phone receiver still in my hand. I'm not sure how long I stood there, but my disbelief must have been showing when I walked back into the kitchen, because Kay and Hazel stopped talking and looked at me with concern.

"You won't believe what I just did," I said. "I called Andrew Wyeth, and he's invited me to come to see him."

"When?" Kay asked.

"Tuesday."

"Next Tuesday?"

"Yes. Do you want to go?"

Tuesday was a school day, she reminded.

"Why don't you see if your dad can go with you?" she suggested.

Five days later, Dad and I were headed toward Chadds Ford with a half dozen of my paintings in the back of the station wagon.

Go confidently in the direction of your dreams! Live the life you've imagined.

—Henry David Thoreau

Chapter 8

Shortly after my father's death at almost ninety-one in 1996, I went to the house on Hillcrest Drive where I had grown up. It seemed empty with both my parents gone. In their bedroom, I opened a dresser drawer. I can't remember now why I was there or what I was looking for. Maybe I was just trying to salve my sadness with the touch of familiar objects from happier times.

A little ten-cent Blue Horse notebook caught my eye. Dad was always carrying these pads around, keeping notes on things he needed to remember. Usually, though, he tossed them away after they'd served their purpose. But this one had been set aside, as if it had some special meaning. I picked it up and opened it to his familiar handwriting. I needed only see the date at the top of the first page, February 11, 1969, to know why he had kept this one. It was his record of our trip to see Andrew Wyeth.

Dad had set down all the details. We left home at nine that morning, stopped at an antique shop in Oxford where I bought some interesting old bottles, had lunch at a restaurant in Petersburg, Virginia, where we'd eaten before. The sky was overcast with high, lazy clouds, and we saw our first snow on the ground at Alexandria, just little patches here and there. The patches grew larger as we passed by Washington, and it excited Dad because he loved snow as much as I do. But by the time we'd reached Baltimore the snow had disappeared.

I hadn't remembered these incidentals because I was too filled with trepidation and nervous energy, my mind racing with questions. What would Wyeth be like? What would I say to him? How would he react? I kept making up little speeches to deliver to him, then dismissing them.

I had pretty much decided that whatever he told me was what I was going to do. If he encouraged me at all, I would find a way to become a painter. But if he told me I had a talent that was little different from thousands of others, I planned to put this thing out of mind, throw out the brushes and the palette, go back to the good life that I'd been living before this dream had seized and shaken me. As we grew closer to Chadds Ford, I'd almost convinced myself to expect that. I almost wanted it.

We arrived about 6:30 and stopped first at the Chadds Ford Inn for supper. We'd eaten there the previous summer and had loved the food. After ordering, I slipped off to a telephone under a stairway and called Wyeth to let him know I'd arrived.

"Can you come on out now?" he asked, catching me off-guard. I hadn't expected to see him until the next day.

"Well, I'm at the Chadds Ford Inn with my father, and we've just ordered supper."

"Come on out about eight then," he said, pushing my tension level up several notches.

After eating ("Had roast beef," Dad wrote in his notebook. "Food delicious."), I drove to the Longwood Motel in nearby Longwood, checked in, got Dad settled into room number eight, then went on to the Wyeths'. Dad had told me that he didn't want to go along, because he might somehow interfere with the visit.

"Bob...is so happy about coming on this trip and now that Andrew Wyeth has invited him to his home tonight," he wrote in his notebook after I left.

"1. He wants to see him paint

"2. He wants him to sign his book

"3. He wants his picture taken with him

"4. He wants him to see his pictures."

All of my planned speeches dissolved into anxiety as I turned onto the long, unpaved driveway down to Wyeth's two-and-a-half-century-old stone house called The Mill. It sat in a bend of the Brandywine River, near an old gristmill that the Wyeth's were just beginning to restore. They must have seen me coming for they met me at the door. Wyeth was fifty-one then, with short, dark hair beginning to go gray. He was wearing a heavy, wool sweater and black trousers.

He offered his hand, and I'm hardly competent to describe my feelings when I took it. I can only call the experience mystical. All I could think was that this hand that I was holding, these fragile bones, these muscles and nerves, this sinew and skin had created so many great works of art, and I could only dream that whatever power was there might somehow flow magically from his flesh to mine.

Betsy greeted me with a big smile, a lovely, friendly woman. You'd have thought I was a long-lost nephew, the way they treated me. I'd never felt a warmer or more sincere welcome, and despite my nervousness and apprehension, I soon felt right at home.

Wyeth had just finished a painting of a young Norwegian girl named Siri, nude, sitting in a sauna with a towel across her lap, her face flush. He called it "The Sauna," and he had just hung it near the front door. I was surprised at how excited he was about it, eager for me to see it. I was reminded of the night I'd painted that cluster of oak leaves, how excited I'd been, and how much I'd needed to show it to Kay. I was entranced that after all these years of painting, and all of his success, he still experienced the same thrill that I had felt about my tiny early effort, still needed to show his work to somebody and get reaction. He talked on and on about it and I was utterly fascinated.

This wasn't the only painting he showed me. He and Betsy took me on a tour of the entire house, showing me paintings in every room, some of which have never been seen publicly. I was practically in a daze when we finished the tour on the second floor. As we came back downstairs, Wyeth turned to me and asked, "Did you bring any of your paintings?"

"They're in the car," I said, and felt my heartbeat leap.

Before we could go on, I needed to deliver one of my little rehearsed speeches. But my brain was scrambling wildly to recall one; I hardly could remember my own name. I must have launched into one, because my mouth was moving and words were tumbling out, but to this day I'm not sure exactly what I said. I remember telling him about the deep need I felt to paint, and about my family and how totally devoted I was to them, and how my father expected me and my brother to take over his businesses, and how all of this had brought me such distress. I also recall saying this: "What I need to know is whether I'm kidding myself or not. I want you to know that I didn't come for false praise, and I won't be offended by whatever you say. I'm just gratified that you were willing to see me at all."

"Well, I can't tell you what to do about your business," Wyeth replied, "but why don't we take a look at your paintings."

He and Betsy helped me fetch them from the car. We propped them up in the light in a room with a huge fireplace, and Wyeth went from one to the next, studying each, silent and contemplative. Not even Alfred Hitchcock on his best day could have created the agonizing suspense that Wyeth was churning in me.

I was fully prepared for him to turn to me and say, "They're good, but..." I suppose I even expected it, and somewhere down deep I may have even wanted him to tell me not to give up my job, to continue painting only as a hobby. It would make everything so much easier.

Instead, I suddenly heard him saying, "You obviously have talent. If you stick to it and have faith in yourself, I think you can make it. Go home and paint the things you know the best and love the best." I could hardly believe what I was hearing, and my heart was dancing with every word.

I'm sure I must have been quick and effusive in my thanks and goodbyes, but I couldn't wait to get back to the room and call Kay.

"Bob called home at 9:30," Dad wrote in his log. "'Happy.' He said Andrew Wyeth liked his paintings, showed him around his house, invited him back Wednesday—and to come back later and bring Kay."

As happy as I was, I couldn't tell Kay or Dad what really was going on in my mind, that Wyeth's verdict had settled everything. My life's decision had been made for me.

I was so excited, and my mind was reeling with so many possibilities, so many conflicting thoughts and emotions that I hardly slept that night.

I was up before daybreak.

I had an appointment with another painter, George Weymouth, who'd been the moving force behind the Brandywine River Museum. I had met him briefly at the museum in August, and Dr. Handy had suggested that I talk with him, too. He was living my dream and she thought he might be a help. He had an all-day sitting for a portrait beginning at nine, but he had agreed to meet me at his home at eight.

The morning was bitterly cold and stunningly beautiful as the sun began to rise. A heavy frost had settled over the hilly countryside during the night. It glittered in waves at first strike of the sun. The earth was winter-brown, the trees bare and bleak, the cornfields stubbled with the residue of last year's crops. But the eastern sky glowed rose and gold, and flocks of cawing crows had taken flight to celebrate its glory. Passing farm after farm, I felt as if I'd driven into a Wyeth painting.

George Weymouth was called "Frolic" by his friends. He was related to the Wyeths by marriage, and his mother was a du Pont. He lived in a four-story, early 1700s house at the end of a long, unpaved road on a farm of astonishing beauty. A three-story barn was just down the hill, along with other outbuildings and elaborate gardens. Many famous people had been entertained in this house.

Weymouth had just gotten up. He was still yawning as he led me to the kitchen but was a gracious and entertaining host. We sat drinking coffee, chatting and laughing for nearly an hour. He was a fine painter but he'd been a businessman before and he'd had to divest himself of those responsibilities so that he could do what he truly loved. We talked about how he had done that, and how I might. He warned that it wouldn't be easy.

"But I've never regretted it one moment," he said, "and you won't either. It's a wonderful life."

That was exactly what I wanted to hear, of course, and I left totally reinforced. I knew now for certain that whatever it took, I was going to become a painter. I knew I could do it. I knew it would happen. And knew I would be successful.

Back at the motel, I called Dr. Handy. I didn't really have to tell her how my visits had gone. She knew by the difference in my voice and mood from my call six days earlier, and she was truly happy about it. She was busy and wouldn't be able to see Dad and me on this trip, but I thanked her profoundly and she made me promise to call and let her know how things were going.

After checking out of the motel, we stopped at a roadside stand to buy fresh mushrooms, then prowled a few antique shops in the area. We had lunch at Buckley's Tavern in Centerville. Then I dropped Dad off at Brandywine Battlefield and went back to the Wyeths' so that I could tour the old mill they were restoring.

I picked Dad up an hour and a half later, and we drove into Philadelphia just to have a look around. We stopped for the night at a Holiday Inn in Media, Pennsylvania, and after supper at a local cafe, we both were in bed by nine. I was exhausted and finally slept soundly.

Dad was up by seven. "Did not sleep good," he noted in his journal. "Too much coconut pie and steak." He discovered that he'd left his razor at the motel in Longwood and we returned there to get it, then, after stopping to buy more mushrooms ("3 lbs. fresh $2," Dad noted), we set out for home.

We didn't talk much on the way back. My mind was completely preoccupied with how I was going to bring about this change in my life. How would I tell Dad and Kay and Tim? What would I have to do to free myself? How long would it take?

Dad may have sensed what was going on in my mind. A couple of times he made attempts to bring up Wyeth's assessment of my paintings. "Maybe you should take off a day now and then just to paint," he suggested at one point.

It seemed clear that he could not think of painting as a life-calling or a reasonable way to make a living and support a family. Equally clear was that he still expected me to continue in the gas business. Yet, years later, I couldn't help but wonder if he hadn't suspected then that he might be losing this son to forces he couldn't understand. Soon after we passed into Virginia, he began to complain of feeling "swimmy-headed." Concerned, I stopped to let him get some air and walk around a little. "I thought I was going to faint," he later wrote in his journal.

A half hour later, we stopped for lunch in Fredricksburg. "I feel better," he wrote afterward, and we continued down I-95 to I-85.

My mind was so centered on my situation that I actually ran out of gas as we neared the North Carolina line. A young fellow picked me up and took me to a gas station, and during the twenty minutes I was gone, a state trooper stopped to ask Dad if he needed help.

We finally rolled into Lexington at 6:30, and I dropped Dad off without ever mentioning the decision this trip had made for me. Nor did I mention it to Kay when I got home. I still wasn't sure how to break this news to the people I loved most.

Years later, as I stood in Dad's bedroom after his death, reading his journal of that trip, I was brought to tears by what he had written after he got home.

"I have had such a good time being with him. I only wish I could do more of it on this basis. He's a mighty fine boy with very high principles and morals.... A real fine trip. Let's go again."

At the time, he clearly still didn't realize that the trip on which I was about to embark was one that would take my life in a different direction than he had planned for me.

Far and away the best prize that life offers is the chance to work hard at work worth doing.
—Theodore Roosevelt

Chapter 9

As it turned out, I never actually had to tell anybody about the decision that Andrew Wyeth made for me. I just quietly began working toward implementing it.

I'd spent almost ten years in the Winston-Salem office, and long before the trip to see Wyeth I'd been mentioning to Dad and Tim that it might be time for me to move on to something else. Subconsciously, I had begun wondering what the gas business had to offer me. I needed challenges and the business didn't present enough to hold my interest. Dad and Tim assumed that I'd be taking another job in the company, and we had begun discussing what it might be.

So it didn't seem unusual when I suggested that we should begin scouting for somebody to replace me. Actually, I already had somebody in mind. Harvey Stoltz was a native of Winston-Salem who was working for a gas company in Fayetteville. I'd heard that he might be wanting to come back home. Within a few weeks, Tim and I had talked him into taking the job. I was to stay on until he was ready to take charge, probably at the end of the year.

Not long after Harvey came to work that spring, I began to find time to slip away for an afternoon and go somewhere to paint. As he got more acclimated, I started slipping off for a couple of afternoons a week. Soon there were days when I didn't come in at all. I threw myself into painting every chance I got.

The more I painted, and the more people saw of my work, the more talk circulated about it. Once again my paintings were accepted for the show at the Gallery of Contemporary Art, and they attracted a lot of attention and sold quickly. My parents went with Kay and me to the opening. I could tell that Mom and Dad were really proud when people came up to compliment my work and chat with them about it.

I'm sure my parents must have suspected that I was moving toward painting full-time, but this was beyond their experience, and they remained cautious. One day I stopped by to see Mom. Somehow, we got to talking about life and I said that in my idea of the perfect life you had to be able to do the work you loved most. She didn't miss my meaning.

"That might not be so easy as you think, Bob," she said. "You don't know what all kinds of things are involved in a life change like that."

For Mom, who'd always taught Tim and me that if we could dream it we could achieve it, this was a sign of concern. Perhaps it was concern for Dad as much as for me. She knew he had to be hurting to see me moving away from his hopes for my life after all the work he'd invested to make things easier for Tim and me.

My biggest concern from the beginning, of course, was Kay and our children. If Kay had thought this was a crazy idea, I never would have attempted it. But it finally dawned on me that she had known from the time I called Dr. Handy what was going on in my mind, and she let me know that no matter which direction I decided to take, she was with me, just as she always had been, my staunchest supporter and booster, then and now.

By this time, it also had become apparent to Tim where I was headed.

One day I offhandedly asked him, "What would you think if I took off a while to see if I could make it painting?"

"I think you've got to try it," he told me. "You'll never be happy if you don't. Why don't you take a year and see what happens?"

Not only was Tim encouraging, he began helping me plan to make it possible.

The first Realist Invitational Show was held at the Gallery of Contemporary Art in Old Salem that fall. It attracted a lot of attention. I had suggested that we borrow some paintings by Andrew Wyeth and his father from Dr. Handy and others for the show and that had worked out. I couldn't believe that my paintings were being shown alongside those of Andrew Wyeth, but there they were. None of the paintings offered for sale sold any quicker than mine. After that, even Mom and Dad began suggesting that I really ought to see what I could do with this painting business. Like Kay and Tim, they had come to realize that it was an obsession that was not going away.

This was the year of the great music festival at Woodstock, New York, and although I was hardly the Woodstock type, I suspect that I may have been affected by its message: live life to the fullest—do it now! I'd set aside enough money to be able to make it for a year without a salary. One thing was firm in my mind: If I did this, I was not going to allow it to hurt my family in any way, particularly financially or emotionally. I'd try it for one year. If it took too much time away from Kay and the children, or if I couldn't make enough money at it to support them at the same level as before, I'd go back to the gas company, and Tim and I would resume building and dealing in land.

I talked this over first with Kay, then with Tim and my

parents, and all endorsed the plan wholeheartedly. So it was set. On January 1, 1970, I would become a professional painter. At least for a year. But deep down, I knew it was forever.

A couple of years after Kay and I moved into our house, I added a carport on the back. The year before, I began a much more ambitious remodeling project (five more would follow this one), adding a whole second story that extended out over the carport. I had something in mind other than making more room for my family, although we needed that. The area over the carport was to be my studio.

I often stopped by a trucking company in Winston-Salem to check over their damaged freight. You never knew what you might find there, and you could pick up some real bargains. One day I dropped by and found, of all things, several tops for blackjack tables. All they needed was a new finish, some legs, and a means for adjusting them, and they would make perfect drawing tables. I bought three of them, brought them home, fixed one to my specifications (later I would do the other two as well), and it became the centerpiece of my new, over-the-carport studio, not to mention the symbol of the gamble I was embarking on. Thirty years later, I still use two of the tables. I think I can mark that in the win column.

Those early weeks as a full-time painter still seem like a fantasy to me. I was so happy and excited to be free to do nothing but paint that I could hardly believe it was true. I was in ecstasy. I painted all day almost every day, usually in watercolors, or tempera (water-based paint thickened with a gelatinous substance), or gouache (water-based paint mixed with gum), often using all three in the same painting.

I wasn't painting with an agenda. I didn't set out to be the Andrew Wyeth of the South, as I later would be called, or to consciously try to capture my place and my memories in paint. I simply was painting by instinct, out of sheer joy. I had no trouble finding subjects. I saw paintings everywhere. It was what not to paint that bothered me. I hardly could wait to finish one so I could start another.

This new life was not without pressure, however. I had to produce. And I had to be concerned about whether anybody would be willing to pay for all this work. I also had a deadline.

When I had told Ted Potter at the Gallery of Contemporary Art that I was going to be painting full-time, he not only offered congratulations, he said, "We'll have your first show." I had little more than four months to get together enough paintings for it.

Two days before the show was to open in May, I hauled twenty-three framed paintings to Old Salem. Ted helped me carry them in the back door of the old bank building and set them around in the basement so he could have his first look at them. He walked around appraising each and when he'd finished, he looked at me with all seriousness and said, "Bob, right now you're just a regional painter, but after Sunday you're going to be more than that. You're going to become nationally famous."

Several years later, after I told this story to a reporter, Ted said he didn't remember saying that and didn't think he did. But I *know* he did. Few words have ever had such impact on me.

I've never told this to anybody before, not even Kay, and I know that it sounds egotistical and maybe even a little crazy, but it's simply true. From as far back as I can remember, I secretly knew that I was going to achieve some degree of fame. I didn't know how much, or for what, or when it might come, but I was certain that it would. And now Ted was telling me that it might happen. I couldn't forget that.

Ted wanted my advice on pricing, but I left that to him. When the show opened, I saw that the prices ranged from $75 for a study of an oak leaf to $750 for a painting of the old cotton mill at Linwood, near High Rock Lake. That was far more than I had ever sold a painting for, and I wondered if Ted hadn't overpriced some of them.

Within thirty minutes of the show's opening, however, eighteen of the paintings had been sold, and the other five were gone after two days. The show brought in nearly $7,000, a big boost to the gallery, which could hardly pay its bills at the time. For my dad, it was an eye-opener. For the first time he truly saw the possibilities of this crazy course on which I'd set myself. Painting, too, could be a lucrative business. From that point on, I should have been paying him as my advance man and public relations person. He was convinced that I was the new Leonardo da Vinci, and he wanted the world to know it. He always had been proud of me, but now he was even prouder.

Unbeknownst to me, that fall he wrote a letter to John Canaday, the art critic for the *New York Times*, sending along transparencies of some of my works and suggesting in a nice way that the *Times* had been derelict for not having already discovered me.

Amazingly, Canaday wrote back, saying that while it was something he'd never done before, he had taken the liberty of forwarding my transparencies to a friend, Milton Esterow, at Kennedy Galleries. Clearly, I wasn't about to make the front page of the *Times'* arts section anytime soon, but Dad recognized an opportunity when he saw one. "You ought to call him," he told me. I did, and he told me to bring some of my paintings and come to see him if I got to New York. I assured him that I would, and that I probably would be getting up that way before too long.

I can't help but wonder whether I would have ever gotten any recognition outside of Lexington if I hadn't been working in Winston-Salem when I started painting. Not only was Winston-Salem the home of the Gallery of Contemporary Art, which gave me my first real break, and was run by Ted Potter, who taught me so much about the art business, the city also was the home of North Carolina's most successful painter at the time, Joseph Wallace King, otherwise known as Vinciata.

Joe was a character unlike any I've ever known. Anybody who ever knew Joe for any length of time could spend hours telling tales about him that would seem so outlandish that nobody ever would believe any of them, yet they'd all be true.

I'm not sure how I first met Joe. It may have been at the gallery. Anyway, I got to know him soon after I started painting seriously, and I became close friends with him and his dear wife, Earline, a gifted sculptor and artist.

Joe had been born on a big tobacco farm in Patrick County, Virginia, but when he was two his family's home burned on Christmas Eve. The family moved across the state line into North Carolina, living first on farms near Stoneville, then Bennett, before settling in Greensboro when Joe was six.

Joe started painting at seven. At eight, when he learned that John Philip Sousa, the bandleader and composer of our best known marches, was coming to town for a concert, he painted a portrait of Sousa and presented it to him when he arrived at the O. Henry Hotel. Sousa, who gave Joe a handwritten pass to his concert that night, was just the first of many famous people whose portraits Joe would paint and whose favors he would win.

Joe sold newspapers, worked in a sign shop, and dreamed of running away to become an acrobat with the circus. But when he was eleven, he fell off a seesaw and broke his left arm. A doctor set it improperly; gangrene set in, and the arm had to be amputated.

At sixteen, Joe moved in with a sister in Winston-Salem so he could attend Reynolds High School, which had a highly regarded program in the arts. At the time he didn't know whether he wanted to be an artist or an actor, and he was preparing for either course, although he knew that his missing limb would make an acting career unlikely for him.

He met Earline when he chose her as his model in an art class. Two years later, they slipped off to Virginia and got married. Joe went on to study at the Corcoran School of Art in Washington, and he was soon on his way to gaining fame as a painter. He always had a fascination with Italy, and he and Earline moved to Florence.

There Joe ceased being a country boy from North Carolina. He grew a goatee, started wearing a cape, affected aristocratic airs and became Vinciata, a name he took from a tenth-century castle called Vincigliata. To call Joe flamboyant would be understatement.

Joe chose the style of the old masters. He painted religious figures, historic scenes, and gamboling nude nymphs. His paintings began showing up in galleries and museums all over Europe, even in the Vatican.

But it was in portraits that Joe made his name and his living. He painted kings and sheiks, generals and movie stars, captains of industry and the children of the rich. Many wealthy men, Joe once told me, wanted him to paint their wives or mistresses in the nude, so many that he had to turn down most of the commissions, although he loved nothing more than painting beautiful young women in their birthday suits.

Early on, Joe learned the secret of successful portraiture: flattery. When he painted President Richard Nixon he made him look almost adorable. And his formal portrait of Queen Elizabeth, for which she sat on three different occasions at Buckingham Palace, once while she was recovering from chicken pox, brought him hosannas from throughout the kingdom and made him the toast of the London tabloids. The dowdy queen had become as glamorous as a movie star, and hardly anybody noticed the three little chicken pox scars Joe had painted on her right forehead.

Eventually Joe and Earline returned home to Winston-Salem, and Joe set up a studio in the old blacksmith shop at Reynolda Manor, the former home of R.J. Reynolds.

Joe quickly involved himself in whatever was going on wherever he might be. He was always into something. At one point, he even got himself elected to the legislature, but he was defeated after only one term when his opponent charged that he wasn't taking the job seriously. Joe had worn a leopard-skin-patterned jacket to a black-tie affair at the governor's mansion, and a photographer got a picture of the governor and his wife greeting him in the receiving line with looks of shock and indignation.

Some people just didn't appreciate Joe's mischievous sense of humor. He would go to any length to pull off a practical joke or an elaborate prank or stunt. More than a few of them got him into trouble.

Joe never got over his theatrical dreams, and when Winston-Salem was celebrating its centennial, he volunteered to put on a big show at Reynolda Park to cap the celebration. The show was held in an amphitheater with tall trees as a backdrop. Joe put up a big screen for showing historical slides and film snippets. He erected a flagpole for the raising of the stars and bars. He got an orchestra to play, and he brought in Metropolitan Opera star Norman Cordon, who then was living in Chapel Hill, to perform.

Joe also called his buddy Jim Womack, a newspaper photographer and fireworks expert in Greensboro, and got him to bury two dozen huge cylinders at the back of the stage and load them with the biggest skyrockets he could find.

The fireworks were to be part of the grand finale, and they were to come as a surprise. Norman Cordon was to close the show by singing "The Star Spangled Banner." As he began, a huge flag would start rising on the pole in the background. When he got to the line "...the rockets' red glare...," Womack was to set off all twenty-four rockets simultaneously. When Cordon got to "...the bombs bursting in air..." precisely that would be happening.

Nobody knew about the fireworks but Cordon, and Joe only told him so they wouldn't startle him and disrupt his singing. As the fireworks blazed the sky, and Cordon reached the line, "...gave proof through the night that our flag was still there..." he was to turn toward the flag pole with one hand raised dramatically as the spotlight rose to the flag.

"Just keep on singing," Joe told him. "Don't pay any attention to the fireworks."

Everything went off without a hitch. The show was perfect right up until Cordon launched into the-rocket's-red-glare line. That was when Joe gave the nod to Womack. Womack pushed the plunger and all twenty-four canisters went off at once. Those who saw it said the explosion was truly spectacular and nearly deafening. It was heard miles away, rattled windows all over town, and prompted hundreds of calls to the police and sheriff's departments. It was perhaps most successful as a surprise.

When the din had diminished and Joe peeked out from behind the tree where he'd taken refuge, he found that the entire audience had fled in panic, along with the whole orchestra, except for the pianist, who was cowering, trembling, under her stool. The stage was strewn with overturned chairs, abandoned instruments, fluttering sheet music, and dozens of limbs from nearby trees. The screen had been blown away, the flag pole had collapsed, but there in the slowly clearing smoke stood Cordon, his face blackened, his clothing tattered, his right arm raised dramatically toward the broken flagpole, singing right on, just as Joe had directed. "...O'er the la-and of the FREE, and the home of-of the BRAVE...."

Joe said that Cordon told him later that when he turned around and saw everybody gone, he didn't know whether to take a bow or not.

I admit that Joe might have exaggerated that tale a bit, as he was often prone to do, but probably not much. I loved to listen to Joe tell his tales. He laughed uproariously all the way through them.

Joe was as impulsive about buying odd things as I am. When he learned that London Bridge was going to be put up for sale, he flew to London and tried to buy it. He wanted to bring it back to North Carolina and put it up over the Yadkin River. Unfortunately, he was outbid by a group who moved the bridge to Lake Havasu, Arizona, and reconstructed it at a real estate development.

When Joe came home after finishing the queen's portrait, I stopped by to see him and he was complaining about the hard time he'd had getting through customs when he arrived in London. He was wearing his cape and putting on his best European airs, of course.

"What brings you to Great Britain, Mr. King?" the customs agent asked.

"I've come to paint the queen," Joe replied regally.

The agent looked at him a little askance.

"Have you ever been to England before?" he asked.

"Just once," Joe said, "when I came to buy London Bridge."

"You know," Joe told me, "I don't think he believed me. They took me back there and strip searched me and asked me all kinds of questions. I think they even called Buckingham Palace before they let me go."

One of the many odd things that Joe did manage to buy was the world's largest painting. It is seventy feet high, 410 feet wide and weighs 12,000 pounds. Think about finding a frame to fit that. Or a nail to hold it on the wall.

This was a portrayal of Pickett's Charge, the climax of the Civil War battle at Gettysburg. It was painted by a French artist named Paul Philippoteaux and sixteen assistants. They started it in 1880 and didn't finish it until two and a half years later. It was displayed in a cyclorama in Chicago in 1883, and it drew 500,000 people in its first year. It was shown only sporadically after that, and it had been in a warehouse in Chicago for decades when Joe came upon it in 1964.

It was a real bargain, Joe said, but once he got it, he suddenly realized that he didn't have the slightest idea what to do with it. He finally had it trucked to Winston-Salem and stashed it in a warehouse, where it remained, costing him rent every month. Joe didn't seem to mind. After all, only one person could claim to own the world's largest painting.

Joe and Earline gave me encouragement and advice from the time I met them, and I always enjoyed stopping by the studio and talking with them. After I talked with Milton Esterow at Kennedy Galleries about bringing my paintings to New York, I went by all excited to tell them about it.

Joe had found great success in New York. He'd had numerous shows at Hammer Galleries, which he said was one of the top three galleries in the world, and he had known Victor Hammer, who ran the business, and his older brother, Dr. Armand Hammer, who founded it, since the beginning of his career.

"If you're going to New York, go by Hammer Galleries first," Joe told me, and it wasn't just a suggestion, it was an order. "That's where you should be. Just tell them I sent you."

Looking back, I can hardly believe how naive I was then, and thank goodness for it, because it turned out to be one of my greatest strengths at the time.

On the morning of January 3, 1971, only a year and two days after I'd begun painting full-time, Dad and I arrived by train in New York. With me, I had two taped cardboard cartons, each containing three paintings, half of which I had borrowed from clients. We arrived at Pennsylvania Station, loaded our bags and the paintings into the trunk of a cab and headed for the Hilton.

When we got there, Dad said, "Why don't you go on while you've got the cab, and I'll take the bags and check us in."

I got back in the cab and told the driver to take me to Hammer Galleries on 57th St. In those days, New York cab drivers still spoke English, or at least a New York version of it, and mine asked where I was from. North Carolina, I told him proudly.

"Are those paintings you've got with you?" he asked.

Oh, yes, I said, going on to tell him that I was hoping the gallery might want to show them.

"So you have an appointment," he said.

No, I responded cheerily. A friend had told me I ought to stop by. The cabbie chuckled and shook his head. We got there a little after 10. The cabbie helped me unload the cartons. I tipped him and thanked him. He gave me such a sympathetic look that I could almost tell what he was thinking: this poor yokel is about to be slapped hard upside the head by big city ways.

But I was brimming with confidence. After all, I knew what I had in the cartons—and I knew Joe King.

"You want me to wait?" he asked, as if he thought I might not even get through the door before I was turned away.

"No, that's all right," I said.

"Well, good luck, buddy."

He left me on the sidewalk trying to wrestle those two big cartons to the gallery door. I was surprised to find the door locked, apparently to keep out the riff-raff, to which I, at the moment, must have borne a striking resemblance from the looks on the faces of the people I saw inside.

A polite fellow came to the door. I introduced myself and told him that I was from North Carolina and that Joe King had told me to come by and show them my paintings. I had an appointment at Kennedy Galleries, I explained, but Joe said I should come by Hammer first. "Well, why don't I take a look at them," he said. His name was Bill Mitchell, the very person Joe had told me to ask for. He helped me with one of the cartons, and once inside we started opening them.

Just as we were getting the paintings out, a dapper little man came walking briskly from the back of the gallery, pulling on a topcoat, clearly headed for the door. He had a high forehead, a bulbous nose, and he wore a boutonniere on the lapel of his pin-stripe suit.

When he got to us, he paused.

"What have we here?" he asked.

"This is Bob Timberlake," Bill Mitchell told him. "He's from North Carolina. He's a friend of Joe King."

"Ah, Vinciata!" the little man said. "Well, any friend of Joe King's is a friend of Hammer Galleries."

He took a quick look at all of my paintings, then turned and said, "Why don't you leave all these. I think we can sell them."

I was so startled I could hardly speak. "I can't leave but three," I said quickly. "The other three are already sold. I had to borrow them."

"Well, leave the three then," he said. "Just give the information to the girl back there. She'll give you a receipt."

With that, he turned and was out the door.

That, Mitchell told me, was Victor Hammer. I was in luck. He'd just come in that day to pick up his topcoat.

When I went to the office to get the receipt, the young woman looked at me dubiously. "You just came in here off the street from North Carolina, and he took your paintings?" she said incredulously.

"Yes, ma'am," I replied.

"It must be your lucky day," she told me. "I've been here seven months. Artists come in here with their paintings every day. You're the first one they've even talked to since I've been here."

Fifteen minutes after I arrived, I was back out on the sidewalk, this time lugging only one carton, wondering how I was going to explain to Kennedy Galleries how my paintings were already spoken for, and wishing I'd asked the cab driver to wait after all. He could have helped me celebrate.

I was eager to get back to the hotel to tell Dad what had happened and to call home. Dad had instructed the desk clerk to have a key waiting for me. I rushed to the room to discover that Dad had gone out somewhere. I called Kay and got no answer. Mom wasn't at home either. I dialed Joe and Earline's numbers and the phone rang and rang. I was bursting with wonderful news and had nobody to tell it to.

Finally, I scribbled a succinct note—"SUCCESS at 10:15 on first gallery. Mr. Hammer wanted them all"—and left it for Dad. Then I went downstairs to the bar. I wasn't a drinker, and it was still well before noon, but I ordered myself a bourbon and ginger ale. It seemed the appropriate thing for the happiest, and most naive man in New York to do.

What thou lov'st well remains,
    the rest is dross
What thou lov'st well shall not be reft from thee
What thou lov'st well is thy true heritage

    —Ezra Pound

Chapter 10

One reason that I had only three unsold paintings to take to New York was that my production had been slowed late in 1970 by health problems. I first had inner ear trouble, then a glandular infection, and it took several visits to doctors to overcome them. The problem was that I had been very active before I started painting full-time, always outside doing physical work, and suddenly I was sitting all the time. My body had trouble adjusting.

By the time I went to New York in January, 1971, I finally had recovered and was painting with renewed fervor. The three paintings I left at Hammer Galleries sold before a month was out and Victor Hammer called asking for more. I sent two in February and promised others to come.

I was slow and meticulous in my work, careful about detail, and I sometimes spent weeks on a single painting. I rarely finished one in less than a week, but with this promising new development, I began painting like a madman. I turned out forty-nine paintings in 1971. Some I sold myself. A few I gave away (one to Joe and Earline King in gratitude for sending me to Hammer Galleries). Ted Potter at the Gallery of Contemporary Art kept asking for more and I sent several to him. But I shipped most off to New York. Every painting sold; the prices were gradually climbing, and the checks were now coming with regularity.

In 1971, I also brought out my first two prints, both to raise money for the Davidson County Art Guild. The first was a snow scene. Snow was one of my favorite subjects. Winter was my favorite season, and from the time I could remember I always looked forward to snowstorms. I was entranced with the incredible beauty of snow and its ability to transform the mundane into the phenomenal. I loved sledding, snowball fights, building snow forts and snow men, and oh, did I love snow cream. There was nothing about snow that I didn't like. I even loved the feeling of warmth and satisfaction I got when I was inside looking out at it.

This particular snow scene was at "Shorty" Garrison's farm in the Cotton Grove community of southern Davidson County. I never knew Shorty's first name because I never heard him called anything but Shorty. He got slabs from nearby sawmills each fall, cut them into lengths to fit his woodstoves and arranged them in long, neat, ascending piles between two huge and ancient cedars, a rampart against the coming assault of winter. Those slab piles spoke to me of comfort and reassurance as soon as I spotted them, and I knew I had to paint them. We produced only 100 copies of that print, and at $35 they sold so quickly that we decided to do another one.

The second was of my mother's antique cupboard, one of its glass doors open, the shelves lined with jars of home-canned vegetables and fruits. We printed 250 of those, and they, too, sold out quickly at the same price. (Incidentally, those who bought copies of "Mr. Garrison's Slab Pile" have seen their investments grow more than 100 times over since then, and "Ella's Cupboard" has appreciated considerably as well.)

I was even more productive in 1972, and on a trip to New York that spring, I was emboldened enough by my output and my sales to suggest to Victor Hammer that perhaps I should have a show of my own. He glanced away, cleared his throat and said, "Well, maybe we can think about that."

Bill Mitchell, the salesman, had become a friend by then. He was standing there and I noticed that he sort of blanched when I brought this up. Later, he told me, "You don't do that. He invites *you* to have a show."

Not a month passed before I got a call from Mr. Hammer. "We've been talking about having a show of your work," he said. "What would you think about that?"

"I would be honored," I said.

I kept sending paintings to Hammer Galleries all through 1972, and they kept selling, but I was holding back the better ones for my first New York show.

As much as I enjoyed working at home, after two years of painting there I decided that it was not such a good idea after all. There were many distractions, and I was constantly underfoot for Kay. Kelly was entering her teens, and she and the boys often had friends over. The phone was always in use when I needed it. But more importantly, painting at home made it too easy to paint too much.

I loved what I was doing so much that often after supper I'd find myself heading back up to my studio to make just a change or two on whatever I was working on, and oftentimes I'd still be at it after midnight, just as I had done when I was working at the gas company.

What I needed, I decided, was a studio away from home so I could make the pleasure I was finding in painting a little more like work, a place where I could set hours as if it were a job, then go home, relax, attend to my family, and resist this obsession until the next day.

I began scouting around for a place near the end of 1972, and it didn't take long to find it. My great uncle Percy Crichter, the lawyer and descendant of Blackbeard, had bought 1,100 acres on High Rock Lake with his friend Thurman Briggs, who had been a member of the North Carolina Wildlife Commission. They had divided the land between themselves and begun selling tracts and lots. I remembered the old log house on the property, and I went down to have a look. High Rock Lake seemed the perfect spot for me to paint.

I discovered that Uncle Percy and Thurman were using the old farm house as a sales office. It wasn't on the water. In fact, you couldn't even see the lake from there, but it was only a few hundred yards away, easy walking distance.

The house sat near the edge of the woods and was such a shambles that Uncle Percy and Thurman did their business from lawn chairs on the front porch. As soon as I saw that house, I knew I had found my studio. It turned out to be one of the oldest houses in either Davidson or Rowan Counties, of which Davidson originally was a part.

The house had belonged to Major Gasper Smith, a Revolutionary War soldier. Another house had preceded it, but it had burned in 1788, and Smith rebuilt it on the same spot, this time of hand-hewn pine logs, eighteen inches thick. The house had been passed to his son David, who later would fight in the Civil War with his own son, David Jr. They were known as Big David and Little David.

Big David had owned slaves and he not only farmed his huge acreage, he ran a ferry on the Yadkin River. After the war, Little David took over the farm and the ferry, and although some of the slaves remained, one man staying until he died at age 104, the farm fell into decline and eventually passed into the hands of others until finally Uncle Percy and Thurman bought it. At some point, somebody had covered the old house with weatherboarding, probably because a log house was thought to be a sign of poverty.

When Uncle Percy and Thurman divided the property, the house ended up on Thurman's land. I'd known Thurman for most of my life, and we quickly struck a deal. I would preserve and restore the house and get a month's rent for every fifty dollars I spent on it. After that, he would keep up the exterior and the grounds and I would maintain the interior, but there were no limits on how long the agreement would last, or how much I could spend on upkeep.

I got my friend Charlie Yow and his son, Tom, to come down and look at the place. Charlie and Tom had worked for Kay's grandfather, Dan Musgrave, who had built our house. Charlie and Tom had added the second story to our house and built my home studio.

This house was twenty-six feet wide and thirty-eight feet long. Originally it had been only a single-story with four rooms plus a loft in the attic. But at some point the roof had been raised and a half-story had been added, creating two low-ceilinged loft rooms. That apparently was when the roof of hand-crimped tin had been put on. The original roof, no doubt, had been of white-oak shakes.

Charlie and Tom began by stripping the rotting weatherboarding from the house, revealing the still-sound logs. They discovered that the logs had been uniquely notched so that they would drain to the outside and to the ends of the house, preventing decay.

The roof was supported by huge beams, and the interior walls were of hand-beveled, tongue-and-groove boards an inch-and-a-half thick, with fine window and door moldings, beading and chair rails in every room, and a beautiful old mantle with hand-cut molding around the main fireplace. Earlier residents had burned logs too big for the fireplace, causing fire damage to the corners of the mantle columns on each side. Underneath all the dirt, spider webs and debris inside the house, though, were wonderful examples of early American craftmanship, and we carefully restored and preserved all.

The heart-pine floors on the main level were uneven and had strange holes in them. When Charlie and Tom tried jacking up the floors to level them, they discovered that it wasn't possible without throwing everything else out of kilter.

Charlie was the one who discovered that at the time this house was built floors often were designed uneven, so they could be scoured with sand and water that would drain to the holes in the middle. We kept the floors as they were supposed to be, although I had no intention of scouring them with sand and water.

We did take out one of the loft rooms so that the main room was open to the second-floor ceiling and the upstairs windows provided more light for my work. There were two fireplaces of hand-made brick, but we had to rebuild the chimneys to make them serviceable. By spring, I could envision what the studio was going to look like, and I could hardly wait to get into it.

That was still several months away as the opening date for the New York show neared, April 14. I was glad to have the studio work to preoccupy me, for I was growing more anxious by the day. This show was a big event for me. It could make or break my career.

Hammer Galleries already had sold fifty of my paintings, and I sent thirty-eight more for the show. The gallery priced them from $1,200 to $4,000 each. That impressed me. You could buy a brand-new Ford pickup truck then for $3,000. It also concerned me. I wasn't sure whether people would pay such amounts. I also knew that a lot of people couldn't afford those prices, including some of my friends. I wanted people who weren't rich to be able to own my work, too. I called Mr. Hammer and told him that I'd like to include some drawings and studies that could be priced much lower.

"We can't do that, Bob," he said. "Somebody will buy a three-hundred-dollar study instead of a three-thousand-dollar painting."

Another reason I wanted the drawings and studies was to show the development of some of the paintings, to let people see how they evolved. I persisted, and finally Mr. Hammer gave in, although reluctantly. I think he changed his mind after the show opened and saw that this made it different, less formal, more personal, and more in keeping with my paintings.

The gallery held previews for special customers, and on Saturday, as Kay and I were preparing to leave for New York for the Monday night opening, Mr. Hammer called and wiped out my anxiety with the news that the show already was sold out, the first time that had happened in the gallery's long history.

I was truly riding high as Kay and I and all the kids flew into New York. Mom and Dad came with us, as did Tim and Teen, and we were all in a celebratory mood. We checked into the Plaza. Kay and I and the kids got a suite so we could entertain.

The opening of the show surely was one of the least formal and most personal ever held at a major gallery in New York, for scores of down-home folks from Davidson County and other parts of North Carolina showed up, including Joe and Earline King. It was almost like homecoming Sunday at church, except that all of my friends, family and neighbors were mingling with the friends and customers of Armand and Victor Hammer and the upper crust of New York society. That so many people from home cared enough to come meant more to me than I could ever express.

Joe King was on home turf at Hammer Galleries, of course, and he spiced up the gathering with jokes and tales. But the highlight for me came when Mom's doctor from Lexington walked in.

Over the din of the whole party I heard her call his name. "I've got to have some more birth control pills," she told him.

"I'll get you a new prescription as soon as I get back home," he answered.

The chatter began to die as people turned to look at Mom in wonder and disbelief. She was sixty-seven.

Mom suddenly realized what was happening and how her greeting had sounded.

"They're for my geraniums!" she cried. "They're for my geraniums!"

The crowd chuckled but I don't know that they were any less baffled by the knowledge that the pills were for her geraniums, not her. I can testify, though, that she did faithfully dissolve birth control pills and put them on her geraniums. Exactly what that was supposed to do for them has never been clear to me, but come to think of it, I don't think I ever saw of any of them having baby geraniums.

Kay and I stayed on in New York for several days after the opening, and every day I went to the gallery and sat for hours chatting with the people who came in to see my paintings. Those several days turned into revelation for me.

The whole world seemed to be passing on 57th Street, and a lot of people from a lot of different places and a lot of different walks of life came in. Among them were the wife of the Brazilian ambassador and the actress Angela Lansbury. There were people who lived in Manhattan penthouses and people who lived in tract houses in southern California. There were people from Peru and Japan, and from other countries and dozens of states. Yet their reactions were all the same. They came up to tell me how the paintings made them think of home, or of their grandfathers, or of a special place they'd gone with their families each summer. They spoke of traditions and important connections lost.

I was overwhelmed by this. I was simply painting my own back yard, the things and the people that I loved, and for the first time it truly dawned on me that what I was doing was important. This wasn't just Lexington and Davidson County and my people, it was all places and all people. I was touching universal truths. No matter who we are, or where we are from, or what our stature in life, we all have essentially the same core values, the same yearnings to connect to beloved people, places, events and traditions, the same needs to know who we are and where we are from. As society grows increasingly more mobile and rootless, these yearnings become even stronger, and people satisfy them in whatever ways they can—from books, movies, or paintings.

A mutual acquaintance once asked my friend Charles Kuralt why his "On the Road" pieces on CBS were so popular, and Charlie said this: "I guess it's because the people I meet on the road have roots....People long for their roots, and I guess they enjoy meeting people on TV who really do have roots, a heritage, and a way of life worth passing on to the next generation."

The responses I got while sitting in that gallery were confirmation that I had made the right decision in becoming a painter, and they gave me even stronger resolve to go on, made me eager to get back home and paint more. They also were affirmation of something Victor Hammer told me before the show. I think he was trying to prepare me for the reaction I might get in the so-called "art world," letting me know that as a realist and a Southerner, I likely would be greeted with indifference or derogation by most critics. "Nobody's going to love your paintings but the people," he told me, "and they always will, because you touch their hearts." Those words have come back to me over and over through the years, and they have served me well.

While no major critics came to my show, people wrote about it anyway.

"New England has its Eric Sloane," wrote James Daniel, editor of *Readers Digest*, "Pennsylvania has its Andrew Wyeth, and the South has its Bob Timberlake. I was born and grew up in the countryside Timberlake captures with his brush and he has caught the feeling of our region as faithfully and beautifully as Sloane and Wyeth express theirs. All three of these prominent artists belong to an American school that will outlast abstract expressionism."

"What he paints makes me remember," wrote Mary Martin Niebold in the *Philadelphia Inquirer*, "and the images are quiet, peaceful and filled with the kind of smiles that slow walks bring."

"I want to step into a Bob Timberlake painting and relive my memory," wrote Bob Talbert in the *Detroit Free Press*.

Good enough for me. After words in print comparing me to Andrew Wyeth and Eric Sloane, and the incredible success of that first New York show, I was as puffed-up as a bullfrog.

In mid-August I finally moved my blackjack-table easel, my boat-seat swivel stool, my fold-top fishing box full of paints and brushes, and a few pieces of furniture into my new studio. I decided to call it Riverwood. I'd spent $11,000 refurbishing it, which meant that I had free rent for more than eighteen years if I never spent another penny.

The months of work getting the place ready had allowed me to acclimate myself and to get to know many of my neighbors.

My nearest neighbors, Dan and Gilley Melton, were just across the pasture. They lived in an unpainted, sagging old farm house with a rusting tin roof. They had lived there rent-free for forty-two years, and they still lived as they had when they first arrived, little different than people in the area had lived a century earlier.

They had no electricity, no running water. They used candles and oil lamps for light when they needed it, but they didn't need it much, for they went to bed when darkness came and rose with the sun. Their water came from a hand-dug well and they raised it with a bucket and a rope attached to a smooth oak log with a hand-crank inserted into one side. They bathed in a galvanized tub, and Gilley washed their clothes in a big black pot over an outdoor fire. They used wood for heating and cooking, and Dan was always tending to his woodpile.

He raised most of their food, using a sway-backed old mule to plow the red earth. Gilley canned and dried much of what he grew, and he mounded up "tater hills" behind the house for storing sweet potatoes, Irish potatoes, as he called white potatoes, turnips and other root crops. They also kept pigs, chickens, goats, cows, and two bulls that loved to fight.

Dan was sixty-nine when I moved to Riverwood, Gilley about the same, and they had been married for more than fifty years. They'd been sharecroppers in South Carolina when they'd first married. They moved to Davidson County so Dan could help a brother-in-law farm. He later bought a team of horses on credit and paid for them growing cotton on rented land. But that ended when the bottom dropped out of the cotton market in the Great Depression, and Dan had to go to work in a rock quarry for ten-cents an hour.

"Hoover times," he'd snort derisively anytime those days came to mind. He didn't have a high regard for Herbert Hoover. "I tell you, he was some dude," he said. "If he'd been president up to now, they wouldn't be nobody but him. The rest of us would've been starved to death."

I met Dan and Gilley soon after we started working on the studio. Gilley was shy and withdrawn and didn't talk much except to fuss at Dan and speak sweetly to her cows. But Dan loved to talk. He'd come to check on the progress we were making and stay to give advice or talk about whatever was on his mind.

After the studio was finished and I started painting there, he often came to watch me work. He seemed fascinated by the process, especially in the beginning. Sometimes he'd sit watching for two or three hours, hardly saying a word. Other times he'd talk my ears off.

Dan told me that he never had taken any kind of medicine and had been sick only once in his life, when he came down with what he called "that furrin flu." That was in the winter of 1918-1919, during the great flu epidemic that killed thousands of people throughout the country. Dan blamed the World War I veterans for bringing it back with them. He was only fourteen at the time, and he was in bed for a week. He might have been there longer, but his room had a view of a nearby cemetery, and during that week he watched seven flu victims being buried, one each day.

"After that seventh one," he told me, "I decided I'd better get up from there if I didn't want to be number eight."

Dan believed that blackberries had a lot to do with keeping him healthy. He was the strongest proponent of blackberries I ever met, and when blackberry season rolled around early in July, you knew just where to find him—at whatever nearby blackberry patch hadn't yet been picked. He thought that blackberries were good for whatever ailed a person and he was always preaching to me about it. I suspect they had their best effect on Dan after being turned into juice and allowed to ferment for a while with a little sugar—great for stomach cramps, he claimed.

Dan had lost his driver's license long ago and rode a bicycle wherever he went. One day I was on my way to lunch and came upon Dan pushing his bike, shaking his head, dejected, muttering to himself. I thought something might have broken on his bike and I stopped and asked what was the matter.

"Comes in threes," he said. "It always comes in threes."

"What comes in threes?" I asked.

"Bad things."

"What's happened?"

"My goat fell in the well."

"Your goat fell in the well?" I said. "How did he fall in well?" I knew that a well house covered it.

"He just jumped up there and those old boards gave way and he fell through."

"Did he drown?" I asked.

"I reckon he did. I don't think he can swim."

"Did you get him out?"

"Naw. I can't get him out. I ain't got nothing to get him out with from way down in there."

"Well, Dan, you can't leave him in there. That's the only water you've got."

"I know it," he said. "Comes in threes. It always comes in threes."

"Well, you go on back to the house and I'll see if I can find somebody to come up there and help you."

I drove on to the restaurant in Southmont, and a couple

of power company guys were leaving in one of those big trucks loaded with winches, hooks, ropes and all kinds of other equipment. I stopped them, told them what had happened, and asked if they could help. They said sure, they'd drive up there.

I went ahead and had lunch, a much longer lunch than usual actually. I didn't want to have to deal with that goat. When I went back, I saw the power company truck leaving Dan's house. The driver stopped when he saw me.

"Did you get it out?" I asked.

"Yeah, we got him."

"Good. Is Dan all right?"

"Yeah," the driver said with a chuckle, "he's up there skinning his goat and talking about things happening in threes."

I decided to go on back to work without stopping. I didn't want to find out what the other two things were. And I knew if I went up there he'd make me take some of that goat meat home with me.

Later, I couldn't help but tease Dan. I said, "Dan, if you decide to get you another goat, you better take him over here to the lake and teach him to swim."

He didn't seem to think that was especially funny. He muttered something that I probably didn't want to hear anyway.

Dan and Gilley had a granddaughter who lived with them. Her name was Tiwanda, but everybody called her Wanda. She was ten, just a wisp of a girl, quiet and shy. She hardly ever spoke, and she lived a life unlike that of any other girl of her age and time. She never saw TV and ranged the fields and woods as free as a wild creature. I never knew why she had come to stay with her grandparents. Neither she, nor they, ever volunteered that information, and I never asked.

Wanda was in the fifth grade and couldn't tell time when I first met her. I taught her to do that. She rode the bus to school every day, and, like clockwork, thirty minutes before the bus brought her back each afternoon, one of the most remarkable sights that I've ever witnessed took place. Every creature on Dan and Gilley's land gathered at the corner of the fence by the road to wait for her, the cows, the bulls, the old mule, the goats, the chickens, the dogs and cats—and they were many, for people were always dropping off puppies and kittens on the rural road, and Wanda took in every stray and cared for it; she would have gone without food herself to feed a stray cat or dog. Only the pigs were denied the opportunity to wait for her, because Dan kept them in a pen behind the house.

And when that bus finally came into sight, you should have heard the cacophony that erupted. The cows were mooing, the goats baaing, the mule braying, the chickens cackling, the rooster crowing. The dogs would be jumping around and barking, the cats mewing, and even the pigs out in the back would be grunting and oinking. When Wanda got off the bus, she went to every one individually, greeting and petting it, even finally working her way back to the pigs.

I never knew another human being with such an affinity for animals. Dan's prize possession was his older bull. That thing looked as if it weighed a ton, and it was an ornery character, always snorting and stamping around, trying to prove its dominance. I wouldn't even get near the fence if that bull was anywhere close. But I'd look out in that pasture now and then and see Wanda, this tiny girl, feeding that old bull corn from her hand, talking to it, petting it, and it would be as docile as a lamb, nuzzling her like a lap dog.

When one of Gilley's cows gave birth to a blind calf, Wanda became its eyes and its caretaker. It followed her everywhere. She willed that calf to live and taught it to survive.

I quickly became a co-conspirator with Wanda and the stray critters. I started buying sacks of dry food for her to feed them. At one time, we had more cats than we could count and eighteen dogs of all breeds and descriptions. Wanda had names for every one and knew all their dispositions. Two of the dogs, Stan and Dan, eventually would appear in several of my paintings. If any of the dogs and cats began to snarl and fight, it took only a quiet word from Wanda to stop them.

It should come as no surprise, I guess, that one of the first paintings I did at Riverwood was of Wanda. It is one of my favorites. Wanda eventually grew up and moved away, and I lost track of her. But I still have the painting, and I treasure it, as I treasure my memories of her and her very special love for all the creatures of the earth.

I walked this land with a dreamer's freedom, and with a waking man's perception—places, houses whispered to me their secrets.

—Daphne du Maurier

Chapter 11

One of the paintings I sold at Hammer Galleries, "My Yankee Drum," was purchased by Wood Hannah, who owned Frame House Gallery in Lexington, Kentucky, one of the country's major producers of offset prints, particularly of wildlife art, which was the hot item in the print market at the time.

This was a sort of sepia-toned tempera of a Civil War drum that Mom and Dad had bought for me, canted in an antique chair before a window in my home studio. Hannah called wanting to talk about producing a print of the painting. He had a vacation home in North Carolina at Grandfather Mountain, and I met him there and signed a one-year contract. When the prints were ready early in 1973, Dad and I drove out to Lexington and I signed all 1,500 copies in one day. While we were there, the gallery held a big party for myself and several other artists and invited art dealers from all over the country.

On the way back home, Dad and I started talking about my print and we agreed that the gallery wasn't doing anything that I couldn't do myself to more profit and satisfaction. I was quite particular when it came to the quality of reproductions. I wanted to be able to control that as well as the price and the number produced.

When we got back home, I talked to Tim about it, and we decided to start a business to market my prints. We called it the Heritage Company. We didn't know the slightest thing about the print business, of course, but we didn't let that stop us. I hadn't known anything about painting when I started either.

My first big problem was finding a printer who could meet my standards. I finally found him in Bill Hall of Hall Printing Company in High Point, who, while sometimes frustrated by my exacting demands, would go on to win every printing award for our reproductions and attract other artists because of them.

We brought out our first print that fall when my contract with Frame House expired. It was called "Rowboat," a scene I'd come across on Bald Head Island, a place I'd come to love almost as much as Lexington and Davidson County.

Bald Head was the infamous "Cape of Feare," the last spit of land where North Carolina's major river, the Cape Fear, emptied into the Atlantic, the entrance to the state's major port at Wilmington. Accessible only by water, Bald Head was the northernmost sub-tropic island in the country, with tall palmettos, wild orchids, miles of sandy white beach, high dunes, a huge maritime forest, fresh-water ponds, and vast marshlands interlaced with dark, meandering creeks.

The island also was a haven for wildlife, and that was what brought me and several of my fraternity brothers from Chapel Hill there on a duck hunting trip in the fall of 1956 when I was a sophomore at the University of North Carolina.

I took time to prowl the island on that trip and found it to be a fascinating place. It had two lighthouses then. Old Baldy was an octagonal structure of stone, brick and masonry which had been put into service in 1818 and had survived many hurricanes. An earlier lighthouse, built in 1813, had fallen during a storm, causing Old Baldy to be built more sturdily. The oldest lighthouse on the North Carolina coast, it sat amongst the trees at the edge of the marsh near the river on the west side of the island, well back from the ocean, its light dampered since 1935. The second lighthouse, built in 1903, was a tall, spider-legged steel tower set atop the open dunes facing the sea on the east side of the island, near the point. When I first visited the island, it was nearing the end of its long service. It would be deactivated and toppled by dynamite in 1958.

At the base of this lighthouse were three identical, white frame houses facing the sea. Here the keeper and his assistants lived with their families until the lighthouse was destroyed. The original keeper had been Captain Charlie Swan, who had lived here thirty years before his retirement. Cap'n Charlie's house, the westernmost, was to be forever known as his, no matter who lived in it after his retirement. In the '50s, he was still alive and made frequent sentimental visits to the island and the lighthouse.

As I stood at the foot of the lighthouse looking down on the keepers' houses and beyond them to the sea I couldn't help but wonder what it would be like to live here in the unrelenting glare of the daytime sun and the unceasing nighttime flash of the big light. I didn't realize it then, but I would eventually express that wonder in several paintings.

After that first visit, Bald Head kept calling to me and I was drawn back many times, especially to Cap'n Charlie's house, empty by then, and to the old, abandoned Coast Guard station. I once took my kids to camp on the beach near Cap'n Charlie's house. We watched the sun set over water from the "Cape of Feare," and the next morning we watched it rise over water from the same spot.

When I started painting full-time, I sometimes spent weeks in the summer with my family at Mom and Dad's house at Myrtle Beach, and I often found myself driving northward on U.S. 17 to Southport to catch the ferry to Bald Head. I'd spend the day prowling, sketching and taking photographs. I was particularly drawn to Old Baldy. I loved its design, structure and textures, loved its history and the stories it held, and I dreamed of leasing it someday and turning it into a house and studio. But that was not to be.

By this time, controversy about developing the island had erupted, and I wanted to set the place down as I had known it, just as I was preserving the disappearing scenes I loved in Davidson County.

Many attempts to tame and develop Bald Head had been made in the past, all of them defeated by nature, but the one that began in 1972 was to succeed. Bald Head is now an exclusive resort community with a beautiful golf course, country club, huge marina, expensive homes, condos, rental units, a bed-and-breakfast inn, restaurants, shops, and ferries making regular runs to the mainland. But I did many paintings of Bald Head before all of that came about, and in those it remains as it was when I first saw it.

Eight of the paintings in that first show at Hammer Galleries were of Bald Head, and they were among the first sold. So it seemed only natural to choose a Bald Head scene for our new company's first print. We printed 750 copies and sold them out of the gas company office, some to individuals, most to dealers who retailed them for $60 each, and they were gone within six weeks. The Heritage Company was off and running.

One of the first dealers we lined up to sell our prints was J. Harold Smith, who had a photography shop and art gallery in Greensboro. I had met Harold at the party when Frame House Gallery released the drum print. He bought

150 copies. "People thought I was crazy," he later told a magazine writer. "Smartest move I ever made." He sold every copy, and Tim and I did not have to work hard to recruit him as one of our first dealers.

Harold went on to become one of my greatest promoters and best friends, buying and reselling my originals as well as my prints. His confidence in my work brought other dealers to us. I might never have achieved the success I did, if not for Harold.

We produced three more prints in 1974, including another Bald Head scene that would eventually involve me in controversy—but more about that later. The other two were Davidson County scenes.

One was called "Afternoon at the Petreas." Mr. and Mrs. Wright Petrea farmed forty acres on Old Highway 64 near the community of Reeds, west of Lexington. I had known them all my life. Mrs. Petrea delivered eggs to our house when I was a child.

The Petreas were in their late seventies or early eighties and still going strong when I first stopped by to visit and ask if they minded if I stayed a while to do a little drawing and painting. I promised not to get in the way. They welcomed me with open arms, as everybody did in Davidson County. I went back many times and rarely found them at rest. Sometimes, though, I would find Mrs. Petrea, an apron around her waist, a bonnet covering her head, sitting in a straight-back chair with a short-handle hoe, working in her garden. She would sit and hoe a while, get up, move the chair, sit back down and hoe a little more.

The Petreas took great pleasure in competing against one another to see who could win the most ribbons at the Davidson County Fair in Lexington, the Dixie Classic Fair in Winston-Salem, and the N.C. State Fair in Raleigh. Both laughingly claimed to have won more than the other. It was hard to tell who the champion really was because both had won so many. They entered different categories from each other, Mrs. Petrea competing to see who could put up the prettiest jar of spiced peaches, the most geometrically arranged jar of green beans, or the best chocolate layer cake or apple pie, Mr. Petrea vying to see who could grow the biggest pumpkin, the prettiest sweet potatoes, or the finest pecans, which he called "pea-cans." They kept at it right into their nineties.

"Afternoon at the Petreas" was a painting of Mr. Petrea's slatted wood chair set under a big oak in his back yard, just as I found it, his hand-whittled walking stick propped against it. It might have given the wrong impression to somebody who didn't know Mr. Petrea. The reason his chair was empty and his walking stick unemployed was because he was out working in the field.

The other print we issued that year was called "Mrs. Leonard's Marigolds." It showed a bouquet in an old enamelware coffee pot, sitting on a watering trough next to an agateware bucket and an outdoor spigot, and it remains one of my favorite paintings.

Almost everybody in Davidson County knew about Mrs. David Leonard's house. She lived on Highway 52, the Winston Road, north of Lexington, not far from Lonnie Smalley's place, where I'd worked all those months on my '31 Plymouth back in high school. Mrs. Leonard was an artist herself. Her medium was flowers. Flowers grew all around the yard of her modest home, and in every imaginable kind of container. The fields adjoining the house erupted in brilliant color every spring and remained that way right into fall, as the great variety of flowers she grew blossomed in waves by their seasons.

The flowers were not only her joy but her livelihood. She cut and sold them fresh at the farmers' market in Winston-Salem. She also dried them and fashioned them into beautiful arrangements to sell during the cold months when the fields were dormant.

I became such a fixture at Mrs. Leonard's that she sometimes hardly even noticed I was there. I especially loved
the unpainted building behind the house that she called
her "shock house." That was where she left the fresh flowers overnight in cans and buckets of well water to get over
the shock of being cut before she sold them. You never
knew what sight might greet you when you opened the door
of that old building with its stepped-board shelves, but you
could count on it being one of dazzling splendor. Mrs.
Leonard never raised a fuss about me poking around in
there rearranging things to suit my painter's eye—or about
my borrowing a bouquet of marigolds to set out on the watering trough for a while.

Eventually, the state tore down Mrs. Leonard's place
and bulldozed her flower fields to build a new expressway.
But whenever I turn off the old Winston Road onto that highway now, in my mind I'm again opening the door of Mrs.
Leonard's shock house and reliving the gorgeous surprises
that always awaited me there. I did a lot of paintings at Mrs.
Leonard's, and I was honored to have been privileged to
preserve some of the fleeting beauty and joy she created
for all who passed her way.

Early in 1974, which turned out to be a full and frantic
year for me, I flew to Los Angeles at the request of Ham-
mer-Knoedler Galleries and checked into the Beverly
Wilshire Hotel at their expense. For a small-town boy, this
was moving in the fast lane. My purpose was to learn the
process of etching in the studio of a master printmaker,
Richard Royce. The gallery had signed up myself and four
other artists, Gloria Vanderbilt, LeRoy Neiman, Don
Kingman, and Salvador Dali to do a special series of prints
by different methods to be issued by a branch of the company called FKH Publications. I had chosen etching, al-

though I had never done it, because it seemed to be more appropriate to the kind of painting I was doing.

I had read about etchings and knew that creating them was a difficult and complicated process and I was eager to learn it. I arrived at the studio early Monday morning, and after a quick tour and a thorough explanation of the process, Richard handed me a sheet of polished copper and told me to go to it.

Each color in an etching is hand-printed from a separate copper plate, and every plate has to be in perfect register. The image is first drawn on the copper, then painted with a substance called sugar-lift. After that, the plate is coated with asphaltum, a protective, then immersed in acid. The sugar-lift pops away, and the plate is washed again, then dipped once more into acid that cuts into the exposed area. You have to know precisely how long to leave it in the acid before removing it. Then you start on the next plate. As I said, not any easy process—greatly time consuming.

I had decided to do a snow scene of Riverwood, mostly in sepia tones, with a blank gray sky, to reduce the number of plates and make my first attempt at etching a little easier. I had brought drawings and photos to work from.

I'd spent two hours drawing on the first plate and was sort of proud of what I'd done when Richard came over to check on me.

"What do you think?" I asked.

"Okay," he said, "but don't you think it would be better if you did it the right way?"

I had drawn it as a positive, forgetting that it had to be a negative to print from it. Just another little detail to make the process even harder. I don't think I'd ever felt so stupid. I wiped my plate clean and started all over.

That turned out to be one of the hardest and most painstaking weeks of work I ever put in. I arrived at the studio early each morning and didn't leave until well into the evening, always exhausted. The only highlight of the week came when I went down to the hotel dining room for a late supper one night and was seated next to Muhammed Ali and his entourage.

But by the end of the week I had a proof of my first etching, and I had learned a lot. I called it "Another World," and the double meaning was intentional, for etching surely was that.

This etching would not be released for two years. Over the next few years I would go to New York to work with Richard on others, one of which would come to be the center of one of the most challenging periods of my life, but more on that later as well.

After doing seven etchings, I decided that I was through with that process. It was too hard, took too much time, didn't allow the detail that painting did, and painting, after all, was my first love. I always thought the etchings looked a little primitive, and I was never fully satisfied with them.

After returning from California, I was scrambling to borrow enough paintings from hither and yon for my first museum show, scheduled at the end of March. But before that I had to take part in another exhibition. Late in 1973, I had been selected as one of twelve artists to participate in the Artists of America '74 traveling exhibit. Another of the artists chosen was Norman Rockwell. Each artist was to select a single painting for the exhibit. The one I chose was called "Mrs. Edna Shoaf Dorsett."

Mrs. Dorsett lived on West Fifth Avenue on the edge of Lexington. I'd hunted squirrels on her property when I was in high school.

As a small child, Mrs. Dorsett had suffered a serious

illness that nearly killed her and left her face disfigured. She had grown up very self-conscious about her looks, shy and withdrawn. Her mother had kept her at home and not allowed her to go to school. Mrs. Dorsett was in her early eighties when I painted her. She was a sweet, dear soul who lived alone and was perhaps the loneliest person I ever knew.

The attic of her little house had been turned into a bare room, lit by a single lightbulb dangling from a cord. A quilting frame was suspended from the ceiling by wires, and there Mrs. Dorsett spent her days making beautiful quilts from bits of cloth salvaged from old clothing and scraps gathered from local sewing plants. She figured she'd made more than 300 in her life.

I'd been interested in quilts from the time Aunt Buff had given me that old family quilt as a boy, and Kay and I had started collecting quilts after Grandmother Raper, as a wedding gift, gave us an unusual quilt called Whig's Defeat stitched by her sisters, Sissy and Lena, about 1860. The quilt depicted the defeat of the Whig Party in North Carolina in the 1850s. I stopped by Mrs. Dorsett's house one day just to see her quilts.

She led me up the narrow staircase to that attic room to show me one she was about to finish. As soon as she sat down by her quilting frame I knew I had to paint that. She loved for me to come to her house to work because she loved company. After that painting, I went back to paint the little Dixie woodstove in her kitchen, where shelves under the windows were lined with potted geraniums. When I told her I wanted to come and paint her kitchen, she said, "I'll get it cleaned up."

"No," I told her, "leave it just like it is."

Even as I was sketching, though, she'd go around pulling the dead leaves off the geraniums despite my admonishments. I loved sitting in that cozy little kitchen on a cold winter day talking to Mrs. Dorsett. It was there I learned that you can uproot your geraniums in the fall, knock the dirt off the roots, hang them upside down in the basement, replant them in the spring, and they will sprout. Honest.

After I finished the paintings, I often stopped by just to visit a while with Mrs. Dorsett. She was always happy to see me, always bustling around wanting to fix me something to eat or drink so I'd stay longer. Sometimes I'd stop by with the kids for a minute or two just to say hello.

"Don't go, Bob," she'd say when we'd start to leave. "Y'all set down and stay a while. I've got some sweet potato pie and grape juice."

I was particularly pleased that people all around the country could now get to know Mrs. Dorsett through my painting, even if she couldn't enjoy their company.

The Artists of America exhibits were the idea of Edward J. Piszek, an art lover and collector who had founded Mrs. Paul's Kitchen in Philadelphia, producers of frozen seafood. The idea behind it was to take art to people around the country who might not have access to art museums or galleries.

The show was to be previewed with an exhibit and party at the Franklin Institute in Philadelphia on March 15. I invited my friend W.C. "Mutt" Burton to accompany Kay and me to the opening. Mutt wrote an art column for the *Greensboro Daily News*, and he had been the first person to write anything about my paintings. In addition to being a newspaper columnist and reporter, he was an artful photographer and a gifted actor who appeared in regional theaters all over the South. Mutt was a warm, charming, humorous man, a great storyteller, fun to be around. Not only had he become a good friend of mine and Kay's but of everybody else in my family.

The preview was a great success. We got to talk with

Grace Kelly's brother, as well as the cardinal of the arch-diocese of Philadelphia, a Pennsylvania senator whose name now slips my mind, and a lot of other nice folks. The only disappointment for Mutt and me was that we didn't get to meet Norman Rockwell, who was then eighty. He'd fallen off his bicycle and gotten banged up and wasn't able to come.

The highlight of the show for me came the following day when it opened to the public at a shopping center in New Jersey. The public relations lady for the exhibit rushed up to me at one point and said, "Come with me, you've got to see this." She led me to the spot where my painting was hanging, and there before it stood a young woman with tears streaming down her face. I had no idea that the PR lady was going to intrude on this young woman but she did. She told her that I was the artist, and we introduced ourselves a little awkwardly, as the young woman dabbed at her tears with a tissue. She told me that she really liked the painting and that it had moved her deeply. I was curious to know why.

"Does she remind you of your grandmother?" I asked.

"No," she said, "it's not that so much as the sense of loneliness I get from her. Yet despite that, and despite her age, and whatever problems she might have she's still determined to create something beautiful and useful for others."

At that moment, I knew for certain that my painting had achieved exactly what I wanted it to.

Less than two weeks after we returned from Philadelphia, my daughter Kelly, Mom, Dad, and I flew to Shreveport, Louisiana, (the boys had other activities scheduled, and Kay stayed with them) for the opening of my first retrospective show at the Richard W. Norton Art Gallery, which sat in the midst of a forty-acre azalea garden with more than 10,000 plants. The azaleas welcomed us in full bloom and they were a spectacular show in themselves. I could hardly wait to get to the museum. Not because of my show, but because amongst the works of great European and American masters in the museum's permanent collection was what was proclaimed at the time to be the world's largest collection of art of the American West, one of my boyhood passions. I spent hours in that museum standing in awe before some of the same works of Charles Russell and Frederic Remington that I'd so painstakingly attempted to copy as a boy.

After my show closed, the museum director called to thank me and said that my paintings had drawn the greatest attendance of any show in the museum's history.

The great works at the Norton Gallery were not the only masterpieces I got to examine closely that year, for Kay and I were soon at the Louvre in Paris, gazing in wonder at the works of Rembrandt, Rubens, Leonardo da Vinci and so many others. For me, that was my turn to stand in front of paintings and cry, and I did just that. I still get emotional thinking about it.

I had come away from the Norton exhibit feeling sort of heady and full of myself, thinking I was a rocket taking off in the art world, but my rocket fizzled and nose-dived only minutes after I stepped into the Louvre. I don't think there's a painter on Earth who won't be humbled by a walk through the halls of that old palace. It tells you things you don't want to hear, puts you in your place, deflates your ego. Yet, it isn't a discouraging or depressing experience. Just the opposite. It drains your vanity, sets you back to basics, makes you yearn to learn more, do better, achieve your best, whatever you think that may be, then move beyond it.

I actually was in Paris partly for work. Two prints that I had done for FHK Publications were being printed in Paris, and I had to go there to check the proofs and make final changes to the plates. One was of Old Baldy, the historic lighthouse on Bald Head. The other was of a century-old house just across the Yadkin River in Rowan County called the Alexander Long House. It had always caught my imagination because its twin, side-by-side red-brick chimneys told a story. In each chimney Alexander Long had designed a big heart of dark-glazed bricks. Beneath one heart was his initials, beneath the other his wife's. I admired a man who proclaimed his love so proudly and publicly.

Since I had to be in Paris anyway, Kay and I decided to make a vacation of it. Some of our friends came along, and we had a great time.

We marched in the inaugural parade of President Valery Giscard d'Estaing (we happened to be on the Champs Elyseès and it happened to be passing by, so we joined in), and I had my international stage debut at the Lido des Paris, the world-famous cabaret. Maybe I should explain how that happened, but first let me say that I was fully clothed throughout my performance.

One night we found a taxi driver who spoke English as badly as I spoke French and told him we wanted to take in some authentic Paris nightlife. He knew just the place. He took us to a seedy little club in a rundown section where each couple had to buy an overpriced bottle of bad champagne upon entry and where the entertainment turned out to be a singing transexual who, for reasons we could never ascertain, was dressed as a tree. Not exactly what we had in mind, and so we ended up at the Lido.

We got there well before the show was to start and were waiting at the front of the line when a fellow came up and whispered that for a few extra francs he could assure us the best seats in the house. *Why not*, we thought. He took us around back, down a stairway, and through a dark hall to the back of the stage, where we were instructed to wait.

156

He left us there and soon returned bringing more people, who also gave him a few extra francs. After a while, others came and ushered us straight to front row seats. We were immensely pleased that we had paid the few extra francs for such privilege. After a while, though, it seemed that most of the audience was entering from the dark, backstage hallway, all of them having paid a few extra francs for the best seats, and the only reason we were on the front row was because we had been at the front of the line to begin with.

Sitting on the front row brought about my stage debut. A pretty young English singer wanted a volunteer from the audience to help her with a number and she picked me. Everybody was egging me on, so I climbed up there, grinning like a hayseed from North Carolina. She put me in a chair, plopped down in my lap, ran her fingers through my hair, and as Kay and my friends hooted and howled, she sang "My Heart Belongs to Daddy." I was only thirty-seven at the time, thank you, not quite ready for the rocking chair, even if my hair was already turning white.

After our trip to Paris, I embarked on the most difficult painting I ever undertook. Perhaps it was the effect of my visit to the Louvre that prompted it, but I wasn't really aware of that.

Dan Melton came over to visit one morning and sat to talk in the open back doorway of the studio. One of the dogs, Stan, had followed him, and he took up a place on the stepping stones at Dan's feet. Dan was wearing an old wool sweater and corduroy pants, and he took off his leather hat and placed it beside him. I was out in the yard working, and when I looked over and saw him with one hand on his knee and the other on the dog's head, I stopped what I was doing and started sketching him.

The painting turned out to be a study in textures, the texture of the old logs and the weathered door frame with its cracks, whorls and knots, the texture of the stone of the steps, of the dog's short hair, the frayed door mat, the stubble of Dan's beard, the wool of his faded blue sweater, the leather of his hat and battered old shoes with the strings missing, and most of all the texture of his rust-colored corduroy pants.

I can't tell you how many long hours I spent on that painting, especially on those corduroy pants. They seemed endless, but I had seized this challenge and I was determined to get every ridge of that fabric, every fold and wrinkle and shadow just right. Dan would come over and watch my slow progress and say, "Why don't you just change my pants?" But I kept at it until I got down every line to my satisfaction.

I was proud of it when I finished, and I am still. It may never hang in the Louvre, but I had the satisfaction of knowing that I had reached beyond myself and achieved the best that I was capable of at that time.

But it was more than overcoming the technical difficulties that I was proud of. The painting had a tone and feeling, a profundity, if you will, unlike any other I'd ever done. I was not surprised that it was Dan who had brought that out in me.

Dan's life had not been easy. He didn't have many options early on, but he'd done the best he could with what he had. He was a man without resentment, bitterness or regret, at peace with himself and with God, as he told me many times. He had come to realize that even if he'd had many other options, he wouldn't have wanted his life to have turned out any differently than it had. The simple life, he had learned, was the best life.

Dan was a man who had known hardship and gained dignity and great wisdom from it, and I think I captured that. It was the least I could do for all that he taught me.

We do not inherit the land from our ancestors, we borrow it from our children.

—Chief Seattle

Chapter 12

Of all the wonderful things that happened for me in 1974, one of the more significant events was a telephone call that came late in the year. The caller was Hugh Morton Jr.

He was from a prominent North Carolina family. His great-grandfather, Hugh McCrae, had developed the mountain resort community of Linville and had bought up huge acreage there, including Grandfather Mountain, one of North Carolina's highest peaks. His grandmother, Agnes McCrae Morton, had started the Highland Games at Grandfather Mountain, a celebration of her Scottish heritage. His father had made Grandfather Mountain into one of the state's major tourist attractions, had been instrumental in bringing the battleship *North Carolina* to a permanent berth in Wilmington to stage sea battles for tourists, and was a well-known figure in the state.

Hugh Jr. was only twenty-six and he was working for a public relations agency in Greensboro that had been started by John Harden, a former newspaperman and author of a popular book about North Carolina mysteries, *The Devil's Tramping Ground*. He had seen some of my prints at Harold Smith's gallery, liked them, and thought that I might be in need of somebody to help promote my work. Could he and John Harden come over and talk about it? Sure, I said, although at that point I didn't have a real idea of what public relations was all about.

Tim and I met with them at the gas company and did our best to act like big shots in the art business. I was impressed with Hugh. He was genial, energetic, ambitious, filled with ideas and enthusiasm, and I liked him immediately. If I allowed him to work on my behalf, his goal was nothing short of making me the most famous artist in America.

I couldn't help but chuckle. I knew that he surely had his work cut out for him if he brought that about. But I saw from his presentation that he thought my work was worth promoting, and I knew that I could use his services.

I had learned the art of selling from my father, and I thought I was fairly good at it. I had no hesitancy about pushing my paintings and prints. I loved what I was doing and believed in my work as much as Dad believed in gas stoves. I was eager to share it and so passionate about it that I'd latch onto strangers on the street, if they'd stop and listen, and tell them how much fun I was having doing it.

I didn't want to be a starving artist hiding in a garret with completed canvases piling up around me unsold and unseen. I wanted people to buy my paintings, hang them on the wall and enjoy them. I wanted as many people as possible to come to know my work and to take the same pleasure from it that I got from doing it, even if they only saw the paintings in a gallery, or a corporate office, or the prints in somebody's living room. I wanted an audience for my work, just as an actor, or a singer, or a writer wants an audience.

But attracting attention to the work required drawing attention to myself. And that was not my nature. I had always felt ill at ease and awkward about that. I didn't even take compliments very well; I'd always slough them off and pass the credit on to somebody else. I love people, and I knew that I could handle attention if it came. I just felt awk-

My grandmother, Lillie
Leonard Raper.

My grandfather, Emery
Elisha Raper.

My grandfather, Edgar A. Timberlake (Pa-
Pa) and grandmother, Dessie Fitzgerald
Timberlake (Gangy).

Mom, Ella Leonard Raper, majored in five sports at Salem College.

Dad, Casper Hill Timberlake, loved sports and played on Lexington High School's first football team.

I was a happy baby—most of the time.

I wouldn't get in the goat man's cart. He turned out to be a Nazi spy.

Uncle Emery Raper was my World War II
hero. When he came home to get married,
he let me try on his uniform.

Dad and me clowning around at Myrtle Beach.

The day I won a bet by shooting dragonflies out of the air with my .22.

A Spanish mackerel I caught at Wrightsville Beach.

My older brother, Tim, took me everywhere in his "Push, Don't Pass" Model A roadster.

On my 13th birthday, I got my first shotgun for bird hunting.

The house Dad built at Myrtle Beach.

Tim, Mom and me at the beach.

My childhood buddy, Johnny Wilson, loved the water, but his mother didn't want him to be around it. He drowned at 16.

Punkin Wallace and I had a wild time at the national Boy Scout Jamboree.

A.B. Hardee was my shop teacher when I won a national award for the Pennsylvania-Dutch chest I built at 15.

I was co-captain of Lexington High's 1954 championship team.

The hot rod I built with the help of Lonnie Smally as a high school junior.

My sweetheart, Kay Musgrave, and I at a German Club
dance at the University of North Carolina.

Kay and I at our wedding rehearsal dinner.

Wasn't she a stunning bride? She still is.

Our first house on Rosewood Dr. after a couple of remodelings.

My first studio was under the skylights at the Rosewood Dr. house.

Our children, Kelly, Dan, and Ed.

Chatting with my dear friend,
Dr. Margaret Handy.

Hard at work in my studio at home on
Rosewood Drive.

Victor Hammer took only a few moments to assess my paintings. "Why don't you leave those," he said. "I think we can sell them."

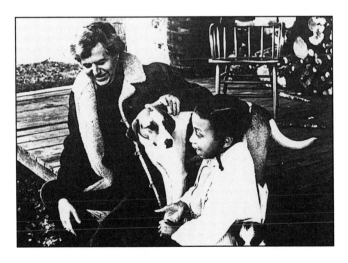

My friend Wanda lived next-door to my second studio, Riverwood, and had a greater rapport with animals than anybody I've ever known.

Making beautiful quilts in her stark attic helped Edna Shoaf Dorsett to overcome her loneliness.

Riverwood was one of the oldest houses in Davidson County, and I loved working there.

Riverwood itself was the inspiration for many of my early paintings.

My brother, Tim, and his wife, Teen, with Kay
and me at one of my shows.

Ron Powers, President of Keep America Beautiful, Iron Eyes Cody, me and my congressman, Steve Neal, in the Oval Office with President Jimmy Carter shortly before Iron Eyes made all the photographers go wild.

President Ronald Reagan and Iron Eyes had appeared in several films together. They argued about who had fallen off which horse in which movie as Ron Powers and my congressman, Gene Johnston, listened.

My dear friend, Charles Kuralt, came to Riverwood to talk about the book we were going to do together.

The privileged few who first heard Charlie read the text of the book on the porch at Riverwood. Front row (l to r): Hugh Morton Sr. and Hugh Morton Jr. Second row: C.J. Underwood, myself, Charlie, and Charles Curtis. Back row: Jimmy Morton, Dad and Tim.

At the White House with Dr. Armand Hammer and his wife, Frances, at the time of the signing of the peace treaty between Israel and Egypt.

Dr. Hammer summoned me to London to tutor Prince Charles, a really nice guy, who would have fit in well at Whitley's Barbecue back in Lexington.

My dear friend, Perry Como, with Kay and me
at one of my New York shows. We continue to
work together for the Duke Children's Center.

Rosemary Clooney sang the songs that Loonis McGlohon
wrote from my paintings for a TV special.

When I built my new studio, I knew it would cause big things to happen. I just didn't expect them to be as big as they turned out to be.

Lillian Carter, the President's mother,
was a great lady. We worked together
to fight cystic fibrosis.

Kay and me with Mom and Dad and Governor Jim Hunt and his
wife, Carolyn, at the opening of my show at the Corcoran
Gallery of Art in Washington.

My new studio offers many isolated and inspiring spots to work.

I love the look on Kay's face here, as Perry Como interrupted a tribute dinner to me to sing to her.

My boyhood chums, Joe Sink, left, and Cloyd Philpott, right.
We called ourselves the three fat boys.

Taking time out for one of my favorite activities.

Fred Craver loved wood as few people ever have. He was the inspiration for my furniture line.

Aunt Sallie Parnell began making hand-loomed rugs at the age of four. She was still at it 100 years later.

Dad carving the Christmas ham with a hug from Mom. They were childhood sweethearts, devoted to one another for as long as they lived.

Kay and I are blessed by our children and grandchildren. At left is our son, Dan, holding his daughter, Evanne. In the center is our grandson, Rob, whose Dad, Ed, is just behind me. I'm holding the hand of our grandson, Dek, Dan's other child.

Here I am in the barn at the studio with all of our grandchildren except for Evanne, who wasn't yet born. Rob is at the left, Kate is just behind my chair. Abby-Liz is on my lap. Ann Claiborne is on the floor. Dek is leaning against the sofa. Carter has her chin in her hand.

My new gallery. I knew if we built it "they" would come.

ward seeking it.

Also I was still in the infancy of this new career and still very naive. I had been so much in love with the act of painting, and the spectacular and almost unbelievable events that it brought to my life had happened so quickly and unexpectedly that I really hadn't had time to think about where I wanted all of this to take me—or how to go about getting there once I decided. I was just beginning to realize all the complexities it entailed.

I hadn't even done basic little things such as preparing a biographical sheet, or having photos of myself printed to send to newspapers or magazines if anybody asked for them. Until this point, the only help I'd had with anything like this had come from my old boyhood buddy, Joe Sink Jr., now the publisher of our local newspaper. I had no mailing lists, and not even any real record of all the paintings I'd done so far. Too many other things demanded my time.

If I intended to continue painting, as I certainly did, and if I hoped to make a decent living from it, as I also did, it was clear that I needed to be better organized, needed to plan ahead, needed to make this love affair I was having with painting more like a business. It also was apparent that I constantly would be needing to make my name and my work better known. I could tell that Hugh truly was interested in me and genuinely liked my work. He couldn't have timed his call any better.

Putting a public relations company on retainer wasn't going to be cheap, but Tim and I talked it over and decided that I had to do it. The prices I was getting for my paintings had been growing steadily, but if I, and they, became even better known, the prices might accelerate more quickly and make the PR company's fees seem a bargain. It was the old business of spending money to make money. We could at least try it for a year and see what happened.

I called and gave the go-ahead. And for the first time since I'd started painting I didn't have to worry about tooting my own horn. Hugh Morton Jr. was now my official, hired tooter. And he turned out to be a virtuoso.

My second show at Hammer Galleries opened on April 16, 1975, and the prices on the paintings were double what they were for the first show. Even at the higher prices, this show, like the first, was sold out in advance. It also brought new and unexpected developments.

One of the people who attended was Roger Powers, president of Keep America Beautiful. We had a nice chat about my paintings, and about his organization, which I admired greatly. Soon after I returned home, Roger called and asked if I would be willing to serve as Keep America Beautiful's official artist. I accepted.

Keep America Beautiful was founded in 1953. Its goal was to establish affiliate groups in every community in the country to protect the environment, fight against litter, clean up blighted areas, plant flowers, build gardens, and generally spruce up and prettify whatever needed it. Millions of people were involved in its projects, and among its most ardent supporters were Lady Bird Johnson, the former first lady, and Lillian Carter—Miss Lillian—the mother of the man who was about to become President. As it turned out, Miss Lillian owned some of my prints, and I would get to know her well later, a wonderful lady.

The first thing that Roger suggested that I might do as official artist was a portrait of Iron Eyes Cody to be used on the first conservation stamp, as well as a poster. I couldn't believe my good fortune. My childhood fascination with all things western was about to move from fantasy to reality.

After decades of appearing in movies and TV shows, Iron Eyes had gained far more fame for a series of com-

162

mercials for Keep America Beautiful that in the beginning he didn't want to do. In the first one, he paddled around in a canoe observing one environmental desecration after another. The final scene was a close-up of his face, a tear forming in his right eye. The tear, incidentally, was a drop of glycerin applied by a make-up man. The commercial had been filmed over six days in San Francisco Bay. The reason Iron Eyes didn't want to do it was because he couldn't swim and was deathly afraid of water. "I told 'em the only way I'd do it," he later told me, "was if they'd have a helicopter with a rescue crew hovering overhead in case I tipped over."

That commercial first appeared in 1971. It became the most frequently aired public service announcement ever and won numerous awards. A poll later showed that ninety-four per cent of Americans recognized Iron Eyes' face, if not his name, as a result of it, and it later was named as one of the top fifty TV commercials of all time.

I was really excited when I flew out to California to meet Iron Eyes. I rented a car and drove up to his house in the hills above Hollywood. It was a modest, white stucco house surrounded by a low cyclone fence in a working-class neighborhood. Iron Eyes greeted me warmly. He was seventy-two then and in robust health, dressed in bluejeans and a western shirt, his still-black hair in the familiar braids. He introduced me to his wife, Birdie, an archeologist, a sweet but reserved woman.

The house was a virtual museum. Every wall was covered with western paintings, antique guns, plaques, proclamations, Indian artifacts, movie posters, photos of Iron Eyes with famous people, hunting trophies, so many things and of such variety that I would have had to take notes to remember it all. The floors were covered with buffalo-skin rugs, and the walls were lined with boxes and stacks of stuff. As Iron Eyes led me around showing off things and talking about them, I learned that we had much in common—hunting, guns, the art of the Old West and cowboy movies at the top of the list.

Like me, Iron Eyes also was a big supporter of the Boy Scouts and still worked with them. I told him about the first time I'd seen him at the jamboree at Newport Harbor in 1954, and he rummaged around and came up with a photo of himself dancing there with 50,000 boys watching from a hillside.

"I was right over here," I said and pointed to a tiny figure high on the hill at the back. "I think that's me right there."

We went on talking and laughing and telling stories for hours. Mostly he was telling stories and I was listening and asking questions, because I was dying to know about all the old cowboy stars. He had known and worked with all of them, Tom Mix, Lash Larue, Buck Jones, Hoot Gibson, Ken Maynard, Gene Autry, Roy Rogers, Gabby Hayes, Clayton Moore, who played the Lone Ranger, and Jay Silverhills, who played his companion Tonto—and, of course, my boyhood hero Tim McCoy, who had been one of his closest friends. He even knew the original Rin Tin Tin, the first canine movie star.

Iron Eyes had been in the movie business since he was eight and debuted in D.W. Griffith's *The Massacre*. He had appeared in more than 200 films and many TV shows since then, including several classics, among them *The Plainsman*, *Sitting Bull*, *Stagecoach*, and *A Man Called Horse*. You could hardly name a western star he didn't know and have stories about. He also became close friends with major stars such as John Wayne, Erroll Flynn, James Cagney, Gary Cooper, Steve McQueen, Richard Harris, even the comedy team of Bud Abbott and Lou Costello, all of whom he acted with at one time or another.

At my prodding, Iron Eyes told me many tales about Tim McCoy. He'd first met him at nineteen when his father, who was Cherokee (Iron Eyes' mother was Cree), had rounded up 500 Indians to appear in Cecil B. DeMille's silent epic *Covered Wagon*. Iron Eyes was one of the 500. In 1926, while filming *War Paint*, Iron Eyes had saved McCoy's life. An over-enthusiastic Indian player had stuck a gun right in McCoy's face and pulled the trigger. Iron Eyes, playing McCoy's scout, hit the Indian's arm just as the gun went off, pushing it away from McCoy's face. The "blank" in the pistol had been overcharged and it knocked McCoy off his horse and left him unconscious and bleeding on the ground with part of one ear missing. If Iron Eyes hadn't hit the gun at exactly the right moment, I never would have had a chance for McCoy to become my hero because he wouldn't have been around to make all those Saturday movies I watched at the Granada.

Early in his career, McCoy had a wild west show that went bust, but in 1934 he started another, this one to tour with the Ringling Bros. and Barnum & Baily Circus.

He called Iron Eyes and asked him to organize an Indian snake dance as one of the acts. Iron Eyes had a deep concern that Indians be portrayed accurately in films and performances. (In his later years, he worked tirelessly for native American causes, and I saw him sign over paychecks to different groups.) He told McCoy that he wouldn't do it unless the dance was authentic. McCoy assured him that it would be. He would get authentic Hopi costumes and, yes, the snakes would be rattlesnakes.

All that Iron Eyes had to do was get together twelve dancers who were willing to handle big rattlesnakes in front of big audiences. He recruited them from among the movie extras he knew, all of them of different tribal backgrounds, all heavy drinkers, and all "bad to fight," as we say in North Carolina. Iron Eyes trained them with a pet rattlesnake named Pete that he kept in his back yard. He had defanged Pete and trained him not to strike, but he still had to sew Pete's jaws shut before his fellow dancers would touch him.

Iron Eyes took his troupe to New York by bus for the big opening at Madison Square Garden (he could spend a whole day telling tales about that trip alone). McCoy was frightened of snakes, even harmless ones, but he had ordered a crateful of big western diamondbacks from Texas for the dancers and had them waiting when they arrived. These snakes were much bigger than Pete. None was less than six feet long. One was nearly seven feet, weighed thirty pounds, and was particularly vicious. All were supposed to be defanged, but when Iron Eyes reached into the crate to bring one out, the big snake struck—its fangs bedding deep into his hand. The rattlesnake dentist had overlooked this one.

Iron Eyes didn't panic. He used a bandanna to make a tourniquet around his hand and did just what we Boy Scouts were taught to do in such a situation. He made a cross-cut over the fang marks and sucked out as much of the poison as he could. He declined to go to a doctor. He was pretty sick for a couple of days and his arm was badly swollen, he said, but he got over it.

When he did, he killed that snake and cured its hide. He had it on the wall of his basement and showed it to me. It brought to mind the big eastern diamondback hide that Archibald Rutledge had on his trophy-room wall.

After Iron Eyes' experience, the other dancers didn't want anything to do with those snakes, even though he demonstrated that all the rest had been defanged. He finally had to design little rawhide hoods with eye holes that fit snugly over the snakes' heads preventing them from opening their mouths. The hoods actually made the big rattlers look even more sinister.

During rehearsals, Iron Eyes noticed that after the snakes had been flung around and thrust about by the dancers, they took off in whichever direction they were aimed as soon as they were released. That gave him an idea for an exciting grand finale for the act.

He didn't tell McCoy or anybody else about his plan.

On opening night, as the snake dance drew to a close, all twelve dancers suddenly rushed toward the audience, stopped short and dropped their snakes. The big rattlers headed straight for the crowd as hard as they could go, just as Iron Eyes had known they would. Iron Eyes had thought that the audience would gasp in fear, then he and the dancers would quickly snatch up the snakes and take their bows, leaving everybody with a thrill to remember.

It just didn't work that way. Screams and pandemonium erupted as people in the front rows broke for the exits. Tim McCoy almost fell off his horse when one of the snakes turned toward him. The snakes were escaping so fast that Iron Eyes and his dancers had to chase them all over the arena before they corralled them. After making page-one headlines, the grand finale got cut in subsequent performances.

Iron Eyes was laughing so hard recalling the story that tears actually came to his eyes. I'm probably one of the few people who ever saw the famous crying Indian actually crying—and it was from mirth.

The next day, I got Iron Eyes to dress in his full, beaded buckskin regalia and took him out into his back yard to sketch and photograph him. At one point, I had him sitting on the ground pretending he was paddling a canoe. I couldn't help but wonder what his neighbors might think if they looked out and saw him.

Later, I produced two full portraits of Iron Eyes and several smaller studies. The one chosen for the conservation stamp and poster showed him in profile, his head slightly bent, the tear in his right eye.

Iron Eyes and I became close friends. I went to California several times to see him. On my second visit, he wanted to take me to his favorite restaurant for dinner. I envisioned a fancy place with palm trees and movie stars dropping by the table to say hello.

Instead, he took me to a joint where the chef had tattoos, wore a greasy apron over his abundant belly, and stood behind a counter, spatula in hand. Motorcycle gang members occupied several booths, making me a little nervous. Then I looked around and saw far stranger looking people who seemed to be making even the motorcycle gang members nervous. Iron Eyes wasn't concerned about any of them. He was wearing his big black Stetson, which he didn't bother to take off during the meal. I was just glad to be with the guy in the black hat.

I traveled a lot with Iron Eyes, appearing at dinners and other functions, and it was always fun. He had a great sense of humor and never ran out of stories. When you traveled with Iron Eyes, you never knew where you might end up, or what you might find yourself doing.

One night we were in New York, and Iron Eyes said, "Come on, we're going to Studio 54." That was *the* hot discotheque at the time. People lined up for blocks hoping to be allowed inside, or just to catch a glimpse of the rich, famous and beautiful people who did get in.

"I'm not much of a dancer, Iron Eyes," I said. "I've never discoed."

"Don't worry about it," he told me. "We'll do Indian dances. They won't know the difference."

Iron Eyes didn't get in any line. We strode right up to the big bouncer standing behind the velvet rope at the entrance. The bouncers at Studio 54 were noted for being overly surly and offensive in exercising their great power over who was allowed in and who wasn't.

"Iron Eyes want to dance," my friend grunted, movie-

Indian style.

He was wearing white buckskins, moccasins, and had a turkey feather in his hair. The bouncer recognized him immediately, and he not only broke into a friendly grin and offered his hand, he was profusely apologetic.

"Man, I would love to let you guys in," he said. "Any other night and you would be in. But it's a private party tonight. I can't let anybody in without an invitation. I'll lose my job. Honest. Come back another night."

Iron Eyes nodded. "May the Great Spirit be with you," he said.

I can't recall where we ended up that night, but it probably was someplace where the cook was wearing a greasy apron. I don't remember doing any Indian dances, or any rattlesnakes being involved, hooded or not.

Twice Iron Eyes and I went to the White House together to be honored for our work with Keep America Beautiful, and both times Iron Eyes did the unexpected.

Jimmy Carter was President on our first visit in 1978. We were ushered into the Oval Office for a little ceremony. News photographers had crowded into the office for a photo opportunity, and this would turn out to be a great one. Iron Eyes was carrying a Sioux war bonnet, a gift for the President. When the time came for the presentation, Iron Eyes walked up the President, but instead of handing him the head-dress, as everybody expected, he plopped it on the President's head. He didn't know that the President didn't like headwear of any kind, hadn't worn a hat since he got out of the Navy, and that although he'd accepted all kinds of hats, caps and other strange head attire during his campaign, he'd never donned any of them.

The head-dress was too big. It came down over the President's forehead and ears. And there he stood, trapped under a mass of feathers and beads, grinning sheepishly as Iron Eyes renamed him Wamble Ska, meaning Great White Eagle. The photographers went wild. You never saw such scrambling and flashing. The President didn't dare take the thing off out of fear of offending Iron Eyes and every other native American.

The next day, of course, photos of the President with that uncomfortable grin and that huge war bonnet dwarfing his head appeared on the front pages of newspapers all around the world. And later that week the comedians on "Saturday Night Live" couldn't resist doing a spoof of the incident. After our visit, I was told, strict orders went out that nobody bearing headgear of any kind was to ever get close to the President again.

This wasn't the only out-of-the-ordinary incident that happened on that visit. Unaware that nobody is allowed to run in the vicinity of the Oval Office, a Keep America Beautiful press agent dashed out of the office into the hallway at full speed to get the news to waiting reporters—and was immediately tackled by Secret Service agents.

Ronald Reagan was President for our second visit three years later. Iron Eyes and I were standing in a White House hallway with a group of dignitaries waiting to be ushered into our ceremony.

All of a sudden, the President appeared down the hallway, headed our way, trailing aides and Secret Service agents. He was wearing a big smile and had a genuine aura of stardom about him. As he got closer, Iron Eyes broke from our group and started toward him. Surely the Secret Service agents had been warned about Iron Eyes after our last visit, and the agents quickly moved to intercept him. The President waved them back, and the two men met in a big embrace.

"Iron Eyes, old friend," the President said, "how are you?"

"Just fine, Mr. President. You're looking great."

They had appeared in several films together, and later in the Oval Office they reminisced about mutual friends and old Hollywood days. I couldn't believe that I was standing in the Oval Office listening to Iron Eyes Cody and the President arguing about who fell off which horse in which movie.

Iron Eyes came to Davidson County to visit me several times. One of those occasions was to film a new set of commercials and short videos for Keep America Beautiful. Some were shot at Riverwood, one in High Point, one in Raleigh, others at High Rock Lake.

At High Rock, Iron Eyes had to paddle around in my new birch-bark canoe. I told him we couldn't afford to have a helicopter and a rescue crew standing by, but I assured him that I'd had a lot of experience falling into High Rock Lake and I could yell instructions to him from the bank on how to get out if he ended up in the water. That didn't seem to comfort him a lot.

He did the shots, but he was awfully nervous the whole time he was in the canoe. The water wasn't deep, but he wouldn't get far from shore, and he kept punching the bottom with the paddle to make sure it was still there.

During most of his visits, Iron Eyes stayed in a two-story log house I'd had restored. It sat on five acres at the end of Wildlife Road on Abbott's Creek south of Lexington. It had been built in 1849 in the Beck's Church community of Davidson County near Thomasville by Henry Hedrick Conrad for his new bride, Rachel Lore. Their nine children were born and reared in the house. Henry Conrad was an opponent of slavery. He became a storekeeper and postmaster, and made a home for freed slaves in the back of his store. He died in 1893 in the house he'd built for his wife and children.

That house had fallen into serious disrepair when Glenn

Fluharty, a Lexington teacher, bought it and had it moved to Wildlife Road. He'd started restoring it when I bought it and let Charlie and Tom Yow finish the job. Kay and I filled it with antique furnishings and used it as a guest house. It had a big living room, a bedroom downstairs, one big bedroom upstairs, two baths, and a kitchen off the back. Iron Eyes loved staying there.

On one of his later visits, I went to the house to pick him up one morning, and after he let me in, he said, "There was a fellow here earlier. Did you send him?"

"No, I didn't send anybody," I said. "Who was it?"

"I don't know. I just heard something early this morning. I got up and came down here and he was standing in the kitchen by the door. I asked was he here to get me, and he didn't say anything, so I said, 'I'll go get ready. I'll just be a few minutes.' When I came back down, he was gone."

"I didn't send anybody," I said. "He didn't say anything?"

"Not a word."

"If that doesn't beat all. Somebody just walks right in."

It had happened to me a few times at the studio, though. Strangers would walk in as if they owned the place.

The day before, we'd gotten together a bunch of posters and other things for Iron Eyes to autograph, and he had them spread out on the kitchen table. Now we noticed that some of the things were missing.

"Isn't that something?" I said incredulously. "Somebody just walks in and carries it right out."

Later, we found the missing stuff back at the studio, but I was so upset that I called my friend Jim Johnson, the sheriff, and told him about the incident. He said he'd try to increase patrols in the area, but suggested that I ought to think about putting up a gate to try to keep people out.

Later, I sold the cabin to my potter friend Clyde Gobble and his wife, Bonnie, a photographer (yes, Bonnie and Clyde), and they moved into it. They hadn't been there but a year or so when Clyde called and said, "This dadgum house you sold me is haunted."

I thought he was joking. "Well," I said, "there's one born every minute, you know. You've got to find just the right guy to sell a house full of haints to."

"I'm serious," he said.

The first time they had an indication of an unusual presence was when they were having a party and Jose Fumero, a weaver who was attuned to psychic phenomena, saw a tall, bearded man with piercing black eyes standing by the fireplace. He was wearing a black coat and had one arm resting on the log mantle. "Do you know you have a ghost in this house?" he asked his hosts, and told them what he'd seen. Later, on New Year's Eve, a couple who were houseguests, Tom Cooper, a potter, and his wife, Kathy, an artist, were staying in the upstairs bedroom. Kathy awoke in the middle of the night and saw a figure of a man standing by the side of the bed. By the time she woke her husband, the man was gone. She described him as being tall, with a mustache and goatee, and wearing a black coat.

Clyde and Bonnie had a scrapbook about their house that included photographs of Henry Conrad and several of his relatives. Kathy immediately picked Henry Conrad as the man she'd seen at the side of the bed. Jose Fumero had chosen the same photo when Clyde and Bonnie showed him the book.

As Clyde was telling me all of this, the incident with Iron Eyes came flashing back. I called Iron Eyes as soon as I finished talking with Clyde.

"You remember that fellow you saw in the kitchen at the log house when you were here last time?" I asked.

"I sure do."

"What did he look like?"

"He was a sort of tall, had a goatee. He had real dark eyes, almost Indian eyes. Had on a black coat like those old coats they wore in those movies I used to make. Why?"

"Iron Eyes," I said. "You may have seen a ghost."

When I told him what had prompted my call, he was convinced that he did.

I never saw Mr. Conrad during any of the time I spent at the house, so I don't know whether he's actually hanging around with Clyde and Bonnie or not. But when people ask me if I believe in ghosts, I say this: I don't disbelieve. I think anything is possible. As Thomas A. Edison once wrote, "We don't know one-millionth of one percent about anything." But whether ghosts exist or not, they usually make good stories.

The last time that Iron Eyes visited, I picked him up at the airport in Raleigh. He was carrying a big bow that he had made from Osage orange wood in 1938. He had hunted rabbits, deer, and buffalo with it and used it in more than fifty movies. An Indian father usually passed his favorite bow on to his eldest son, he said, but he wanted me to have this one. He'd already inscribed it to me. It was a very moving moment in a very public place, and I was so overwhelmed that I could hardly say, "Thank you."

Somehow, I think Iron Eyes knew that we never would see one another again. After that visit, we kept in touch by telephone, but his health began failing badly. When word came of his death on January 4, 1999, I got out the copy of the Great Spirit Prayer that he had given me and read it again. I had heard him recite it many times. I thought the last two lines were particularly appropriate to the moment:

Make me ready to stand before You with clean and straight eyes.

When life fades, as the fading sunset, may our spirits stand before You without shame.

Iron Eyes gave his heart and his talents to many causes in the ninety-five years he spent on this earth. He did much for many people, especially native Americans. And he became the very symbol of our country's efforts to stop the despoliation of our land and save it for future generations. He was my dear friend, and I have no doubt that he stood before the Great Spirit with clean, straight eyes and no hint of shame.

Before my portrait of Iron Eyes became a stamp, a poster and a print to raise money for Keep America Beautiful and to draw attention to its programs, I did another painting for them called "Daisies." It was of three different enamelware coffee pots, red, white, and blue, filled with wild flowers, and it raised $350,000 for Keep America Beautiful in short order.

Hugh Morton Jr. had a lot to do with that. A year after Tim and I had signed a contract with John Harden and Associates, Hugh came to me and said he was planning to leave the agency and start his own company. Would I stay with him? I did so without hesitation. He had become my friend and adviser as well as my business associate and I had become dependent on his energy and ideas. Since that time he had gotten stories about me in newspapers and magazines, had booked me on TV shows, always had me going somewhere and doing something, always was coming up with new and better ideas. And the prices of my originals had continued to rise dramatically. The year before I painted "Daisies," one of my paintings, a mountain scene called "Near Boone," had sold for $21,000, a sum I couldn't have dreamed a few years earlier.

For the "Daisies" painting, Hugh came up with the idea of selling 1,000 signed prints at $350 each, more than twice what we were getting for prints at the time. But with each of these prints would come a chance to win the original at a drawing. The original was valued at $20,000. Because of the lottery aspect the print got wide attention and sold out quickly. When the drawing for the original was held at Keep America Beautiful's national convention in Denver, a man from Salisbury, almost in my back yard, won it.

Hugh saw potential for my work with Keep America Beautiful that wouldn't have crossed my mind. And even if it had, I wouldn't have been able to bring myself to try to capitalize on it. But Hugh had no such hesitancy.

He thought I should be appearing in public service commercials for Keep America Beautiful and told them so. I never would have thought of that myself, but they considered it a grand idea. I ended up making quite a few, several with Iron Eyes, as well as a few short videos for which Hugh oversaw production.

I well remember the first commercial I made. I thought I was going to freeze to death. The day we chose for the filming turned out to be the coldest day in January. I was to be filmed working on a painting that I eventually called "The Ritual." It was of a flock of geese that returned each year to a friend's pond near Linwood.

This friend was Charlie Smith, and he had quite a way with geese. He got it naturally. His father had been known as "Goose Will." Goose Will got his name back in the late '20s after he found a crippled goose at High Rock Lake and nursed it back to health. He trained that goose to do all kinds of things, but one thing in particular got him written up in newspapers everywhere. The goose flew alongside his Model T Ford wherever he went. People came from all around to see it.

I once took my friend C.J. Underwood, a TV reporter from Charlotte, down to meet Charlie so Charlie could tell him about his daddy and the goose and show him the news-paper clippings.

Finally C.J. got around to asking what became of the goose.

"Well, Daddy was going somewhere and the goose was flying along beside him, and daddy made a right turn, and the goose flew smack into the windshield of a Star Laundry truck from Salisbury," Charlie told him.

"Oh, my goodness," C.J. said, "did it hurt him?"

"Killed him deader'n a duck."

"That's awful," C.J. said. "What did he do with him?"

I could see that C.J. was thinking that there might be a little goose tombstone somewhere that he could film as an ending for his story.

"What do you think he did with him?" Charlie asked. "Those were Depression times. We had him for supper!"

Charlie took up his daddy's love of geese. He even learned to think like a goose. He was the best goose caller I've ever known. He could set geese to honking all over the county, and he could do a perfect imitation of a goose in flight. I can't give an apt description of it. You sort of had to see it to really appreciate it. Charlie had trained a flock of geese to respond to his commands, and that gave us an idea for one of the commercials. I would be sitting outside painting the geese, and they'd fly by just as I was painting them.

The director and cameraman who were to film this seemed dubious when we told them that the flock would appear whenever we needed them. I think their exact words were, "Surrrre they will."

You should have seen their faces when Charlie honked and here came the geese.

The problem in filming that commercial was not with the geese but with me. It was so cold that my fingers kept going numb and the paint was freezing on the palette. I kept having to go to the car to hold my hands in front of the heater fan to get my fingers to work. The geese came every time Charlie called them, though. The cold didn't seem to bother them.

That commercial, as well as the others we did, was shown hundreds of times on TV stations throughout the Southeast and I was especially pleased when North Carolina became the national leader in organizing groups to keep our state's highways free of litter. The commercials had the added advantage of making my face and voice, as well as my work, familiar to millions of people.

I wasn't the most famous artist in America by a long shot, but I was a lot better known than I was before I met Hugh. And we were about to undertake a project that would attract even greater attention, nationally and internationally.

They do not die, the old homeplaces of the South. They have lives of their own as vivid and tenacious as kudzu.

—Anne Rivers Siddons

Chapter 13

A year after I began sending paintings to Hammer Galleries, Bill Mitchell, the salesman who greeted me when I showed up unannounced, told me, "Bob, you've got to do a book."

Not until 1976, however, did I begin thinking seriously about publishing a collection of my paintings. One thing I knew from the start was that if I did it, I wanted it to be the finest book ever produced, a book unlike any other, a work of art unto itself, a book to be cherished as much for its physical properties as for its content. That required the finest content, too, of course, and demanded a writer of stature to produce the text. When I mentioned this idea to Hugh Morton Jr., the first two words out of his mouth were, "Charles Kuralt."

I knew instantly that he was right, but would he agree to do it?

Hugh was certain that he would. He knew him. His father was a close friend of Charlie's.

America, of course, knew Charles Kuralt for his warm and moving "On the Road" pieces on the CBS Evening News, for the specials that had been made from them, and for the news reporting he had done before he started roaming America recording the extraordinary lives of so-called ordinary people. But those who knew him well knew that he was writer first, TV correspondent second. And everybody in North Carolina knew that he was one of us, downhome born and bred, and that in his heart he'd never left us. He knew the people I was painting without meeting them, knew the scenes without seeing them.

Born in Wilmington in 1934, Charlie had lived in several North Carolina towns in his early childhood, including two years in nearby Salisbury, until his father, Wallace, finally settled in Charlotte and became director of the Mecklenburg County Social Services Department. Charlie entered Alexander Graham Bell Junior High School and took his first journalism class there in the eighth grade. He graduated from Central High School in 1951 and was senior class historian. That fall, he entered the University of North Carolina and eventually became editor of *The Daily Tar Heel*, the campus newspaper. We barely missed each other at Carolina. He graduated in the spring of 1955 before my arrival that fall.

Charlie took a job as a reporter at the *Charlotte News* and soon was writing a column about local people that quickly became popular. In 1957, his column won the Ernie Pyle Memorial Award, and he got a letter of congratulation from the head of CBS Radio News. "If you mean it," he wrote back, "offer me a job."

His first job at CBS was as a radio newswriter. Two years later, he moved to TV and at twenty-five became the youngest person ever named a correspondent by CBS. He worked in Latin America and on the West Coast and reported from Africa and Vietnam before moving to New York, from where he first set out on the road in the fall of 1967. The "On the Road" series had transformed him into a beloved American figure.

Hugh called Charlie and told him what we wanted to do,

and he agreed to fly down to talk with us. We picked him up at the airport in Greensboro, and I quickly saw why he was so successful at what he did. He was one of those people who made you feel completely comfortable the moment you met him. He never attracted attention to himself; he turned his attention to you and made you feel as if you'd known him your entire life and could confide anything to him.

On the way to Riverwood, we filled him in on our plans for the book. It would be big, thirteen-and-a-half inches by eighteen-and-a-half, containing seventy-five of my paintings printed on the finest rag paper, bound in the finest leather. It would be published in a limited edition of 2,125 copies. Two-thousand of those would be priced at $600 each and would come with a signed, limited-edition print. The other 125 would come in a specially designed cherry-wood box, a miniature, though unlacquered version, of the chest I'd built in high school. Ten signed, limited-edition prints would be in the bottom drawer. These books would be numbered and signed by Charlie and myself. Each would sell for $3,500.

"What do you want me to do?" he finally asked.

"All I can tell you," I told him, "is that I want this book to be something that you would want to give to your daughter on her wedding day."

He didn't press me beyond that, and I was grateful because I couldn't have told him more. It wasn't until after he had done it that I realized what I wanted was for him to step inside my paintings and set down the feelings that had caused me to paint them.

We drove on to Riverwood where I had some originals ready to show him. The Heritage Company had produced another half dozen prints by then, bringing our total to thirteen, and those were there. We also had made large transparencies of all the paintings that would appear in the book, and we had those for him to take with him.

But first I wanted him to see the places and meet the people. We prowled the land around Riverwood, talked to Dan and Gilley, who had no idea who Charlie was, for they never watched TV. I drove him all around the county—to the Petreas' farm, to Charlie Smith's goose pond, to Mrs. Leonard's house, and by the house where Shorty Garrison once lived. We called on Mrs. Dorsett. We drove to the upper regions of the county to see an old farm house that I had recently painted. The house was sided with brittle, weather-beaten boards and had a rusty tin roof like many of the old country houses, but the occupants had prettied it up with shutters, a wooden bench, chair and swing on the front porch, all painted a luminous blue. Not until after my painting of that house was framed and hanging at Hammer Galleries in New York did somebody notice that I'd failed to paint the chains that held up the swing. I left it that way, the blue swing forever suspended in mid-air. I called the painting "Route 6, Mocksville." Maybe I should have named it "Levitating Swing."

I'll never forget a comment Charlie made as we were crossing the ever-muddy Yadkin River on our way to see the Alexander Long house, which had been restored after I painted it.

"Looks too thick to drink and too thin to plow," he observed.

I felt good when Hugh and I took Charlie back to the airport. I knew that he was going to produce exactly what we wanted for the book. But beyond that, after only two days together, I knew that I had made a friend for life.

Months passed before we heard from Charlie again. Then he called one day and said he had finished something and wanted to come to see if it was what we had in mind. We set aside a weekend to spend together. Hugh's father drove down from Grandfather Mountain with his son, Jimmy. We gathered for an early supper at Whitley's Barbecue with Dad, Tim, my friend C.J. Underwood, also a friend of Charlie's, and Charles Curtis, who was to design the book. Later, satiated with barbecue, hushpuppies and peach cobbler, the seven of us sat on the front porch at Riverwood enjoying the warm, early fall evening.

Charlie began talking about his manuscript. He'd done the whole thing on the road, he said, taping the transparencies of the paintings to the windows of the motor home and motel rooms for inspiration as he wrote. Each of the passages was written to stand beside a specific painting.

"Why don't you read it to us?" Hugh Sr. said, and we all chimed in with encouragement.

We gathered around, and Charlie began to read:

Here, come and sit just here beside me for awhile, my daughter. There are some things I have forgotten to tell you.

Do you know those old houses that stand alone in the fields?

They are fewer than they used to be, those houses alone. The old folks die away; and their children bunch together in brick suburbs, where they cannot hear the screen door of the homeplace banging in the wind.

But, if you pause at the fence line before a house on a sandy road in the Coastal Plain, you may notice that somebody still keeps the place up, that the tobacco barn seems to be still in use. If you glance up in your passing down a back road in the Piedmont, you may see such a sight as a woman washing her long white hair over a tin tub in the side yard, as she must have done on sunny mornings in this side yard for seventy years. If you look away uncertainly toward a house standing alone in the early dusk of the foothills of the Blue Ridge, wondering whether it is occupied, you may have a reward: a dim light flickering, flickering, and then growing brighter, and then glowing steadily in a ground floor window. The old houses are not all empty, not yet.

I know you have a feeling for line and proportion; so I know it has not escaped you, my daughter; that these houses are invariably beautiful. They are as satisfying to me as the Acropolis must have been to the Athenians who cultivated the valley below its hill. But it is not the houses I have been meaning to tell you about. It is the people in the houses.

They are people, most of them, who have remained a little apart from the asphalt and billboard world we have made for ourselves. They have disdained it, or have been passed up by it, and have remained in a slower and gentler and more deliberate world of their own. They share a recollection of a day when people did not move so much or so fast, when families and neighbors meant more, and money somewhat less. They are not as intrigued as we are by the accumulation of machines and gadgets; they feel that old ways of doing things serve them as well. They are not as eager as we are to get out and see the world; they appreciate the surprises to be found in their own woodlots. They are not in such a hurry as we; they know the satisfactions of being still.

"How 'do?' the people in the houses would say to you if you walked up to the porch. "Light and come in. Come in and set a spell." And when you left, "Come back when you can stay longer." And, in between the greeting as strangers and the parting as friends, you would learn something about our home country, something about the woods and the farms

184

and the seasons, something about life on the earth in a time when people lived farther apart than we do—and closer together.

What happened is this: I met a painter, also a North Carolinian, who, like me, has known some of these old things himself, and heard tell of many others, and has felt within himself the strong urge to get it down, as much as he can, and pass it on.

His paintings have reminded me of the homely beauty of ordinary things, of the careless perfection of nature, of the richness of human talk and song, the value of friendship and neighborliness.

His urge became my urge. These are fragments of stored memories.

These are things you could discover if you walked up to the porch of one of the old houses, and came in, and sat a spell:

That the thunder is God walking, the lightning is God winking, and the snow is the old woman shaking her featherbed.

That if you ask a Daddy Longlegs, "Where are my cows?" he'll raise a leg and point to them.

That, when you hear the whippoorwill, it is time to go barefooted.

That you must make soap on the full of the moon.

That you must put pennies in apple butter to keep it from sticking...

That, if you wash your face in dew the first morning in May, you'll be pretty.

Oh, there was a world of such good and useful things to know, and all known to the people in those houses, and half-believed. I myself was young in such a house, and therefore knew how to make a bamboo peashooter or a reed whistle, how to make a slingshot from the fork of a dogwood or a doll from cornhusks, with the silk for hair: I knew how to turn a thick stick into a horse for riding, and a thin stick into a launcher suitable for slinging a crabapple at a cow. I knew how to turn a double page of *The News and Observer* into a kite held together by flour paste, and I knew how to fly it on a length of tobacco twine above the barn, above the fields, high enough, as I imagined, that God could read the headlines if He wished.

I could plow a mule; yes, even I could plow, or rather follow the mule as he plodded the route he knew, preparing the furrows for alternating rows of corn and black-eyed peas—the patient long work of the wet spring.

Of work there was plenty, there must have been. And hard, hard work, as any man knows who knows the mule, the turn plow and the one-man harrow, as any woman knows who has washed clothes over a fire in a cast-iron pot, turning the steaming mess of overalls and lye soap with a hoe handle. There was hard work, little rewarded, which often led to an early grave. The typhoid fever came one year; another year consumption, the bad flu, the double pneumonia. I do not mean to say there was not work or grief. The old people in the old houses remember many funerals.

But, when they could, they eased the work by doing it together. In the earliest days, there were logrollings, and, while the men cleared the new ground, the women cooked dinner for the hands. There were corn shuckings, a competition; and, if you found a red ear, that gave you the right to kiss whichever girl you pleased. There was tobacco stringing; there was cotton chopping, often done together, neighbor helping neighbor.

And there was quilting.

The women sat around the quilting frame, young and old together, the young ones straining to learn the intricate skill, the old ones so experienced that no intricacy could interfere with their talk. Piecing and talking, a quilting bee:

"Sally, they tell me that Sarah Alexander is bound and determined to marry that boy from Dunn."

"Yes, and he cares no more for her than a crow cares for Sunday."

"I don't know what she sees in him, anyhow. He brags on himself, but he's empty as air; don't you think so, Betty?"

"He is. And her mother needs her home. Honestly, I saw that woman at the Meeting a week ago Thursday and she's grown so thin she can't make a shadow..."

And so, through the afternoon, piecing and talking, and creating nothing less than patterned masterpieces for their grandchildren to handle reverently. The afternoon's talk fades away in our memory, but we can still say the names of the patterns:

Grandma's Tulip...

Bear's Paw...

Four Hands Around...

Lazy Girl...

Log Cabin...

Cherokee Rose...

Old Woman's Puzzle...

Drunken Man's Path...

"I know that boy's daddy, Sally; and he was always bad to drink. Always looking for work and praying not to find it! He'd just set around the house, and he'd throw more out the back door than his poor wife could tote in the front..."

Golden Stairs...

Spider Web...

Hen and Chickens...

Star of Bethlehem...

Jacob's Ladder...

*Rising Sun...*Oh, how could they ever have kept track of that pattern while piecing and talking?

Lover's Knot...

"Yes, but I suppose Sarah will have him if she sets her cap for him. And they say he does have work. She may look farther and fare worse..."

*Rose of Sharon...*Always for a bride.

On the warm days, when the stiffness is out of their fingers and they feel up to it, solitary women still sit down in quiet rooms in lonely houses to finish up quilts alone. They remember the piecing and talking with the neighbor women. There are few neighbors anymore and rarely a quilting bee. The piecing goes slower without the talking.

On the warm days, old men also remember the coming together of neighbors to clear a field or to raise a barn and remember how, afterwards, in the kitchen, in the over-warmth of the woodstove, somebody would open a fiddle case and tune up to much encouragement, and remember how they danced then with the young girls to "Turkey Buzzard" or "The

Miller Across the Ridge" or "Goin' to the Wedding." They danced until the sweat rolled down them, and rested, laughing, and roasted apples and popped corn and drank cider and then, somehow, went back to dancing again! These are men who are hardly able to get up and go in to supper without their walking sticks, my daughter. I just wanted you to know what they remember.

I have been thinking of practical and useful things that are now held to be curiosities.

This kerosene lamp. Try to think of it not as an antique but as a steady light for reading. Try to imagine the feelings of the girl your age who read by the light of it; and wonder, as I have been doing, what she read in the still night before sleeping. The Bible? Byron? And what long thoughts did she think after reading, before sleep came?

This basin. Did she use it for washing next morning? This horn comb. Did she put it in her hair hoping the neighbor boy would notice?

And this blacksmith's hammer, much used. How many nails did it make, how many links of chain? How many ax heads did it repair, and whose hand wielded it?

This bean pot. Whose beans did it cook, and was there often more to eat in that house than beans and sow belly and cornbread dipped in molasses? We cannot know, but this bean pot works on the imagination.

These kitchen scales. Whose kitchen did they rest in, and for how many summers have they weighed out the rewards of the land?

This drum. What boy carried it into battle and where and when, and was the sunlight flashing from the bayonets of the enemy, and was the boy very much frightened? Listen to this chair, this drum.

"Antiques" are the slightest thing they are. They are the artifacts of a time so close to our own that we still can feel the breathing presence of the people who owned these things, almost hear their voices in their possessions.

Listen to this coat.

The people who lived in the old houses were more grateful to God than we are; I am sure of that, and I think I know a reason: they knew His work better than we do. They knew the uses of everything that grows.

They knew that a sassafras root, if boiled, makes a fine kettle of tea and, if boiled longer, makes a pretty orange dye for a bolt of homespun or a cotton dress.

They knew that the youngest leaves of the poke plant, gathered in the spring while they are tender, and washed and boiled and seasoned with salt and bacon, make a salad. And, if it was a red dress they wanted, and not an orange one, they knew they could go back to the same plant in the fall for its berries, which boil out to a beautiful red. This is the plant we call a weed and spray poison to kill.

I know you are thinking, "Yes, but what if they wanted a blue dress?" Elder. "Black?" Sumac. "Yellow?" Marigolds or hickory bark or buckhorn or plum root, depending on the shade of yellow. They knew God's gifts. In the autumn leaves or in the sunsets, we sometimes appreciate His vivid colors. They wore them on their backs.

They were more patient than we. Do you remember the time you sampled a persimmon in September? A persimmon in September is a mistake. A persimmon in October is a benediction. Persimmons make you wait until after the first frost. Persimmons teach patience.

This was a ritual of the fall: One pail of persimmons, one pail of milk, a double-handful of flour, two eggs, a teacup of sugar, two pinches of soda, a piece of butter the size of a walnut, and a sprinkling of nutmeg. It was called persimmon pudding; and it was worth waiting for, until October.

Here is what you could make from a persimmon tree: a shuttle for your loom, a mallet for your toolbox, a section of floor for your back bedroom.

Here is what you could find in a persimmon thicket: a wild turkey, a fox or possum, a pair of bobwhite quail, a white-tailed deer, and after the frost, when they were missing from the field where they were supposed to be shocking corn, your own children.

"Use it up," they said, "wear it out; make it do, or do without."

Making it do was much on the minds of the people in those old houses. Even young boys were familiar with auger and plane and bucksaw and caseknife. Even young girls were wonderfully skilled with needle and watering pot and butter churn and mixing bowl. From the time they were children, if they wanted a rabbit box, they made it; if they wanted a layer cake, they baked it. Whatever they wanted, a fence or a wagon tongue or a counterpane, they were likely to make it and ever afterwards, to make it do.

If they wanted a bucket, they cut the staves and beveled the edges and cut a bottom out of solid oak and soaked split vines or splines of hickory to serve as hoops. Making things for themselves this way required considerable time and patience, but time and patience were always in greater supply than cash money, and a finished handmade bucket was for more than holding water. It was for being proud of when they'd finished it.

Oh, many things were different then, and among them time itself.

A day passed in three parts: "morning," from sunup to noontime; "evening," from noontime to dark; and "night." "In the morning" meant tomorrow, but not necessarily tomorrow in the morning.

A week passed in a prescribed order: Saturday for going to town, Sunday for giving to the Lord, Monday for doing the washing. There were variations from house to house, but on those three days no variation. You could ride out in a horse and wagon on a Monday afternoon in those old days, and, if you spied a yard without clothes hanging on the line, you could be sure the folks were sick or away.

Holidays were different. Whitsunday. Reformation Sunday. Twelfth Night. (Have I ever mentioned to you that the animals kneel and talk in their stalls on Old Christmas morning?)

The seasons, too, were different, a matter not merely of solstice and equinox, but of the heat of the sun, the gathering of clouds, the rain of bright leaves on the cooling earth, the coming of storms and the still, chill nights, and then the miracle of crocuses and jonquils breaking through the dried crystals of the last snowfall.

Some of their seasons we have misplaced altogether: The warm days after the killing frosts, the shirt-sleeve November days before the hard cold set in. Indian summer.

The warm spells in January, tempting schoolboys to leave their sweaters home, and woods flowers to press their luck. Sham spring.

The cool snaps in April when the berry vines were blooming. Blackberry winter.

As for the seasons that are left to us—well, you have always been sensitive, my daughter, so you have sensed the wonder of the seasons. But you are a child of your time, living so protected from the hot sun and the cold rain and the drifting snow that you have had no chance to discover all that the seasons are good for.

I am trying to remember.

Summer.

Do you remember the time we went to the Daniels family reunion? The church service in the hot morning, the people in the pews fanning themselves with the funeral parlor fans until it was time to stand with brown-backed hymnals in the hands and sing "Amazing Grace" together, and then walk out under the shade trees, all happy and hugging one another, the children playing noisy games of tag around their mothers' skirts while their mothers tried to hear the news of Aunt Ella and Uncle Nick and how Willard's boy was doing up at Raleigh? Do you remember the dinner on the grounds that day, the long table set up on the sawhorses and covered with white tablecloths and dishes of fried chicken, ham biscuits, potato salad, coleslaw, pickles and preserves, slices of watermelon, apple pies....

cherry pies....

blackberry pies, pecan pies, lemon pies, and

chess pies and several kinds of chocolate cake? Do you remember the tub of pink lemonade with chunks of clear ice floating in it? Do you remember how warm a day it was, in every way a day can be warm? That is what summer was for.

Summer was for punching holes in the lid of the Mason jar you kept your lightning bugs in. Summer was for tying a string to a June bug's leg and following him around the yard.

Summer was full of work—keeping the weeds out of the fields—and full of hazard: stubbing your toe on a sycamore root, stepping on a sand spur, meeting up with a moccasin while swimming in the creek, getting stung by a wasp or bitten by a spider or scratched by a briar or eaten up by chiggers (real) or bears (imaginary). What with the work and the hazards, it's a wonder so many youngsters survived the summer.

Summer was for seeking out dark, cool, and secret places.

Summer was for swinging in a swing and hiding in a hayloft and finding a Venus-flytrap to tickle closed in a dry clearing under longleaf pines. Summer was for racing a shower to the safety of the porch, then watching the flashes of lightning and counting, "one thousand, two thousand, three thousand..." until the crack of the thunder told you how many miles away the lightning bolt had struck.

Summer was for drawing cool water from a deep well and drinking it from a gourd.

Summer was for fishing, for catfish in the brown river or for flounder in the sound or for sea trout in the surf.

Summer, then as now, was for visiting the sea.

Oh, there were excursion boats and ferries, forgotten craft, carrying gay blades and honeymooners and farm families on their first holidays ever, forgotten vacationers, to old hotels and houses on the banks and capes and beaches, long-forgotten hostelries.

There were houses and people in the houses—occupants of Lifesaving Stations, lighthouse keepers, fishermen, whole villages of houses and people now gone. The wind sandblasts the old shingles; the storm waves rise and pound the protective dunes; the houses where men and women lay together in the night listening to the sea yield to the sea. The blowing sand sifts into the shallow foundations; the beach grass and sea oats cover all.

The summer memories of old people are nothing to the sea. Men may claim their bit of shoreline. Sooner or later the sea will have it back.

But in their time the old people were young here, as you are, my daughter. They, too, felt the blown spume and smelled the northeast wind. They, too, tramped the broad white beach and watched the plovers skimming the breaking waves and laughed at the sandpipers scampering up the beach away from the swash line, and saw the ghost crabs scuttle into their holes.

They in their time watched the dark-blue storm clouds build up to seaward and felt the mystery and power of the place, this deceptively sunny and impermanent meeting place of land and water.

Summer was for falling in love at the seashore with a girl you'd never meet again.

Fall.

The sun shifted slowly to the south, and slanted

down through the thinning red leaves of the maples in the side yard, and cast the shadow of the axe upon the chopping block. Fall was the end of something, and you felt it in your bones.

But there was a joy set against this melancholy, like bright pumpkins in the dead grass.

Fall was the smell of hams hanging in the smokehouse, the dry smell of fodder in the fields, and fall was the pungent smell of apples.

If you go for a walk across the fields or through the woods in autumn, you may find a stand of twisted apple trees. Right there, you can be sure, was a house or a sawmill or a camp.

The folks in those old houses put in their apple trees before they put on their roofs. How else would they have dried apples, eating apples, and apple pie and apple butter and applesauce and brandy and vinegar?

How else would they make cider in the fall? They would be amazed to know that some of us today live in houses without apple trees. Fall was for apples.

Fall was for boiling and jarring and waxing and sealing and filling the cupboards and pantries. And, oh, those cupboards! Oh, the feeling of wealth and accumulation within them, the abundance of butter beans and sweet corn and field peas, of beets and greens and red tomatoes, of jams and jellies and pickles and relishes and watermelon-rind preserves, of red berries and silver pears and spicy golden peaches standing in bright glass rows upon the shelves of the cupboards of long ago autumn! I suppose you will never see a filled cupboard, my daughter, and never quite know fully the satisfaction of the fall.

Fall was the last geranium.

Fall was the last of the marigolds, accepting the last of the sun.

Fall was the last shower of gold and crimson from above, a brownness coming upon the earth, and a chill. And then, one morning when the mist was rising, a faint clamor in the sky and a "V" so high and far away it seemed traced by a pencil. The geese coming south!

Fall was the familiar wooden contours of the decoys and the worn stock of the shotgun and the wet cold of the morning, seeping through two wool shirts, and the thrill of the whistling wings.

Winter.

In winter, every room of those old houses was cold, except the kitchen. I remember waking early in a featherbed under piles of quilts, waking so early that the cold moon shadows of the sycamore limbs outside my window still danced on the narrow boards of the tongue-and-groove ceiling. I lay there in my cocoon of warmth, building up my courage for the moment when I would throw back the covers, grab for my clothes, and dash breathless and barefoot through the door, down the stairs, and through the cold house to the warm kitchen! Everybody dressed in the kitchen in winter.

Winter was for having breakfasts of grits and eggs and sausage and country ham and clabber biscuits and wonderful warmed-over bits of last night's good supper, with sorghum and honey always on the table, and crackling bread so hot and hard that the butter melted and ran off on your fingers. The milk in your glass was cold in the winter.

Winter was for baking cookies and filling the

cookie jars and thinking of Christmas.

Winter was for walking in the frozen ruts in the barnyard and on the lumber roads in floppy galoshes that let your toes get cold. Winter was silence, and a silent snow that came in the night.

The snow was almost unbearable. I mean it was an event of almost unbearable excitement and of agonizing doubt: Would it "stick"? Then, when it had covered the ground, would there be enough to mix in a bowl with sugar, milk, and vanilla to make snow cream? Then, when the snow cream had chilled your belly, would there be enough to go sledding in your mother's second-best big dishpan? Then, while sledding, would there be enough to make a snowman? Then, when the snowman was made, with lumps of coal for eyes, would there be enough to make them close the school tomorrow?

The snow changed everything, muffled sound and amplified light and, by outlining bland and formless trees, hills, fences and gullies in bold relief, showed you things right around you that you'd never seen before. I thought, I remember thinking, upon climbing back into my bed on a snowy night, knowing how pure and puffy white the world would appear in the first light of morning, that the snow was a present from God to children, that He sent it to make me happy.

The winter was for sleeping. I knew the toads and coons and snakes were sleeping; the possums and squirrels were sleeping, warm in their burrows under the snow. And soon—I was sleeping, too.

The winter was for sleeping and waiting for the spring.

Spring.

At first you couldn't be sure. You *thought* the naked branches of the old oak tree in the field seemed, in a certain light, to be dusted by the palest green. That was how it started, sometimes when the snow still was on the ground. Spring was for watching the snow melt away, for watching the brown branches turn green, for listening for the first tree frog, and smelling the earth again.

Spring was for plowing and planting, of course, for traveling a distance down muddy roads to visit neighbors and shut-ins, for watching the old men in overalls gather again on the Courthouse lawn to swap knives and tell stories and talk about who had died. For the living, it was a grateful season.

Spring was a stirring of the people, and not of the people only. The ants and the caterpillars and the garter snakes were out and around. Mushrooms appeared in the morning where there was nothing the night before. The world waking up seemed quite amazing.

Spring was for walking the edges of the fields to find wild flowers to bring home to your mother.

Spring was for sitting down in the moist pine needles, studying a patch of forest floor, and seeing the universe down there in a robin's egg, moss, and bluets. Spring was the nameless yearning of sitting there, feeling the weak sun on your shoulders, feeling reborn amid so much rebirth.

Spring was for feeling and breathing and seeing. It was the time color returned and was welcomed—the fragile pastels of the woods flowers and the hopeful, youthful April color of the fields and ditch banks and the bright splash of the flower gardens.

Spring was the smell of cherry pies baking in the

oven of the woodstove.

Spring was for finding wonders in the grass.

The seasons change, winter after winter has blown by and yielded to soft spring after spring, and the old houses in the fields of home appear weatherbeaten and rejected. There is little you can do about that, my daughter. The seasons have passed, and it is a different time.

You could not exchange your youth and perception for the life of a girl brought up in one of those old houses, and you should not if you could. Your horizons lie across oceans, not merely across fields to the edge of the woods: that is all to the good. Your understanding of the world is more complete than hers by far; your hopes rise higher; and you will do things in your life beyond her expectations, or even her dreams.

But our existence is in the past, as well as in the future. Unless we know very well where we have been, we cannot see where we are going. That is why I wanted you to have these glimpses of simple verity and unselfconscious beauty—because they are growing rarer as we rush to pave the forests and subdivide the meadows and find substitutes for natural things. Those old houses and the people who lived, and still live, in them have something of value to tell us, something satisfying to show us.

We say that truth and beauty cannot be substituted for, that they are eternal.

But, if we never listen to the quiet knowledgeable voices of the past, which of us can ever distinguish between the truth and shallow illusion?

If we never pause to notice such a thing as the sky reflected in a pail of water, where will we find beauty then?

As Charlie read in that sonorous and embracing voice so familiar to millions of people, those of us on the porch fell into an enthralled silence, suddenly aware of how privileged we were. All we had to do was to look across the pasture in the gathering twilight to see one of those old houses Charlie was talking about, lantern glow flickering in the window as Gilley and Dan went about getting ready for bed, still living the life Charlie was so eloquently describing. Each of us knew that we were involved in a moment so special that we never again would experience anything like it. And when he had read that final line, we sat in a reverent silence that nobody wanted to break. If any of the others were like me they were stifling tears. I was overwhelmed at how adroitly Charlie had moved into my paintings and how beautifully he had given them voice.

In our silence, the evening song of the crickets, the katydids, and the peep frogs, unnoticed during Charlie's performance, welled like an orchestra. Over by the fence, one of Gilley's cows lowed, and down at the edge of the woods, an owl hooed.

I was the one who finally broke the silence. "We've got to record that," I said.

And we did. Each copy of the book came with a thirty-three-rpm recording of Charlie reading the text.

The book was called *The Bob Timberlake Collection*. It came out in the fall of 1977, timed to coincide with my third show at Hammer Galleries. Tim and I had formed a separate company, Riverwood Press, to publish it, and we had taken in as a partner my childhood buddy Bob Grubb, my attorney.

Hugh had gotten Jerry Bowles, a New York writer for major art publications, to write the introduction. Scott Hyde, chief photographer for the Brooklyn Museum, formerly of the Whitney Museum, photographed the paintings. Charles Curtis, who designed it, had been the head designer of the Sierra Club books. I bought the leather for the cover at Bruce Fullbright's upholstery shop south of Lexington and had it shipped to the Case-Hoyt Company in Rochester, New York, where the book was printed and bound. I went there to oversee the job and spent three consecutive shifts in the plant as it was being printed.

When I finally held a copy in my hands, I knew that we had accomplished what we set out to do. We had created an heirloom, and I was proud of it.

Later, Charlie told me that he did give a copy to his daughter on her wedding day. He told me, too, of how deeply touched he had been when his friend at CBS, Eric Sevareid, told him that upon reading the text, he had immediately called his own daughter and asked her to come over so that he could read it to her.

We marketed the book out of the gas company, and all 2,150 copies were sold before anybody ever saw it. Dee Michael, one of our employees, filled most of the orders. Remarkably, the $3,500 copies were the first to go. Among the owners were Frank Sinatra, Henry Fonda, Perry and Roselle Como, Kathy Lee Crosby, Tennessee Ernie Ford, Loretta Switt, Bill Murray, Buddy Hackett, Jim Ryan, and former President Gerald Ford and his wife, Betty.

The book drew a tremendous amount of attention. *Readers Digest* excerpted it and used many of the paintings, as did *Audubon* magazine. It truly made me into a nationally recognized artist and brought me many pleasant surprises. Letters came from all over the country, among them a personal note from Henry Fonda with a reproduction of a painting he'd done of the old hat he'd worn in his film, *On Golden Pond*. Fonda wrote the week he won the Academy Award for the film.

But I was hardly prepared for one development that the book brought. Without doubt, it was one of the most unbelievable events of my life.

This royal throne of kings, this scepter'd isle...

This blessed plot, this earth, this realm, this England...

—William Shakespeare

Chapter 14

Dr. Armand Hammer may have been the most intriguing and remarkable person I ever knew. I met him on a trip to New York before my first show at Hammer Galleries in 1973. I couldn't believe that I was shaking the same hand that had shaken the hand of Vladimir Ilyich Lenin.

A man of immense charm, Dr. Hammer was seventy-five when I met him, nearly twice my age, but we took to each other immediately. I would come to feel that he treated me almost as a grandson. For certain, he treated me differently from most of the people around him, and from some who worked for him I sensed resentment and jealousy because of it.

Actually, we had much in common. He was a strong believer in salesmanship and a terrific salesman. In that, he made me think of Dad; in fact, he and Dad got along great together, probably because each saw some of himself in the other. I've met few people who had as positive an outlook as Dr. Hammer, and, of course, I admired that greatly. He truly believed that anything he set out to achieve was possible, and his accomplishments were phenomenal. By the time I met him he had done more than most people could dream, and he had narrowed his ambitions to two major goals: finding a cure for cancer, and bringing about peace throughout the world.

The amazing thing about Dr. Hammer was that to him these were not meaningless, rhetorical goals. He had the associations and the resources to make them reality, and he worked steadfastly toward that end

Dr. Hammer was born in New York City. His mother was a Russian immigrant, his father the son of Russian immigrants. His father was a physician and socialist leader who started a successful pharmaceutical and chemical company and eventually lost his medical license and served time in prison for manslaughter after performing an illegal abortion on a patient who died.

The eldest of three sons, Armand became a physician, too, although he never practiced. He took over operation of the family business while his father was in prison. In 1921, he became concerned about the famine and epidemics of typhus and cholera that were sweeping through Russia in the wake of World War I and the Russian Revolution, killing thousands. He purchased a surplus army field hospital, had it loaded onto a freighter bound for the Baltic port of Riga, and set out for Europe on a humanitarian mission, his eventual destination Russia.

Within a few weeks, thanks to his father's socialist contacts, he was in Moscow, where he found deplorable conditions, little food and few comforts. Frustrated by petty government officials and despairing of being able to do anything to help, he was planning to return home when a friend of his father who had been put in charge of the metals industries for the new Bolshevik government invited him on an inspection tour to the Ural Mountains in western Russia.

That trip changed Dr. Hammer's life, and the stories he later told me about it reminded me of scenes from the movie *Dr. Zhivago*. On it, he saw bodies of the victims of famine and disease stacked like cordwood, buzzards feasting on the emaciated carcasses. He told me that mothers stood alongside the tracks, throwing their babies up to people standing between the cars, hoping that the babies would be caught and saved.

He also saw vast resources going untapped, or stockpiled and unused, lumber, furs, precious stones, metals and other minerals. He saw great industrial complexes standing idle, closed by an unworkable economy, the workers going hungry. Why not exchange these resources for food and medicine? he asked. America had great stores of wheat and other grains going unsold. Not possible, he was told.

He could do it, he said, and would. He cabled his family business to begin trying to set such an exchange in motion.

Back in Moscow, Lenin, the leader of the revolution and head of the new government, heard of Dr. Hammer's proposal and summoned him to a meeting. Lenin had just initiated new economic policies, a return to some capitalist methods, and he not only approved Dr. Hammer's proposal, he put him in charge of a closed asbestos mine and later granted him the license to work out other trade agreements and bring foreign business to Russia. Dr. Hammer journeyed to Michigan to meet with Henry Ford and arrange the shipment of tractors to Russian farmers. To pay for these and other goods, he shipped caviar, furs and valuable minerals back to the United States, funneling much of it through his family's company and turning a handsome profit.

Dr. Hammer settled into a mansion in Moscow, married a Russian cabaret singer, had a son. He also brought his brothers Harry and Victor to Moscow to work for him. Victor had a strong interest in art. During the revolution, the great art treasures owned by the czar and the Russian aristocracy had been seized and were being sold in Moscow at bargain prices. Victor began buying paintings, tapestries, china, religious icons, jewelry, Faberge' eggs (at one time the Hammer brothers owned more Faberge eggs, fifteen, than any other collector; the Queen of England was second with ten). Armand quickly saw the potential in these treasures.

After Lenin's death in 1924, a power struggle ensued between Joseph Stalin and Leon Trotsky, with Stalin eventually winning. Stalin cancelled Lenin's economic policies and Dr. Hammer lost his trade enterprises. Still he was allowed to start and operate a lucrative pencil company until he was forced out of the country in 1929.

In 1928, Dr. Hammer had gone into partnership with a New York art gallery to sell some of the art he and Victor had been accumulating. They opened a new gallery on 52nd Street called L'Hermitage after the famous art museum in Leningrad. It later moved to the Waldorf Astoria Hotel, then to 5th Avenue. The Hammers took control of the gallery and Victor was put in charge, but selling art was tough when the Great Depression began, and the gallery showed steady losses.

Dr. Hammer had been living in Paris while disposing of his Russian business interests, but he returned to try to save the gallery and began selling the Romanoff Treasures, as he labeled them, with much hullabaloo in major department stores around the country. The works sold and he was hailed as a marketing genius. He later was commissioned to sell the vast art collection of publishing tycoon William Randolph Hearst, and handled the estate collections of President Franklin D. Roosevelt and primitive painter Grandma Moses, whose works I adore and collect. He and Victor also came to control the entire works of one of my idols, the Western painter Charles Russell. During the '30s, Dr. Hammer changed the name of L'Hermitage to Hammer Galleries and nearly four decades later, he would buy out the prestigious Knoedler & Co. Galleries in New York, America's oldest art dealer, and merge the two into a single company.

Although he maintained his interest in art and kept assembling a vast private collection of masterworks (in 1980, he paid $5 million for a 470-page manuscript of Leonardo da Vinci's handwritten notes and sketches), he left the operation of the gallery to Victor, while he moved on to other enterprises. He foresaw the end of prohibition and began importing white-oak staves from Russia and having them assembled into barrels. He knew that brewers and distillers would need them when prohibition ended, and he was right. That enterprise brought him a fortune, and he moved into the spirits business himself, taking over the J.W. Dant Distillery in Kentucky, where he made another fortune. He restlessly moved from one endeavor to another, buying part of Arm and Hammer Baking Soda Company just because it already bore his name. He also bought the Mutual Broadcasting Company and started a cattle venture with Senator Albert Gore of Tennessee.

In 1956, he made a $50,000 loan to a small California Oil Company that was about to go under and soon got caught up in the excitement of the hunt for oil. He eventually took control of Occidental Petroleum and turned it into the twelfth biggest industrial corporation in America with operations throughout the world.

Dr. Hammer's interest in Russia never waned and after Stalin's death he reestablished contacts there. He went on to work with Nikita Kruschev, who succeeded Stalin, and every Russian leader who followed. He also knew and worked with every American President from Franklin D. Roosevelt on. He became a sort of ambassador at large between Russia and the United States, always promoting trade and peace. Russian authorities gave him Lenin's apartment to stay in on his frequent trips to Moscow.

Few people, if any, can claim to have known as many world leaders as Dr. Hammer. When China began to open up to the West, he was the first American invited to Beijing by Deng Xiaoping to do business there. He was instrumental in seeing that Russian Jews were allowed to emigrate to Israel, and he worked ardently to bring about peace between Israel and Egypt.

Even now it is hard for me to believe, but I was visiting Dr. Hammer in his suite at the Madison Hotel in Washington at the time of the signing of the peace treaty by Menachem Begin and Anwar Sadat. The city was practically an armed camp. People carrying machine guns were inside and outside the suite. Our conversation was interrupted by an urgent call from Begin about a snag in the agreement. Dr. Hammer had invited me to be his guest at the signing, and I couldn't believe that I might actually be present for such an historic moment, but higher authorities intervened, and I was bumped at the last minute.

Throughout his life, Dr. Hammer had given millions to various charities. In 1968, he saw Walter Cronkite interviewing Dr. Jonas Salk, the producer of the polio vaccine. It caused him to remember his father's great frustration in fighting the epidemics of that deadly and crippling disease early in this century. That got him thinking about cancer and how millions of people die from it each year, and how frustrating it must be for the doctors who have to deal with it.

He went to see Dr. Salk and asked if he thought a cure for cancer was possible. He did, said Dr. Salk; it was simply a matter of funding research enough to find it. That set Dr. Hammer on a mission. If a cure could be found, he was determined that it would be. He gave $5 million to Columbia University to start a cancer center in memory of his father and mother and established an annual prize of $100,000 for the researcher who made the greatest advances toward a cure. Wherever he went he encouraged others to get involved in the cause. It was largely because of Dr. Hammer that I joined the fight, working to support the cancer center at Duke University, for which we've helped raise more than $2 million so far. It's a fight to which I remain committed.

Dr. Hammer's relationships with so many world leaders and his many missions for peace led him to start an annual international conference on peace and human rights in 1978, and he never gave up the idea that people of all kinds and all beliefs could live in harmony with one another.

I was astounded that a person who had known so many important people and done so many important things would take an interest in a painter from Davidson County, North Carolina, but he did, and I never doubted that his attention was genuine. I would have many shows at Hammer Galleries, and he flew in for almost every one, no matter where he was. I was humbled when I learned that he had told many people that he considered me to be America's best living watercolorist, even though I knew that wasn't the case. He always wanted to know about my work and questioned me closely about North Carolina and Lexington. I think he was intrigued by the beauty and simplicity of the rural life that he saw in my paintings. I always wanted him to come for a visit so I could show him the places and let him meet the people, but his unrelenting schedule never allowed that.

He did invite me to his townhouse on West Fourth Street in Greenwich Village, and I'll never forget my first visit there following one of my shows. A bodyguard who wore a pistol in a shoulder holster took me there in a van. Dr. Hammer's block was sealed off at each end with tractor-trailers that blocked the street, their wheels on the sidewalk. It was as if the President, or some world leader, were visiting. The guard drove onto the sidewalk to get around the truck. Other guards and business associates were at the house, but I was ushered right in and immediately saw why guards were necessary. I felt as if I'd walked into a movie set. Never had I seen such opulence. There were Tiffany lamps, Faberge' eggs, magnificent paintings, tapestries and sculpture, items fashioned of gold and silver, and other priceless works of art. Dr. Hammer took me on a tour of the house showing me this small part of his vast collections, telling me how he'd acquired each item. Many were among his favorites.

Afterward, we talked for a long time and he gave me the feeling that he valued my opinions and enjoyed nothing more than sitting and chatting with me, and I saw why he'd been so successful as a businessman, negotiator, and peacemaker.

Dr. Hammer bought several copies of *The Bob Timberlake Collection*, but it wasn't until later that I learned that he had given one of those to Prince Charles for his thirtieth birthday when he visited Los Angeles in 1978.

I learned this early in 1979. Kay and I were planning to build a vacation house on the sound at Figure Eight Island, north of Wilmington. We had bought a lot at Bald Head but had decided against building there because it was so remote. We were just getting ready to start our house at Figure Eight and we had rented a place there for the New Year's holiday. Few people knew where we were, but early on Saturday morning, the day after New Year's Day, the telephone rang, and an assistant said, "Please hold for Dr. Hammer."

"Bob, how are you doing?" Dr. Hammer said when he came on the line. "Happy New Year."

"Fine, Dr. Hammer," I said, "Happy New Year to you."

"Listen," he said, "I need to meet with you Tuesday morning."

"Okay," I said, a little uncertainly. "Where?"

"In London."

"In London?"

"Yes, Prince Charles wants to meet you, and I told him

I could arrange it. I can count on you, can't I?"

"I'll be there if I have to walk and swim," I told him.

"Try the airlines first," he said with a laugh. "We'll take care of the tickets."

I hung up the telephone and turned to Kay.

"That was Dr. Hammer," I said. "I've got to go to London."

"What for?"

"Prince Charles wants to meet me."

She laughed. She thought I was joking.

I don't think she really believed it until I called our daughter, Kelly, who was then a student at Wake Forest University in Winston-Salem.

"How would you like to meet the world's most eligible bachelor?" I asked. This was two years before the prince married Diana.

"Who?" she said.

"Prince Charles."

"Do you think he could help me with Brit lit?" she asked.

I called Joe King to find out what to expect. He was excited about my trip and assured me that I was in for a memorable experience.

"Be sure to tell Liz I said hello," he said with a chuckle.

Much of the East Coast had been socked in by a snowstorm, but I managed to get to the airport in Raleigh, made it to Atlanta, and caught a delayed flight. An unhappy and restless child in the seat behind me kicked my backside all the way to England, and I got no sleep at all.

When we finally landed in London Tuesday morning, all I could think about was Joe King's experience with customs. Would they really believe I was coming to meet the future king? But I must have gotten into the wrong line, or something, when I got there, because I never saw anybody from customs. Nobody stopped me; nobody asked me a question. I went straight to the hotel where Dr. Hammer's office had instructed me to go.

No sooner had I got to my room than the telephone rang. It was Dr. Hammer.

"Bob, we're in the lobby. Are you ready?"

"I just got here," I said, "but I'll be right down."

I didn't have time to shave, change clothes, or even brush my teeth. I splashed some water on my face, swept a brush through my unruly hair, and rushed downstairs in the rumpled clothes I'd been flying in for hours.

Dr. Hammer and his third wife, Frances, were waiting, and we climbed in the limousine at the hotel entrance and were off to Buckingham Palace. On the way, Dr. Hammer filled me in on the reason for my trip. That was when I learned that he had given a copy of my book to Prince Charles. I didn't know until then that they were friends, but I guess I should have expected it.

The reason he'd given him the book, Dr. Hammer explained, was because the prince enjoyed painting with watercolors. Only recently had Dr. Hammer coaxed him into letting him see some of the paintings. They were quite good, he said, so good that he wanted to exhibit them at Hammer Galleries. The prince demurred, saying that he wasn't good enough to let others see his work, that what he really needed was a good tutor.

"Your Highness, I could get Bob Timberlake to come and instruct you, if you'd like." Dr. Hammer recalled telling him.

He had loved my book, Dr. Hammer said. "You'd have

thought I'd given him another crown," he told me. He wasn't above a little hyperbole now and then.

"Do you think he would?" he recalled the prince asking.

"He'd be honored, I'm sure."

I must admit that I was a bit uneasy after getting this information. I'd never instructed anybody in art before, I told Mr. Hammer, much less the Prince of Wales. I'd never even had any instruction myself.

"Don't worry," he told me. "You'll do fine. You're going to like him."

So here I was, feeling like Alice in Wonderland, arriving at Buckingham Palace with one of the world's richest and most famous men, and as Japanese tourists peered into the limousine windows, snapping pictures, trying to figure out who was inside, we whisked right through the gate past the stiff, red-coated guards with their beehive hats. It was too late to turn back now. We were tumbling down the rabbit hole—and what a wonderland we fell into.

We were ushered into the office of the prince's private secretary, a friendly captain of the Welsh Guard, who greeted us warmly. He knew Dr. Hammer well, and we all chatted amiably. On the wall was a huge board on which every minute of the prince's day was mapped—we had thirty minutes, I noticed—and I began to get an idea of what a regimented life a future king had to live. At the moment he was sitting for a formal portrait.

As we waited for our audience with him to begin, I kept thinking about mine and Kay's great-great-great-great grandfathers, Wooldrich Fritz and Valentine Leonhardt. They had been murdered by men in service to the crown of England, and here I was waiting to have a friendly chat with the man who would one day wear that crown. I couldn't help but think what a small world this really is.

When our turn came, we were ushered down a great hallway, and the prince suddenly emerged from a doorway in full royal regalia, bedecked with braids, sashes and epaulets and weighted with medals. He was smiling a little self-consciously, and he greeted Dr. Hammer and his wife affectionately, apologizing for his formal attire. Dr. Hammer introduced me, and he welcomed me with the same warmth, thanking me for coming and telling me how much he'd enjoyed my book and how much he admired the paintings.

One thing that stuck in my mind was that we were the same heighth, eye-too-eye. I don't know what I had expected him to be like, reserved, I guess, perhaps a bit haughty, the way I pictured the queen. But he was not that way at all. He was completely disarming, charming, wry, even humble. He put me immediately at ease, and as incongruous as it sounds, he made me feel right at home. As we exchanged chitchat, I couldn't help but think that he would fit right in at Whitley's Barbecue, even if his accent was a little different. Everybody would love him. I could picture the two of us fishing for crappie at High Rock Lake, or hunting ducks at Knotts Island. I could see him sitting on the porch at Riverwood with a group of my friends, all of us with our feet propped on the rail, laughing and telling tales.

He had clearly boned up on my book, because he began discussing individual paintings, calling them by name, and asking specific questions about techniques I'd used, and I quickly saw that he knew more about painting than he let on.

"I have trouble with clouds," he told me. "I can never get my clouds right. How did you do the clouds in 'Snow World?'"

"Oh, easiest thing in the world," I said. "It's a wet-on-wet process. You just wet the sky area, put on the color, watch it run and mottle. Then you smooth it out with a Kleenex and you've got clouds...."

He chuckled. "I must try that," he said.

We went on to discover a mutual interest in architecture, and he expressed his disgust about so much of the building that had taken place in London since World War II. His next meeting was about that, and he really got warmed up on the subject.

He truly seemed to be enjoying himself. I surely was, and I could tell by the happy expression on Dr. Hammer's face that he loved hearing the two of us discussing subjects that we both clearly felt passionate about. When the secretary appeared to remind Prince Charles of his next appointment, I had the feeling that he was reluctant for the conversation to end.

"Would you like to see the rest of the palace?" he asked.

I certainly would, I told him.

"Give them the royal tour," he instructed his secretary with a laugh.

And that was what we got. We even ventured into the private quarters (the queen was not in, so I couldn't pass on Joe's greeting). Taking the tour with Dr. Hammer was even more instructive and gratifying, because he knew more about the palace's art than our guide.

Before we departed, the prince reappeared to thank us for coming and bid us farewell, and I must admit that I left with a wistful feeling.

I guess I hadn't expected to have such a good time, or to feel such a connection to a royal personage, or to like him so much on a human level. I couldn't imagine what his life must really be like, or how it would be to live in Buckingham Palace, which seemed more like a corporate headquarters than a home, and I felt a little sad for him. I sensed that he might prefer to be more like other people, that he probably really would enjoy laughing it up at breakfast with the crowd at Whitley's, just another one of the guys, or fishing for crappie at High Rock Lake without guards and crowds watching and snapping pictures. I told this to Dr. Hammer when he asked me my perception of the visit as we were being driven away from the palace.

Funny I should feel that, he said, for the prince had confided to him that at times he wished he could shed his identity, move about without all his trappings, mingle with people who did not know him as the Prince of Wales and the future king, who did not seek favors from him, or expect him to behave in any particular manner, who would accept or reject him for himself, not for his royal birth.

Then Dr. Hammer made it clear that he considered this incredible experience I'd just had as a mere get-acquainted visit.

"How would you feel about traveling some with the prince?" he asked.

I was taken aback by the question. It was a complete surprise.

"What do you mean?" I asked, and he spelled out his plan.

He not only wanted me to become a tutor to Prince Charles, but a companion and friend, a connection to a world he didn't know. He wanted me to spend time with him regularly.

"I'd have to think about that," I said, although I already knew the answer.

Later, of course, I had to tell him that the answer was no, that I simply didn't want to be away from my family, my home, and my work for extended periods. Too many exciting things were happening for me then. A new book was in the works. A retrospective show of my paintings was scheduled to open at the North Carolina Museum of Art in late summer, only the second show ever to feature a North Carolina artist. And, indeed, on the day after my visit with Prince Charles, Dr. Hammer and I had to go to the Royal

Academy of Art in London to talk about having a show there.

Only recently I learned that one of the many books that have been written about Dr. Hammer claimed that he was using me to court Prince Charles in the hope that the prince might influence British Prime Minister Margaret Thatcher to nominate Dr. Hammer for the Nobel Prize for Peace. That's ridiculous. I always found Dr. Hammer to be sincere and forthright in all his dealings with me. I really think that he saw two very different people for whom he cared very much, who had one important thing in common—a love of painting—and he thought we could become friends and complement one another, so he put us together to see what would happen.

Even from the short time I spent with Prince Charles, I could see that under different circumstances we might very well have become good friends. I hope that he has come to terms with his life and his future, but I want to make this known: If sometime years from now I hear in the news that King Charles has abdicated and mysteriously disappeared, I'm going to keep an eye on the door at Whitley's. And if he shows up wearing bluejeans, a plaid shirt, an old hat and a big grin, we'll make a place for him at the table, order him a big tray of chopped barbecue, and afterwards we'll head down to High Rock with a couple of cane poles and a bucket of minnows—and crappie beware!

The credit belongs to those who are actually in the arena, who strive valiantly; who know the great enthusiasms, the great devotions, and spend themselves in a worthy cause; who at the best, know the triumph of high achievement; and who, at the worst, if they fail, fail while daring greatly, so that their place shall never be with those cold and timid souls who know neither victory nor defeat.

—Theodore Roosevelt

Chapter 15

If my trip to Buckingham Palace at the beginning of 1979 had seemed like a visit to Wonderland, I can't imagine what to call the bizarre realm that I innocently wandered into later that year, for it truly was the domain of the Mad Hatter.

In hindsight, I know that I should have seen this unsettling experience coming. Perhaps it was my old and faithful companion Naivete that kept me from it. I remember telling reporters at the time that I sometimes felt almost guilty about all the fun I was having. I should have realized that some people would want me to pay a penalty for that—and especially for the successes that were coming my way.

After all, Victor Hammer had warned me years earlier, but I suspect he thought that the attack would come sooner and from a different quarter. Perhaps because it hadn't, I lulled myself into believing that it wouldn't. I was startled that it came at home, and at one of my proudest moments—the opening of my retrospective show at the North Carolina Museum of Art in Raleigh on September 16, 1979.

The museum had not yet moved to its current modern

building and spacious campus near the fairgrounds on Raleigh's outskirts. It was still at its original site in an old building downtown. And it had never seen such a crush of people as appeared at my opening. More than a thousand people crowded inside, actually raising the temperature to an uncomfortable level. I know I was sweating. So many came that they couldn't all fit into the auditorium where I was to give my little talk and I had to do it twice.

We had a preview for a select group the night before and the press was invited. A reporter from *The Fayetteville Times* trailed around behind me at the preview, and she showed up again at the opening on Sunday. At least I thought she was a reporter. It turned out that she was the staff artist, who occasionally wrote about art.

I tried to treat all reporters alike. I was friendly and open with them and attempted to answer all of their questions as fully and honestly as I could. But my answers didn't seem to please her, and her questions became increasingly antagonistic. She seemed to be offended that I actually sold my work, that I could think of myself as a painter *and* a salesman. "Commercial," she sniffed with scorn in her voice.

"What do you expect me to do?" I asked, but got no answer.

She appeared to be especially irritated that people liked my paintings and prints and wanted to see them. When people came up to talk with me, she edged in close to hear the conversation and constantly interrupted. If somebody complimented me or said that he, or she, liked my paintings, she asked why.

It was an awkward and uncomfortable situation, and frankly, I was relieved when the opening ended and I no longer had deal with her obnoxious presence. I didn't concern myself with what she might write. I couldn't do anything about that, after all. Not surprisingly, a week later, she published a scathing review of my show, blasting it with a full arsenal of vituperation. I was a "paint-by-numbers artist" producing "sleazy, cheap...plastic nostalgia."

"It's not real," she wrote. "Everything is so perfect. It's overly sentimental."

Fine. She had every right to think whatever she wanted about my work, and every right to publish it. And I had every right to ignore it—you can learn from genuine criticism, but not from scurrilous invective (other reviewers, incidentally, wrote very favorably of the show). I would have ignored this particular review if I had known about it, but I didn't. Not until other reporters started calling a week or two later did I learn about it.

These reporters were calling about a petition drawn up by two Fayetteville artists, William C. Fields, a portrait painter, and Nick Lloyd, the head of the art department at Methodist College in Fayetteville. I didn't know either of them, in fact had never heard of them. The writer who assaulted my work in the Fayetteville paper was first to report about this. She did that in a story about my show that accompanied her review. In the story, incidentally, she even found fault with my looks—"too fleshy to be handsome," she called me. Apparently, my paintings were too pretty, and I wasn't pretty enough. The petition was circulated among "professionals" in the art field, and the attack apparently had been planned with the reporter's knowledge and involvement, because it was sent out with a copy of her review attached before the review appeared.

The artists who started the petition proclaimed themselves to be outraged at "the debasement of our state art museum by...Timberlake's work." They professed themselves to be appalled and vehemently protested "the abrogation of all professional standards" by the museum. They wanted my paintings yanked from the walls and consigned to the trash heap, or better yet, tossed into a bonfire. I didn't measure up to their high artistic and so-called ethical standards.

"His achievement is solely commercial," proclaimed the petition, "the result of clever promotion. His commercial success, moreover, has been based on deception."

Here they went beyond criticism, claiming that I was exploiting "the gullibility of an ignorant public" with my "so-called 'prints,'" which were "nothing more than inexpensive photo-mechanical reproductions." This simply wasn't true. We had never represented our prints as being anything other than that, but they were the finest photo-mechanical repro-ductions available (believe me, there are differences) and they were printed on the finest rag paper to be found.

Reporters wanted me to respond. But how do you re-spond to something so blatantly petty and ridiculous? If you do, don't you put yourself on the same level as your accus-ers? Doesn't it just fan the fires and draw more attention? If you dwell on personal attacks, doesn't it pull you into the snare of your antagonists, draining your energies, turning you from creative endeavors, diminishing your powers and assisting your attackers in accomplishing their goal—your downfall?

This whole thing was so alien to my nature that I couldn't believe it was happening. No matter what I thought of an-other artist's work, I never would attack him or her, not even privately. I always promoted other artists and crafts people, especially other North Carolinians. Two years earlier, Tim and I had bought the old Chamber of Commerce Building next to the YMCA on West Third Street in downtown Lex-ington and opened Heritage Gallery. One of our purposes was to display and sell the work of other North Carolina artists. Indeed, we had exhibited paintings by another of the instigators of this very petition.

That was Claude Howell, who was head of the art de-partment at the University of North Carolina at Wilmington. He was a fine painter. I like his work. But he was a headstrong and highly opinionated man who thought that things should be done in a certain way—his way. I think he also saw himself as the guru of art in North Carolina and looked upon me was an untrained interloper outstripping him in success and popularity.

For whatever reasons, he clearly did not like me. I had met him, and on several occasions we had attended the same functions, but he avoided me like the plague. He literally would get red-faced and start to tremble if I walked into a room where he was. When I was invited to speak at the university in Wilmington, I was told that he advised his students not to attend.

Howell was the only other North Carolina artist who'd had a one-man show at the North Carolina Museum of Art, and ironically I may have had something to do with that.

My old friend Stuffer Myers, the watercolor painter who sold art supplies from his auto parts store and who organized the North Carolina Watercolor Society, loved everybody who attempted to create or perform art of any kind. He wanted everybody to appreciate and enjoy art, and he was an unslacking promoter of North Carolina artists. After the governor appointed him to the board of trustees of the state museum, he came to me and expressed his concern that the museum didn't do enough for North Carolina artists. He wanted me to go with him to a board meeting and urge them to do more, and I agreed.

"We might get blackballed for this," he warned me with a laugh, but he thought it was worth the risk.

We went in 1972, and when Stuffer introduced me, he pointed out that my paintings were being sold at Hammer Galleries, that the gallery was planning my first show, yet I'd received no encouragement or support from the museum. I got up and made my pitch for North Carolina artists, and later Stuffer told me that it at least got some board members talking about stressing North Carolina art.

A couple of years later, Howell was invited to have his show, which was held in 1975, and I felt good about it. Sadly, Stuffer died before I had mine; I know he would have been bursting with pride because of it, and he would have been as unable to understand this attack on my work and my character as was I.

I can honestly say that I held no enmity for Howell or the other two artists. I had trained myself to concentrate only on the positive, and I had perfected the ability to close out the negative, and that was what I did with this. I simply assumed that these folks would have their little fit of pique and it would pass.

But that was not to be the case.

Partly, this was because so many people—members of the supposedly gullible and ignorant public—responded to this absurd situation with indignation and rallied to my support. Newspaper editorials, columns and letters to the editor denounced the petitioners as arrogant elitists who were envious and resentful of my success and therefore wanted not only to censure me but censor my work, depriving people of the art they enjoyed and condemning and ridiculing them for wanting it. More than a few of the letters sent to newspaper editors called me an artist of the people, not of the critics, echoing what Victor Hammer had told me years earlier and proving his wisdom. This was more than heartening to me. It was almost overwhelming.

When shows closed at the state museum, they sometimes were offered to other museums around the state, but newspapers reported that two, the Fayetteville Museum of Art, of which W.C. Fields once had been president of the board of directors, and the Southeastern Gallery of Contemporary Art, the gallery where I first exhibited my paintings and had my first sold-out show, had declined to host my exhibit because it did not meet their standards. The Winston-Salem gallery had received a large endowment upon the death of businessman James G. Hanes in 1972 and had moved into the posh mansion on his thirty-two-acre estate since my paintings had helped pay their rent, but Ted Potter was still the director, and he quickly issued a statement saying he'd been misquoted and that the only reason my show wasn't being offered was because of scheduling problems.

Angry calls and letters inundated the Fayetteville Museum. Raymon Yarborough, the publisher of the Fayetteville paper, who owned one of my originals, wrote a letter to the editor of his own newspaper denouncing the local museum and urging people to go to Raleigh to see the exhibit before it closed on October 14. To calm the storm, the museum director quickly retracted her statement and said that the museum would attempt to schedule a show of my paintings as soon as it could be worked in (it finally will happen twenty-one years later in the year 2000).

All of this brought more news stories and whipped the petitioners into a greater and angrier frenzy. They now claimed that my show had been scheduled only because of political pressure. This apparently was because Governor Jim Hunt and his wife, Carolyn, had attended my opening, and the governor had been quoted as saying I was his favorite artist. Earlier in the year, Governor Hunt had presented me the North Carolina Award for Public Service for my work with the Cystic Fibrosis Foundation, the Duke Comprehensive Cancer Center, and other charities, but if that and the governor's fondness for my work endowed me with political clout, somebody surely failed to inform me about it.

The petitioners also demanded the resignation of the museum director not only for having the poor judgment and bad taste to schedule my show, but for submitting art to political machination.

My detractors were even more disturbed that people

had come to my defense and the news media had taken note of it.

"Timberlake was getting equal billing in each news story and public opinion seemed to be on his side, as shown by a spate of letters to the editor from artistic illiterates from all over the state," they wrote to their supporters.

How dare the great unwashed mass of artistic illiterates contradict the edicts of the self-appointed Art Gods! And what audaciousness for newspapers to present both sides of an issue!

More seriously, the petitioners filed a formal complaint that the museum was committing a criminal violation.

My show had consisted of forty-seven original paintings. Not until I arrived at the museum for the preview did I know that the museum's gift shop had ordered some of my etchings from Hammer Galleries to offer for sale, although they were not part of the show. Now the petitioners were claiming that these were not genuine, that I didn't have the ability to create them, and that the people who had purchased them had been defrauded.

The museum director, Moussa Domit, halted the sale of the etchings two days before my show was to close and hired an expert to determine whether they were genuine. One particular etching was called into question. I still had four of the five copper plates used to make this print (the other had been destroyed) in the basement at the gallery, and I made them available to the museum's authority, Ben A.G. Bern, a university professor who had worked for many years in lithography.

My show closed on October 14, and newspapers reported that it had drawn record crowds. They have not been matched since.

Five days later, Bern issued his findings: the print was my work and it was authentic.

I figured that would be the end of the charges and ha-rassment and I was relieved. I had a new book coming out, and I had to turn all of my attention to it. This was another big, handsomely produced collection of paintings, with text written by myself and edited by Hugh Morton Jr. It was called *The World of Bob Timberlake*, published by Oxmoor House, a division of the company that produces *Southern Living* magazine, and it was not a limited edition. More than a few people had complained to me about the price and limited number of my first book, and I wanted to make sure that any future books were available to more people and more affordable. The publisher had scheduled me to make a tour of many cities, speaking and signing my book, and wher-ever I went, people turned out in droves. Few mentioned the museum controversy, and those who did simply ex-pressed disdain for my critics, or offered support.

The controversy didn't go away as I expected, however. My critics vowed that the fight had just begun. They an-nounced that they were getting their own experts to "deauthenticate" the museum's authentication of my etch-ing. Wherever I went on my book tour, reporters turned out seeking quotes to keep the brouhaha stirred.

Up to this point, Hugh Morton Jr. and I had thought it best to say as little as possible about this preposterous situ-ation, and that had not been easy. But we discussed it and decided to issue a statement. Hugh was even angrier than I. He wrote the statement and issued it from his office in Greensboro in my name with my approval. In it, he called my critics' complaints "childish whining."

"It is high time for this insecure little group of academic 'experts' to realize that the public is sick and tired of being told what it ought to like," he wrote. "It is, therefore, in the spirit of brotherly love that I challenge these folks to put away their mud pies and go back to painting."

Looking back, I realize that our instincts were right in

the beginning, that the statement did nothing to help us, but it was a time of great frustration, especially for Hugh.

For a while after that, things settled down. The news stories diminished and died away. Christmas came and passed in peace. My book did great, becoming the country's number-one bestselling art book of 1979. But all the while tension still seethed beneath the surface.

In February, Hugh told me that a reporter for the *Greensboro Daily News*, a newspaper which came to my front door every morning, was "investigating" me and wanted an interview. Let him investigate away, I said. What could he possibly find? My naivete obviously was still hard at work. I hadn't yet discovered that a reporter who is determined to assassinate a person's character doesn't really have to find anything to do it, and that a supposedly responsible newspaper will allow it. I know better now.

I should have known better then. The reporter who was conducting this so-called investigation had come late to the museum controversy, but he revealed his techniques in the story he wrote about it. This is how it began:

"He is accused of being primarily a businessman, at best a commercial artist; a charlatan in afficionado's disguise; a clever promoter, not a humble craftsman; a master of the emotional device rather than the creative talent.

"Still, the paintings and etchings of the popular Bob Timberlake hang today in a one-man retrospective exhibition at the North Carolina Museum of Art in Raleigh...."

Did he offer proof of any of the scurrilous charges in his opening paragraph? No. Did he allow anybody to refute them? Only partly. But the effect was that of asking if I'd stopped beating my wife. No matter what I answered, I was still a wife beater. Why would a newspaper allow a reporter to fling about unfounded accusations that label a person a cheat and a fraud? You tell me.

I certainly had no intention of talking with this reporter even if I had time, but when he requested—almost demanded—an interview, I was in the middle of a crisis. I had been invited by the U.S. Postal Service to design the Christmas stamp for 1980, the first Southern artist ever so honored.

My design was of a Raggedy Ann doll lying atop a tiny quilt on a handmade doll bed set on a window sill beneath a Christmas wreath. Six-hundred-fifty million of the stamps were being printed when the company that owned the copyright to Raggedy Ann raised an objection. In March, I got a frantic call saying that all the stamps printed so far had to be destroyed and I had to come up with another design, preferably without a copyrighted item as a subject. I gave strict orders that I was not to be disturbed for ten days and retreated to my studio. I came up with several proposed designs. The one that was approved showed an antique child's top, a toy horn and drum on a window sill. I finished the painting on my son Dan's seventeenth birthday, March 20, 1980.

Six days earlier, while I was holed up working, the under-the-surface seething about the museum controversy had erupted again in the newspapers. The director of the North Carolina Museum of Art, Moussa Domit, resigned. He had many critics and had been drawing fire well before my show, and many people thought that his enemies had latched onto me as the means to finally bring him down, but I was told that he resigned for personal reasons. Whatever the situation, I felt bad being even peripherally involved in causing somebody to be forced out of his job. Domit certainly had treated me well and defended my work unflinchingly.

But the critics still weren't through with me either. Not by a long shot.

Nine days after I sent off the painting for the new stamp,

I went to my front porch, picked up the Sunday morning *Greensboro Daily News* and found that I was page-one news. If I had been caught holding up Lexington State Bank, or making off with the tithing plates at First Methodist Church I wouldn't have rated the display that I got in this edition, and this was just the first of a three-part series, the kick-off of the results of the so-called "six-week investigation."

The reporter started off, of course, with his most powerful ammunition, his major finding: that I had "mislabeled" two of my prints. The implication was that I had deliberately defrauded people. The explanation was simple and far less sinister. Hugh had given it to the reporter, but he chose not to include it. It would have been inconvenient to his thesis.

One of the prints to which he was referring was the second print I did, shortly after I began painting, well before Tim and I started the Heritage Company to produce our own prints. It was of my mother's cupboard, and the print was done to raise money for the local arts group. When we did the first print for the arts group, we numbered each consecutively, and we had a lot of people scrambling to get the lower numbers and grumbling because they didn't.

All of the prints were exactly alike. The only difference was the number scribbled on each. When we did the second print I suggested that we number all of them 1/250, meaning one of 250, and eliminate that problem. That was what we did. I didn't know anything about the print business. As far as I know, no artists in North Carolina were producing prints at that time. I had no guidelines to go by. It didn't cross my mind that anything would be wrong with doing it that way. Not a single person complained, I might add.

When Tim and I started issuing prints through the Heritage Company we numbered each consecutively up until the fourth print, which came out near the end of our first year of operation. That was my painting of the Bald Head

Island Rescue Station. We were issuing 1,000 prints, but we were setting aside 250 of those exclusively for property owners at Bald Head. We numbered the 750 prints consecutively, as we did for "Rowboat," but then the question arose: how do we number the others? They would be no different from the other prints except for a Bald Head seal that would be embossed in the paper. If we numbered them consecutively as a special edition we'd have two identical prints bearing the same number up to 250. That was when I remembered how we'd numbered the "Ella's Cupboard" print so that all 250 were the same. We'd had no problem with this method, so that was how we decided to do these. I actually thought it would make everybody happy.

A few weeks after the prints went out, we got several calls from Bald Head property owners complaining that they thought they had number-one but discovered that others also had it. Only then did I realize that I'd made a mistake. We offered to replace the print with a consecutively numbered one, or to take it back and return the money, as we have always done. Nobody, as I recall, took up the offer.

Never again did we number a print in that way, but now that mistake, made five years earlier out of inexperience and an intention to please, was being made to appear criminal. The reporter sought out people to say that prints numbered in that manner could be printed in numbers far beyond the stated edition, the implication being that that might have happened, although no evidence was presented to show that it did. And, of course, no evidence existed because it didn't happen.

Naturally, the story reported that I "refused" to be interviewed, the implication being that I had something to hide, that declining to submit yourself for evisceration by a reporter is a crime in itself.

The second day's story was more or less a rehash of the museum controversy and the complaints of my critics, but the reporter managed to dredge up a few more people, mainly less-than-successful painters and failed gallery owners, to vilify me further as talentless and interested only in money.

It was clear that to these people my real crime was that I painted images that people actually recognized and liked, and I had gotten attention and money for it. For some people that could not be abided.

By the third day, astoundingly, I was being accused of depriving all upcoming young artists of the counsel and wisdom of Andrew Wyeth. This report began thusly: "In 1975 an airline magazine carried an article about North Carolina artist Bob Timberlake under the headline, 'Move Over Andrew Wyeth.' Not only hasn't Wyeth moved, but Timberlake's critics suggest that if anyone moves it should be Timberlake—off his self-promoted pedestal."

The thrust of this article was that I was constantly comparing my work to Wyeth's and exploiting his reputation for my own ends. An outright, total lie. Never had I compared my work to Wyeth's. Never would I have even thought to do such a thing. Writers for *Reader's Digest*, *The Detroit Free Press*, *Acquire* magazine, *The Charlotte Observer* and other publications had done so, but I never encouraged such a thing, never drew attention to it, and haven't since. When reporters asked me how and why I started painting, I told them about my visit with Wyeth and how nice he and his wife had been to me, and that was all. It was simple fact.

Hugh told me that when the reporter interviewed him, he questioned whether I'd actually even visited Wyeth, indicating he believed that I hadn't and had simply latched onto his name to promote myself.

Wyeth himself wasn't quoted, so he apparently declined to talk with this reporter, too, but a brother-in-law told the reporter that Wyeth paid no attention to his imitators or "the many painters who try to exploit his name," the implication, of course, being that I was one of them. (Andy, incidentally, has never mentioned any of this to me, causing me to wonder if he ever even knew about it, and we remain friends.)

The article went on to say that "some local artists and at least one dealer," all unnamed, "had been told either by Wyeth's representatives (unnamed) or a relative (unnamed) that he was shaken by Timberlake's use of his name and that he has since adopted a policy of not seeing young aspiring artists."

On such flimsy and despicable reporting was the newspaper attempting to destroy me.

Until you have fallen under intense daily fire by a newspaper's big guns, you don't know what it's like to wait to see what the next day's shelling will bring. You feel so helpless and defenseless. You can't stop it and you can't answer it. It bothered me most because I could see that it hurt Kay, Mom, the kids and others close to me. It really devastated Hugh. As he saw it, his job was to bring good attention to me and to protect me from the bad. He felt that he had failed me, even though I assured him that I didn't feel that way. He was particularly angry and flustered when the newspaper refused to publish a letter to the editor from him answering the charges, and he paid from his own pocket to have it appear as an ad. I honestly believe that Hugh never got over this.

People who knew me knew that there was no foundation to the charges and implications in these articles and tried to reassure me.

"The higher you get in the tree, the better shot you make," Dad said. "Somebody will always be trying to bring you down."

"When you're a public figure, you have to expect things like this," my friend, attorney and business partner, Bob

Grubb, told me.

That was rather startling to me, because until then I never thought of myself in those terms. I was the same person I was before I started painting. I was just a guy enjoying his work, not attempting to cheat or harm a soul, but because I had gained attention, that somehow made me a valid target for lies and vilification.

As had happened before, though, people rallied to my support. Letters to the editor decried the newspaper's series. My former minister, friend and hunting companion, Howard Wilkinson, then the president of Greensboro College, wrote a guest column calling the reporting astonishing. "...The net effect was accusative and the dark suspicion was left that Timberlake might very well be, after all, a fraud, a cheat, a deceiver and a fake....I have known Bob since he was 12....I will state here that his character is unimpeachable, that he is indeed a wonderfully fine individual; and there is not a dishonest bone in his body. On the subject of Bob's motives, I am prepared to 'deny the allegations and defy the alligators!'"

My friend Mutt Burton, who still wrote a weekly column for the *Daily News* editorial section after his retirement, was a sweet and generous man who rarely said an unkind word about anybody. But of my detractors he wrote: "Having had such witless fun in the first round, they have devoted much of their kinetic energy and spleen since then to dancing around their surviving target, waving their pointless spears, screeching equally pointless and hysterical aspersions and urging one another on to more and more idiocy in the obvious hope of discrediting, and, if possible, destroying Artist Timberlake. It is a very sad and shameful performance. More than that, it is, first and last, the most unwarranted and mean-spirited campaign of calumny I have ever witnessed."

None of this deterred the detractors, though. Since the fall, they had found an expert to say that the etching they had questioned was not genuine. Whereupon the museum hired another expert who found that it was. The critics had then taken it to still another expert of their own. I could see this going on forever, a perpetual dance of authenticators whirling in meaningless circles. But after the *Daily News* series, the critics demanded that the state attorney general launch an investigation, hoping, no doubt, that I would be indicted and sent to prison for life, since the death penalty does not yet apply to painting that which does not please the self-appointed art gods.

I welcomed such an investigation. It was something I had wanted from the beginning. Bob Grubb drove to Raleigh to offer our help in any way that we could. Not until August, nearly a year after this whole asinine business began, did the attorney general issue his report absolving me of wrongdoing from any of the accusations. After that, I was allowed to paint and go about my business in relative peace.

But the reporter who was so intent on assassinating my character did not give up easily. Two years later when I had a one-man show at the prestigious Corcoran Gallery of Art in Washington, he dredged up the whole mess again, reporting suspicions that my Washington show might also have been brought about by political pressure, presumably because I had twice been honored at the White House for my work with Keep America Beautiful. He failed to note, however, that the presidents who had honored me had been from two different political parties.

It has been difficult for me to go back through all of this, because I had put it completely out of mind. Looking back, it almost seems as if it happened to somebody else. It still is beyond belief to me that it occurred. But as with almost all bad things in life, good did come from it. It made me more careful about how I treated people and more cautious of what I said about them, made me more aware of the hurt and damage words could wreak. I learned a lot and grew a lot as result. Sadly, one of the things I learned was that I could no longer trust everything I read in the newspaper.

As it turned out, though, art itself seemed to benefit from my endurance test, as several newspaper editorials pointed out. People who had never been to an art museum were drawn to the North Carolina Museum of Art during my show, no doubt partly because of all the attention this brought to it. And the whole controversy caused people in the state to talk about and debate art as never before or since. Just the same, if I could have had my druthers, I would have preferred promoting art and artists in North Carolina in a calmer and less conspicuous way, as I had always done, and continue to do.

A few years after all of this happened, I was at the Duke cancer center for the announcement of a new research development. I was introduced, and who should I see in the audience taking notes but the *Greensboro Daily News* reporter who had attempted to destroy me.

Later, I saw him sitting alone, going through some materials. I walked over to him, held out my hand and introduced myself. He was completely taken aback, too startled to speak. He attempted to stand but settled back in his chair as he shook my hand.

"I'm glad to see you writing about something positive for a change," I told him.

He mumbled something that I couldn't understand.

"There's something I've been wanting to tell you," I said. "I have forgiven you for what you did to me."

He didn't respond, but the stunned look on his face was the only reply I needed.

I'd learned long before that forgiveness doesn't just bring

peace to your soul. It's far more satisfying than striking out angrily ever could be.

A little kingdom I possess, where thoughts and feelings dwell.

—Louisa May Alcott

Chapter 16

My year of imposed controversy had no detrimental effect on my career. After it passed, my paintings sold at ever higher prices. The resell value of earlier paintings and prints continued to rise as well. Every print that Heritage Gallery produced still sold out in advance (as our prints still do).

If anything, the controversy helped me, because most people saw it for what it was, an unwarranted attack, and sympathized with me. It also made many more people aware of me and my work. I was reminded of what Dad had told me long ago: "When things seem to be going against you, they're really working for you." But in the midst of the assaults that wasn't easy to see.

The eighties were to be a decade of ongoing success for me, but also of great change and enormous loss.

In 1980, my friend Loonis McGlohon of Charlotte, one of the country's finest jazz pianists and composers, asked Hugh and me if he could do a TV show of music built around my paintings. I was not only willing to do it, I was immensely flattered. Earlier Loonis had composed a song called "Nobody's Home" based on my painting of two houses in the Alamance County cotton mill village of Glencoe.

"When I looked at that painting, I had seen that same

scene as a kid," he told a reporter. "I just had to write a song about it. He really pulls some of the best work out of me."

Loonis wrote many more songs based on my paintings for the TV special, including "Blackberry Winter," written with the great Alec Wilder, "Wine of May," and "Cardboard in My Shoes." The show was called "Sketches in Jazz." It featured singers Rosemary Clooney and Johnny Hartman, and it was shown on public TV stations all across the country.

In the summer of 1981, I became the first Southern artist ever to have a one-man show at Corcoran Gallery of Art in Washington. That was followed by my first Christmas show at Hammer Galleries. My second Christmas show at Hammer came in 1984. Both, as always, quickly sold out. In 1985, I had one-man shows at the Charles and Emma Frye Museum in Seattle, Washington, and the Huntington Museum in West Virginia (where another show is scheduled for 2000). I was particularly honored when the Isetan Gallery of Art in Tokyo held a two-man show of graphics— mine and Andrew Wyeth's.

Mom and Dad were no longer able to attend my shows. Mom's health had been growing worse. In addition to having suffered five heart attacks, she also had rheumatoid arthritis and lived in constant pain. She never complained, but she wasn't able to get around as much anymore. She and Dad stayed at the Myrtle Beach house for much of the year. Dad was in semi-retirement and spent a lot of time playing golf.

Mom and Dad always came back to Lexington just before Thanksgiving so we all could be together for the holidays. Nothing was any different at Thanksgiving of 1985, except that Mom seemed to be talking more about the past. She kept pointing out belongings that had family history or special sentimental value. I remember her showing me a cup and telling me that my great-great grandfather Roberts, whom I'm named after, used to drink his buttermilk from it.

Tim and I dropped by the house almost every day, and almost every time I saw her, Mom showed me different possessions saying, "Now I want Kay to have this...and Teen to get this..." She had picked out special items of sentimental value for everybody.

"Mom, I can't remember all of this," I told her. "Let me bring a camera over after Christmas and take pictures of everything. Then you can write on the back what it is and who you want to have it."

I didn't understand why she was doing this, but if it was something she felt a need to do I wanted to help her.

Christmas was Dad's favorite time of the year, as it is mine. Mom always put in a big effort to make sure that everything went just right at Christmas. She wanted everybody happy, especially at that joyous time of the year. Kay and Teen did most of the work on the big Christmas dinner, but Mom was right there helping. It was, as always, a great Christmas. Not until later, when I was looking through the snapshots we made that day, did I notice just how much Mom had deteriorated in the few weeks between Thanksgiving and Christmas.

Three days after Christmas, my phone rang early in the morning and I heard Tim's distressed voice.

"Bob," he said, "Mom's gone."

He was at the house when I got there, along with Mom's doctor, Ray Strader. Dad was in a daze. Mom was in her bedroom. She had gone to sleep the night before and had not awakened. She still looked to be sleeping.

I hugged her and told her that I loved her. I promised her that Tim and I would take care of Dad. I knew she would be worried about that. She was not yet eighty. She and Dad had lived together for more than sixty years, and they had adored each other for all that time.

Later, Dad told Tim and me that Mom had him to get her jewelry and everything else out of the lock box at the bank in Myrtle Beach before they came home for Thanksgiving. He didn't understand why she wanted to do that. They were to go back to the beach in January. But now her actions became clear.

She knew that she was going to die. She prepared herself and she attempted to prepare us. She got us through Christmas, made sure we all were happy, and then she let go and went to her rest.

Four months after Mom's death, Kay and I were blessed with the birth of our first grandchild, Elizabeth Carter Ellis, called Carter, named for her great grandmother, born April 27, 1986, to Kelly and her husband Ace. I was only sorry that Mom was not here to cry at the news and later to hold her great-granddaughter and coo to her. Our second grandchild, James Roberts Timberlake, born to Ed and his wife, Lisa, arrived only seven months later on November 28, 1986. He's called Rob. In the years to come, we would have five more—one, Kate Timberlake Ellis, born to Kelly and Ace in 1989 on Kay's birthday, June 7, and another the very next day, Abby Elisabeth, born to Ed and Lisa. Ace and Kelly gave us our fifth grandchild, Anne Claiborne Ellis, on October 6, 1991. Another grandson, Roberts Decatur Timberlake, called Dek, was born to Dan and Rhonda on February 27, 1992, followed by another granddaughter, his sister, Christopher Evanne, on March 8, 1995.

By the time our grandchildren began arriving, I was engrossed in an extensive new project: building a new studio.

I did not want to leave Riverwood. It had played a major role in my life and work and commanded a big chunk of my heart. But I had been frustrated there for several years. I wanted to buy it and had tried several times, but that had proved to be impossible. My landlord, Thurman Briggs, had died and ownership had passed to his son, Paul, who did not want to sell it to me. I needed more room. I wanted to expand the studio itself, to build a guest house and other structures closeby. As it was, I couldn't even make repairs to the outside of the building. For a long time, the roof had leaked and I had to set pots and pails around whenever hard rains came.

I kept thinking that Paul might change his mind and stayed year after year on that hope, but he never did. When I discovered that he had offered the property to others for less than I was willing to pay, I didn't understand it, but I finally realized that for whatever reasons he just didn't want me to have the place. Not until much later would I come to believe that the real reasons for this may have lain beyond the understanding of either of us.

Only when I realized that Riverwood never would be mine did I begin to think seriously of leaving. But I had no idea where I would go until a piece of land that I had coveted since I was fourteen or so became suddenly available.

Fleeta Burke was the paternal grandmother of my daughter-in-law Lisa, Ed's wife. She was in her eighties, and she owned a seventy-acre farm on Shemwell Highway, just a few miles south of Lexington off N.C. Highway 8, not far from the Junior Order Home, where I first laid eyes on Kay. The property was beautiful and I'd tried to buy some of it from Fleeta over the years, but it was family land and she wanted to hold onto it. She lived across the road from the farm in a lovely house built in 1948 and set in the woods far back from the highway. One day she fried chicken for lunch, but before eating, she got into her car to drive to the mailbox by the road at Lebanon Lutheran Church. The accelerator jammed; the car lurched into a wild circle and slammed into a tree in front of the church. Later it was detemined that Fleeta had suffered a stroke before the crash. After her death, her children, Dr. Jim Burke (Lisa's Dad) and Belinda Wilburn, decided to sell the farm.

I bought thirty-three acres in the center of the property, which included an old two-story farm house, a big barn and other outbuildings (later I would buy the remainder of the property). The house stood on a ridge under huge oaks, behind a line of ancient cedars. It had been abandoned for many years and was a shambles that could not be saved.

Where the house stood was where I wanted my new studio to be. And I already had the structure that I wanted to be the heart of it. I was drawn to old log houses and barns, and I found quite a few as I prowled the countryside painting. I had restored and sold two log cabins, and I had found an old log barn just off U.S. Highway 64 west of Lexington. It had been built in 1809 by Henry Shoaf III, whose grandfather had come from Germany to settle in Davidson County (then part of Rowan County) in 1765. Henry Shoaf III was known as Rich Henry. He had acquired more than 2,000 acres, including much of the western end of what would become the town of Lexington. He owned many slaves to farm his fields.

He also bore the same name as his first cousin, who loomed large in Davidson County folklore. Big Henry Shoaf was a giant, said to stand seven feet tall and weigh more than 400 pounds. He was a blacksmith and could toss a huge anvil for a great distance. It was claimed that he had lifted a 950-pound boulder and set it in place to become the cornerstone for a house he built. He could knock a mule to the ground with a single blow, and he delighted crowds by inviting groups of men to try to wrestle him off his feet. No group ever did. At festive occasions, he would ask two grown men to sit in the palms of his hands, hold them aloft and parade them around to whoops, cheers and great laughter.

Among the many tales about Big Henry was that he would go to his hay field at daybreak with an oversized scythe, a gallon of buttermilk, and a gallon of brandy. By the time he quit work at the end of the day he had consumed both the buttermilk and brandy and had cut so much hay that it took five slaves to stack it.

It was also told that, unarmed, Big Henry single-handedly killed three Yankee soldiers he discovered raiding his house during the Civil War.

I had painted the barn that Big Henry's cousin, Rich Henry, built. In the '50s, when new Highway 64 was constructed, the Shoaf barn had stood in the right-of-way, and it was about to be destroyed until some family members raised objections. The state then slid the barn 200 feet to another location.

For at least ten years I had tried to buy the barn, but it was in an estate situation, making negotiations difficult. In 1985, I finally convinced the heirs to let me have it to ensure that it would be preserved, but I would have to disassemble and move it. I paid $3,500 for it and began looking for a place to put it.

Not long before I acquired the barn, Renè Swing came into my life. He was a creative genius, an artist with a chainsaw, a man born to build log structures. A story about him and the house he had built from old logs for his family appeared in the *Lexington Dispatch*. I called and told him of my interest in log structures. He invited me to come see his house and we instantly became friends.

Renè went with me to look at the barn, and he was eager to help me turn it into a new studio. I just couldn't find the right spot for it. When the Burke farm became available in 1986, I found my place. I called Renè and told him we were ready to start.

We tore down the old house in a matter of days and hauled it away except for the handmade bricks from the chimney, which, we discovered, were far older than the house. We dug and poured footings. Then we began disassembling the Shoaf barn, using a crane to lift off the logs one by one.

All but the top logs were oak, some fifty-five feet long. As trees, they had been growing in the 1600s. Renè and his brothers, Dirk, Shaun, and Kim (called Sue) carefully numbered and labeled each, loaded them onto two flatbed trucks, hauled them to the studio site, and erected them anew. We found the year the barn had been built, 1809, carved into one of the logs, along with Henry Shoaf's initials and lots of other things, including a Masonic emblem in one of the poplar top logs. On some loft logs were notches used to count the bales of hay stored there.

The barn measured fifty-five feet by twenty-eight and had a wagon-way, sixteen-feet high and sixteen-feet wide through the middle. The logs were simply the frame on which we would create the giant sculpture that I wanted the studio to be.

The creation of it would take three years, and essentially Renè and I designed it as we went. It was like embarking on a long trip without a road map, and it made the journey all the more exciting. I loved working with Renè. He had a positive nature like my own, and our ideas reacted well off each other. A lot of contractors, if you come up with an idea that's different or difficult, will tell you that something just can't be done. Renè was never like that. He was always looking for ways that things could be done. He'd never tell me that an idea wouldn't work, even if I came up with a stupid one. Often when I came up with a good idea, it only provoked a better one from Renè. "Hey, that's a great idea," he'd say, "but what if we did it this way?"

The studio literally was designed day-to-day. Sometimes I would sketch out ideas while I was having breakfast at Whitley's. Other times I'd rip pages from magazines when I saw something I liked and take them to Renè. We drew plans right on the walls as the work progressed around us, then plastered over them.

The barn's basic structure and my particular needs determined the overall plan. I wanted the building to be much larger than the barn, so we added a wing across the whole width of the back. I also wanted to add a third level as my work area, my actual studio, and for that I wanted large amounts of natural light from the east and south, making large windows in those areas a necessity. The third level and the additional wing caused the shake roof to be high, nearly forty feet, and steeply pitched, especially in the front. Across the front, facing north, we added a wide porch with huge cedar trunks as supports and Adirondak-looking cedar pickets for railings.

Some of the old barn logs were bad and sections had to be cut out of them. A huge chimney on one end of the house filled a big gap and took care of that problem. Stonemason Dale Frank and his crew built the chimney. It was fifteen-feet wide at the base and more than forty feet high. It was constructed of two parts local blue slate to five parts brown-and-white field stone brought to the site in seven-ton loads from a quarry in the southern part of the county. The foundation and the walls of the back wing also were built of this stone.

This wing contained a kitchen, a dining and seating area, a sleeping loft and library loft. It faced south and had huge windows to collect the winter light. The wagon way served as the high-ceilinged center of the house, a display area. The main room, with a huge fireplace, occupied one wing off the wagon way. The other wing had a bath, a stairwell, and a smaller sitting room with a big bay window facing east. Bedrooms occupied the space above each wing on the second level, and the whole third floor was my studio and work area.

When finished, the studio contained 4,000 square feet of floor space. Old brick provided the floor for the kitchen and dining area, even for the counter tops. The floor of the wagon way was of wide flat stones and polished slabs cut from the trunk of a massive oak still bearing its bark, and in one spot a walnut that had fallen into a crook of a limb long ago, causing the trunk to eventually grow around it. Floors on the other two levels were of broad hardwood boards. Renè asked what I wanted him to do about the knotholes.

"If you don't fall into them, don't fill them," I told him.

All the doors were built on site, some of wood salvaged from old farm buildings, some of new wood designed to look old. Hinges, latches and locks were made by wrought-iron artist Jerry Darnell of nearby Seagrove, as was the huge chandelier in the dining area. All the window panes were hand-blown at Blenco Glass Company in Milton, West Virginia, and in many of them I etched quotations so that if the scenery outside did not provide inspiration, the words might. Perhaps my favorite of the lot is this:

Imagination is more important than knowledge.

—Albert Einstein

I can't think of anything more applicable to me. Imagination determines everything I do. If I can imagine it, I can do it. Imagination created this new studio, and I wanted it to be a center for the imagination, a place where creative juices flowed freely. I wanted it to be more than just a place for me to paint. I wanted books to be written here, sculptures carved, videos and movies made, photographs taken, tales told, music performed.

I wanted this to be my own special world. I knew I would spend the remainder of my creative life here, and I knew that the place itself would be an ongoing creation, as indeed it has been. As we built the studio, we also erected next to it a small cabin from logs salvaged from a house in the northern part of the county built in 1765. This served as a guest house in the beginning. Later, I added a lake and two small ponds, and a fish camp, made from left-over logs and other materials, on one of the ponds. A few years later, I turned the big barn into a place where I could hold dinners, fundraising events, and other activities for large numbers of people. It also would provide more work areas for creative endeavors and more space for what Kay and some other family members and friends call my "stuff." In fact, I have been accused on more than one occasion of constructing this entire complex just to have a place to keep my stuff.

I admit that I am an inveterate and incurable pack rat. Mom told me that when I was only three or four, I'd go out to play and come back with my pockets filled with pretty stones, the shells of bird eggs, dead insects, acorns and other items that caught my eye. Later, I collected arrowheads and developed an instinct for where they might be and a talent for spotting them. That led to collecting other tools and pottery shards left by the native people who had populated our area thousands of years earlier. As a boy, I also collected coins, stamps and model airplanes that I built and painted myself.

Dad loved antiques and loved hunting for them as much as he loved bird hunting. He was a trader. He'd never buy anything unless he could get the price down. Antique dealers would see him coming and rush around putting higher prices on the items they thought might interest him so he could talk them down to the price they originally wanted. If my Aunt Buff was the inspiration for my early love of antiques, Dad was the source for my love of searching for them. He led me into an unending treasure hunt that's always intriguing, at moments terrifically exciting, and sometimes intensely gratifying.

I even began acquiring a few antiques and collectibles while I was in high school and college—unusual bottles, pottery and small things that I could afford. Mom and Dad were great pottery collectors. Seagrove, an area first settled by potters from England in 1740, was only thirty-five miles from Lexington, and Mom and Dad often went there to buy pottery and took me with them. They were friends of Ben Owen, one of the country's most famous potters, who had been influenced by the great Oriental masters, and whose work had been exhibited at the Smithsonian, the Metropolitan Museum of Art, and other major museums, and they had quite a collection of his work. (Although Ben is now gone, I count as friends his son, Wade, and his grandson, Ben III, a very talented potter.) Mom and Dad often bought me gifts of pottery and antiques for birthdays and Christmas, and those became the beginnings of my own collections.

After Kay and I married, Grandmother Raper's wedding gift of a family quilt started us collecting old quilts of unusual designs and histories, and that collection has grown to well over 100 guilts with the years. I became greatly enamored of enamelware, or agateware, or graniteware, as it also is called, brightly colored metal pitchers, bowls, cooking pots, pans, pails, coffee and tea pots, cups, saucers and plates. These were especially popular during the Depression for their economy, durability and simple beauty. We built a huge collection of enamelware, and I often used pieces in my paintings, as I did other items from my collections. Oftentimes, if I used a piece as a prop, I would later give it to the person who bought the original painting as a Christmas or anniversary gift.

My love of bird hunting led to my collection of decoys. I got my first set of decoys when I was twelve years old, and I used them for duck hunting. Later, especially as I hunted more and more along the North Carolina coast, where many talented decoy makers lived, I began acquiring many more, but these were not for hunting. I collected decoys of swans, geese, ducks of every type, and I chose them for their character. If something was really unusual about them, I bought them. If they were cracked, or worn, or in really rough shape, I wanted them even more. Anytime I was at the coast, I'd ask hunting and fishing guides, boat captains and country store owners if they knew anybody who had old decoys, and often as not, they did. Sometimes I'd just see some decoys in a shed beside somebody's house and stop and ask if I could look at them. I bought many that way. Now such decoys are hard to find and extremely expensive when you do find them. But in past years I found many at bargain prices at places such as Knotts Island, Swan Island and Currituck. And some guides gave me decoys right from their rigs when I hunted with them.

I am told that I may have one of the finest canoe collections in the country. I loved canoes from the time I was a boy, but I didn't really begin collecting them until my good buddy and hunting companion Gene Whitley and I took our sons on a camping and canoeing trip down the Sioux St. Marie River in Canada with a group of other Lexington fathers and sons in 1975, when Ed and Dan were still in the Scouts. While we were there, we stopped by a trading post that had birch-bark canoes made by an old trapper who lived nearby. I'd heard about birch-bark canoes all my life, but I'd never seen one, and I was absolutely fascinated by these. I wanted one but I had no way to get it back home. I talked to the trading post owner, and he said, "Well, I tell you what. When winter sets in up here, there's not much to do. I'll just drive one down there for you." I didn't think he meant it, but, by golly, the next January he showed up with a birch-bark canoe sticking out of the back of his Volkswagen van. This was the canoe that Iron Eyes Cody later paddled in some of his TV spots, and it hangs now in my studio with the red-mud stains from High Rock Lake still evident on its bottom.

From that beginning, I have collected about ninety antique canoes, everything from toy canoes, to three-foot salesmen's samples, to a century-old, 16-foot, double-sailed, mahogany racing canoe from Maine, to a hand-hewn Crusoe Island dugout made from the trunk of a cypress tree in the Green Swamp of southeastern North Carolina, one of our state's wildest and most impenetrable wildernesses.

This is just the beginning of my collections, though. I also collect Civil War and native American items, antique drums, toys, bird houses, children's furniture, miniatures of every type, old illustrated papers, old fishing tackle (which, of course, I keep in the fishing camp) and many other things.

As I became better able to afford it, I began collecting original works by my favorite artists. Kay and I have paintings and drawings by Winslow Homer, Grandma Moses, Norman Rockwell, Frederic Remington, Charles Russell, Albert Insley, Frank Schoonover, and, of course, the Wyeths, N.C., Andrew, Jamie, and Henriette Wyeth Hurd and Carolyn Wyeth, Andy's sisters. We now have twenty Andrew Wyeth originals.

Kay and I also began collecting antique furniture. Usually, these were unique pieces, the only kind that appealed to me, solid and beautifully crafted. As we gathered more and more pieces, we had difficulty finding places to keep it all. A house, or even two houses, will only hold so much. So it only made sense that I would want the new studio to be big enough to accommodate some of my collections. And it was to these collections that Kay and I turned when we began decorating soon after Rene and his brothers and the other work crews finished the studio late in the summer of 1989.

During the three years that it took to build the studio, I did much less painting because the construction took so much of my time. Still, important things had happened for my career. In 1987, Hammer Galleries held a show featuring my paintings along with those of my friends Andrew Wyeth, Eric Sloane, and David Armstrong. I also designed the U.S. postage stamp commemorating South Carolina's 200th year of statehood, which was issued in 1988. That year, I created the stamp commemorating the same anniversary for North Carolina, and it came out a year later. Early in 1989, an exhibit of my original paintings was held at the Greenville Museum of Art in South Carolina, and later the same year I was awarded the only Albert Schweitzer Medal ever presented to an artist. In the fall, I had a new book of my paintings coming out, *Somewhere in Time*. It was especially significant to me, because it was the last project on which I got to work with Hugh Morton Jr., who edited it. He gave up his public relations business in 1987 to become director of the North Carolina Division of Travel and Tourism in Raleigh. Early in 1989, he resigned to take over his family's business, Grandfather Mountain Inc. Only seven years later he was dead by his own hand at the age of 48, the victim of severe depression, a condition my beloved friend never allowed me to see in all the time I spent with him.

I had to go on the road to promote the new book in October. Fortunately, the new studio was completed before that. I moved my drawing table, supplies and other equipment and belongings the few miles from Riverwood to the new studio in September.

That was not an easy move. My creative energies had been invested in Riverwood for sixteen years and I knew that I would be leaving a big part of myself there forever. But I had wonderful memories to take with me. And I was only leaving physically. Riverwood would always remain in my heart, and it would be just down the road whenever I needed to go back.

If somebody had told me then that the new studio to

which I was moving would take me away from painting, I'd have said they were crazy, utterly insane. But, strangely, that was exactly what was to happen.

Build a chair as if an angel was going to sit in it.
—Thomas Merton

Chapter 17

All through my childhood, Dad bought Mom a fine piece of handcrafted furniture for Christmas every year. He always bought it from the same person, a remarkable man named Fred Craver, and he had a standing order so he'd be sure of getting it.

Only the piece changed year by year, and Dad would stop by now and then to check on it. Fred was notoriously slow and careful, and if something he was working on wasn't going exactly as he expected, or if some other project struck him as more interesting at the moment, he'd put a job aside and leave it until the mood struck him to get back to it.

Some people waited years to get furniture from Fred Craver, and they waited without complaint. They knew that when they got it they would have something special and enduring.

Stopping by to check on his Christmas order was just Dad's excuse for visiting Fred. He enjoyed talking with him and watching him work. Dad, of course, was an amateur woodworker, and he admired Fred and envied his abilities.

Fred's shop was in what once had been the exhibit building at the old Lexington fairgrounds. He bought it for $450 in 1938, when he went into business on his own. The shop was just behind Fred's house on West Sixth Street, a house built of walnut, his favorite wood.

Dad usually took me on his visits with Fred, and I always looked forward to them. Fred's shop truly was a magical place to me, dusty and cluttered, ripe with wood scent, curiosities and creative possibilities. The curiosities included Fred's tools, marvelous, intriguing devices, unlike any others, because he made most of them himself. There also were carvings, pieces of furniture and other items in various states of completion, none the same, for Fred never made any two items alike. And there were racks filled with wood of every type. If an old building was being torn down anywhere nearby, Fred likely would be there to see what kinds of wood were in it and what might be salvaged. He usually marked the boards so he'd know where they came from.

I doubt that anybody ever loved wood more than Fred Craver, and I've known nobody who could transform it into more beautiful creations.

"There's nothing that can't be made from wood," he'd tell me. "As long as you can see it in the wood, you can make it."

Fred was tall and lean and wore big-rimmed glasses. He was notoriously taciturn, didn't care all that much for being around people, for that matter, strangers anyway, but he kept a few round-back oak chairs by the pot-bellied wood stove in his shop for the occasional callers he enjoyed. For the most part, though, he was a man of habit who loved his work and didn't care for interruptions.

He always seemed to take pleasure in Dad's visits, and for some reason he took an interest in me. He made me feel special, perhaps because he knew of my interest in Dad's basement woodworking shop. Or maybe he just saw in me the same instinctive love for wood that he felt.

Fred had two daughters but no sons, and I sometimes

felt almost as if he thought of me as a surrogate son. He always took time to talk with me. He explained the qualities of all the different woods to me. Every piece had a distinct character, he told me, even pieces from the same tree. He actually could read wood. He would show me a chunk, point out the growth rings and explain when the tree had experienced wet years, droughts, fires, diseases, or insect invasions, talk about the grain and how it was formed, demonstrate how it would cut or polish or take a finish. He treasured every piece of wood and saw beauty in it, no matter if it was decayed or laced with worm holes. Green wood, raw wood, aged, worn, weather-beaten, it didn't matter to Fred. He had a reverence for wood. Period. And he passed it on to me.

I can close my eyes and see Fred's bony, scarred fingers caressing a piece of wood as if it were velvet, or a child's hair.

Fred was a child himself when he began working with wood. As a teenager, he took a job at Hoover Chair Company, now long defunct. He was a pattern maker for thirteen years, and in his free time he refinished and restored furniture in a little building behind his house. He also made furniture of his own design for his family and found that it gave him double pleasure, first in its creation, then in its use.

Fred was more than a craftsman. He had an artist's soul and a sculptor's instinct. He carved horses into the first set of bookends he made of walnut at age fifteen. Some of his furniture had elaborate, hand-carved decorative flourishes. He also carved wall hangings, trays and bowls. In 1936, he carved a set of elephants that caught the eye of a local furniture executive who bought them and gave them to Alf Landon, then the Republican candidate for President.

Two years later, Fred went into business for himself as a maker of custom designed furniture. His first major order came from John Hanford of Salisbury, a florist and the father of a two-year-old daughter named Elizabeth, later to be known as Liddy Dole. Hanford was so pleased with his set of mahogany chairs that he spread the word about the quality of Fred's work. For the next fifty-three years, until illness forced him to stop, Fred never was without a waiting list of customers.

In the beginning, he made his furniture only with hand tools. Then he designed tools with foot pedals. Later he used motors from sewing machines and other small appliances for power.

No matter the job, or the way he did it, he set his own deliberate pace.

"Never hurry," he used to tell me. "Only causes mistakes."

In 1955, thanks to a prominent local Democrat, Fred came into possession of some wood from a copper beech tree planted by Thomas Jefferson at Monticello. The tree had been killed by a lightning strike. Fred transformed the wood into two gavels and a frame for an information board. One of the gavels was used to open the session of the U.S. House of Representatives on Jefferson's 212th birthday, and the frame still hangs in the Democratic Cloakroom of the House. Fred was always proud of that.

He was proud of me, too, when I won the Ford Industrial Arts award at age fifteen for the Pennsylvania Dutch chest that I built, and his early influences no doubt had something to do with that.

After I married, got out of college, and returned home, I still went by to see Fred regularly. I got him to build furniture for Kay and me. I took him ideas and he always added his own touches to improve them.

After I began painting, I could see Fred's influences on my work, because I was absolutely fascinated with the textures of wood, especially aged and weather-worn wood, and it showed up in painting after painting.

But I had no idea what a major influence Fred eventually would exert on my life until I built my new studio.

Anybody growing up in Lexington, or living long enough in the town, absorbs the furniture business. You actually breathe it, for it literally is in the air. Lexington sits in the center of America's premier furniture-making area, and furniture has been the heart of the town's commerce throughout the 20th century. Many people I knew in childhood took jobs in the furniture plants. Some of my family worked there, as did Kay's, and many of our friends still do. I grew up in the furniture business, of course, working in Dad's store, but after I helped close out the store as my first job after college, I never thought I'd be involved with furniture professionally again.

After I started painting, though, people from furniture companies would call now and then wanting to use prints for one of the big, international furniture markets held each spring and fall in our area, or wanting me to paint something for one of the shows, or to ask my help in some special project.

One out-of-town company bought two original paintings at $25,000 each, and later one of the company executives asked if I'd ever thought of starting my own furniture line. I hadn't, but I was willing to discuss it. We had a couple of meetings that didn't seem to go anywhere. Then I got so wrapped up in trying to finish the new studio that I put off future talks.

But after I moved into the studio, furniture presented itself again. It happened—no surprise to me—at Whitley's Barbecue.

* * *

258

Here I must digress to tell about Whitley's. But to do that I must first tell about Gene Whitley. He was quite a character and a special, devoted friend.

Gene loved to laugh and had a sharp wit. He truly was one of those guys who would give you the shirt off his back if you needed it. He grew up on a hard-scrabble farm in Georgia and liked to say that he was spending the rest of his life trying to get over it. "Bob, you don't know what poor is...." he'd tell me and launch into a litany of poor jokes.

Gene started out as a car salesman and eventually went to work at the Ford place in Lexington, where he became the country's top salesman of Edsels, that car from the '50s that was too far ahead of its time. He sold so many that Edsel Ford himself came to Lexington with several of his executives to find out how he was doing it. The reason he could do it, of course, was because he was Gene.

Gene and his wife, Sylvia, who had been the bookkeeper at the Ford place, took the money they'd saved, bought Taylor's Barbecue on Highway 8, south of Lexington and changed the name to Whitley's. I met Gene by stopping there to eat. About the time I started painting full-time, Gene built a new and bigger building just down the road and moved the restaurant there. After I began working at Riverwood, I ate breakfast there almost every morning and often returned for lunch.

Gene and I became hunting buddies. At one point we and some of our other hunting pals got to talking about all the game we had in our freezers that our wives were threatening to throw out. So we decided to hold a critter dinner at the restaurant. We had it on the second Wednesday night in March and it was so much fun that we held it again the next year. It became a tradition and grew every year. First dozens came, then scores, then hundreds, and we had every imaginable kind of food: wild boar, deer, turkey, quail, duck, geese, dove, pheasant, every kind of seafood, alligator, rattlesnake, cooter stew, frog legs, fried rabbit, squirrel dumplings, possum pate. We had a lot of fun in addition to the food, and for quite a few years, we used the event to raise money for the nearby Junior Order Home. But it grew so big that it got out of control—we didn't know half the people who came—and we finally had to stop it.

A lot of people aren't aware of just how big a role a restaurant can play in the life of a small town. Gene, for example, loved sports and was fanatically devoted to the Clemson University Tigers in whatever sport they happened to be competing, but particularly to the football team. He didn't attend Clemson, or any other college; he just liked the Clemson teams' determination to win. He was a big booster of area high school sports, got to know many of the players and all of the coaches. If players were particularly good, he called college coaches on their behalf. Soon, he got to know the coaches and assistant coaches of all the Atlantic Coast Conference teams, and they frequently met prospective players at Whitley's, or they'd just get together there with one another to gossip, talk shop, jaw about sports with Gene, some of them spending the night at his house across the road.

Whitley's was a place where things got done. Business deals were closed. Land, pickup trucks, all kinds of stuff were traded and sold. Gossip, news and jokes got spread. Politicians on the local, state and national levels came to shake hands and campaign. If you wanted a rock wall laid, a house built, your yard mowed, or a muffler put on your car, you could arrange it over a tray of barbecue at Whitley's. You could even get a Bob Timberlake print to hang on your wall if you were determined enough.

Sadly, Gene died of cancer in 1989, and Sylvia sold the restaurant to new owners in 1998, but they kept the Whitley's name, and little has changed. To this day, I gather there almost every morning with my assistant, Dave Hastings, my property manager, Charles Johnson, and others to plan our day over eggs and grits. We're often joined by Kay and some of our friends, Preacher Lamar Moore, his wife Louise, former Sheriff Jimmy Johnson, and others. We get to chat with all the regulars and with those who just happen to be passing through. It's a pleasant and productive way to start the day.

You never know what the topic of conversation might be at Whitley's, or what might happen. Your life can even be changed there, and mine was.

My studio was a great topic of conversation around the county as we finally neared completion after three years of work. It certainly was impressive perched up on the hill. People could catch glimpses of it through the trees and were wondering what it was like inside.

Not long after I finally moved into it, I was at Whitley's for lunch and Jay Young, the vice-president of marketing for Lexington Furniture Industries, was there. LFI, as the company is called for short, had been bought a year earlier by a group called Masco that was on its way to becoming the world's largest home furnishings company, but LFI still was run by local folks. Started by Henry Link as Dixie Furniture, his nephew, Smith Young, Jay's dad, was now president, and Jay's brother, Jeff, was vice-president for design, and only a few years from becoming president. I ran into Jay at the cash register. I had known him all his life. We started chatting about the studio.

"I'd sure like to see it sometime," he told me.

"Well, why don't you come on now," I said. "I'm going straight back there. Have you got time?"

"I could take a little time," he said.

"Just follow me then."

As we stepped inside the back door, Jay said only one

261

word: "Wow!"

After I'd shown him the place, he said, "We really ought to do something with this."

"What do you mean?" I asked.

"I mean a furniture line built around this concept."

"If you're serious, you need to let me know, because I've been talking with another company about doing the same thing," I told him. "Nothing would please me more than to deal with a hometown company, especially one I own stock in."

"I'm serious," he said. "Let me get Jeff down here."

Jeff came the next day, and he was not just impressed, he was excited about the idea. But the big fall market was coming up, the busiest time of the year in the furniture business, and we had to wait to begin talks until after that.

Not until January, 1990, did we finally get together and agree to move forward. Soon afterward, Jeff sent two designers to see me, Mike Black and Ed Ball. I showed them everything in the studio, told them the stories behind all the pieces, and we had long talks about what we should and shouldn't do. Later, I took them out to meet Fred Craver and see his shop and house. I'd asked him if it was okay, and he said sure. He loved to show off his furniture and was happy to share his ideas.

After that visit, Jeff Young later told me, Mike and Ed came back bursting with enthusiasm. "We've got it!" they said. "We know exactly what we want to do."

Early on I had taken a tour of one of the plants to see how things were done. I noticed one man whose job was to inspect every board as it came into the plant and saw out any knots, cracks, or bad spots. I emphasized to Jeff that I wanted those left, designed into the furniture. Knots, burls, cracks and worm holes would make each piece distinctive.

I told him what Fred always told me, "Let the wood speak for itself." If it had dents or worn edges, I wanted them to show. And I didn't want slick, shiny, immaculate finishes. I wanted the finish to be *in* the wood, not on it, so the patina would grow more beautiful with time. Perfect furniture is standoffish. I wanted furniture that would be just a little flawed, like most of the people who would own it. I wanted it to be welcoming and personal. I wanted it to look as if it were already loved when it came out of the plant.

Jeff listened. I don't know how much trouble he had getting that concept past his corporate bosses, but somehow he managed it.

Every meeting we held to work on designs was more exciting than the previous one. The line was going to be called "The World of Bob Timberlake," and in the beginning, we thought it would include twenty or twenty-five pieces. One was to be a replica of the chest I'd made in high school, another the glass-topped table I'd designed for displaying the book Charles Kuralt and I had done together. We also were going to do my mother's cupboard from my painting, as well as Aunt Nona's pie safe, and my favorite bed. Also some chests and other pieces actually bearing reproductions from my paintings. Several pieces would be straight from Fred's designs, for which, much to my delight, LFI was going to pay him a royalty.

After we got the wood furniture well underway, we began to talk about upholstered pieces, which would have to be manufactured by another North Carolina subsidiary of MASCO, Hickory Craft Furniture, which made Ralph Lauren, Henredon, and five other lines.

A meeting was set in High Point for executives and designers from both LFI and Hickory Craft, as well as from corporate headquarters. These were some of the leading professionals in the business, and my only experience before I got involved with LFI was building a chest when I was fifteen and helping my dad in his furniture store.

I wasn't expecting to have to make a speech, especially to such an august group, but that was what I was called on to do. They wanted to know what kind of furniture I wanted to bear my name.

I told them first of all that I wanted it to be really high quality, sturdy, lasting, built of the finest materials. I wanted individual pieces, too, not suites, so people could put it together anyway they chose. And I wanted it to be not only comfortable but comforting.

As I talked, a story popped into my mind, and I started telling it.

It was about a fishing trip I'd made to British Columbia a few years earlier with my friend J.B. Lopp. We had flown to Vancouver, left our wives there to tour and shop, then went on to Port Hardy, where we caught a floatplane to a lodge run by Craig and Deborah Murray way back in the boondocks near Nimmo Bay. The lodge floated on logs at the edge of a crystal-clear lake. In Port Hardy we met a couple of guys from Atlanta who were going to be our fishing companions. We hadn't known them to this point, and we discovered that one had been second in command to Oliver North in Vietnam, the other third in command to Ollie.

The appeal of this lodge was that you fished by helicopter. If the fish weren't biting in one spot, you got back in the helicopter and went to another.

On our first day, we hopped all around, fishing almost from dawn to dusk, catching at least a ton of salmon, all of which we released. We got back to the lodge just at supper time, all worn out, and had the most wonderful dinner of fresh trout, hot homemade bread, a great wine, and freshly picked raspberry cobbler.

After supper, I was really feeling fat, sassy and happy, and I went into the main room of the lodge to relax. It was decorated eclectically—what I'd call "early attic"—with hunting and fishing trophies and old and bulky furniture. What drew me was this big, worn, mohair chair that looked as if it had come right out of the '20s. It was wide and accommodating and had huge arms. I sank into that thing, and it enveloped me. I felt as if it had its big arms around me. Semi-classical music was playing softly on a stereo. Rain had begun falling, drumming on the roof and splattering on the lake. For the first time in my life I had the sensation of being back in my mother's womb. I'd never known such comfort as I felt at that moment, warm, protected and content, and I was thinking, *Wouldn't it be wonderful if at the end of the day, everybody could feel just what I'm feeling right now?*

When I got back home, I looked everywhere trying to find a chair like that—furniture stores, antique shops, junk places—but I never found one.

"What I want us to do," I told these executives, "is to make that chair and all the things that go with it so I can have that feeling again and share it with as many people as we can."

Afterward. Tommy Black of LFI told me that as the president of Hickory Craft was leaving the room after that meeting, he put an arm around Tommy and told him that he'd been waiting thirty years for this, that he'd never been so excited about the prospects for a furniture line, and that he would be willing to work without pay, if he had to, to bring it out. His excitement would be borne out. Within two years, this new line would be taking up sixty percent of Hickory Craft's total production capacity.

Having spent so much of his life in the furniture business, Dad was as excited about all of this as was I. He couldn't wait for me to tell him what had happened at every meeting. But at the end of March, 1990, just as we were really getting started planning the line, I got a call that Dad had been taken to the hospital in Myrtle Beach.

Dad had a tough time after Mom's death. He was filled with remorse that he hadn't been able to do something to help her, to save her, filled with guilt because he was still here and she was gone. He missed her profoundly and was unbearably lonely. For the first two months after her death, he didn't want to be apart from Tim and me. One of us stayed with him every night during that period.

Actually, those turned out to be good times, because we had some wonderful conversations, reminiscing, talking about our regrets and disappointments, our hopes and dreams, saying things that needed to be said but might never have been spoken otherwise.

Dad had lots of friends who sought to help him, and he slowly reemerged into life. He started playing golf again, going to antique shows now and then. More and more he stayed at the beach house. Eventually, he seemed to find some pleasure in life again, but he was never the same without Mom.

A couple of years after her death, I got a call at the studio from the gas company saying that Dad was in trouble. He had gone to Chapel Hill to visit a friend and called the gas company from a phone booth to say that he thought he was having a stroke. He was going to the hospital, he said, but hung up without saying which one. I set out for Chapel Hill immediately. I'd told the people at the gas company to call the hospitals and find out where he was. I was just hoping he could get to a hospital. I could picture him in a wreck, or unconscious on the side of the road. I stopped at a rest area near Burlington, called the gas company and learned he was at Duke University Hospital. Some of my friends from the cancer center were with him when I got there.

He was hospitalized for a while and eventually recovered from most of the effects of that stroke, but it had been a jolt to him. A warning shot.

Now he had been dealt a devastating blow. For a while it was questionable whether he would survive. Dad had become close friends at the beach with Bobby Porter, a retired Army general, and his wife, Sue, who looked after him. They got him to the hospital. He spent five weeks there, and I was with him every day. This time it was clear that he would not recover. He was completely paralyzed on his left side. He was conscious and would try to talk but couldn't. Tim and I finally brought him back to Lexington on a medical evacuation plane.

The doctors recommended nursing home care, but we knew that wasn't possible. Dad had a tremendous fear of being in a nursing home. Many times he'd laughingly warned Tim and me that if we ever put him in such a place, he'd make us pay. He'd told his lawyer to cut us out of his will the moment he was admitted, he joked.

We had a hospital bed installed in his bedroom, hired nurses to attend him twenty-four hours a day, and took him back home. We had no way of knowing how long he might live like this, and it was even harder for him because he was aware of his situation. He'd always been so active, so vital, and now he was trapped by his failing body. Seeing him like this was tough. Everybody in the family spent time with him regularly, and we did our best to make things better for him, but we were depressingly limited. I bought him a portable stereo and a stack of CDs of big-band music from the '30s and '40s. I put one of the CDs into the slot, fitted the earphones over Dad's head, and his right foot started tapping. He looked up at me and smiled with his eyes.

In the weeks that I'd been attending to Dad, the planning for the furniture line had continued without me, but I soon got back into it. From the beginning, the intention had been to recreate the whole look and feel of the studio, not just the furniture. That meant lamps, rugs, quilts, decorative accessories such as pottery, decoys, wall hangings and the like. In the beginning, LFI had considered farming out the production of such items to other companies and marketing them with the furniture. But soon after I returned home with Dad, Jeff Young told me that LFI could not handle the complemental products after all. If I wanted to continue with the accessories, it would be up to me to see that they got made, but LFI would help me in any way possible.

This actually was far better for me. It would allow me to control both the choice of products as well as the design and quality. But LFI was planning to launch the furniture line at the fall market. That was only five months away. And I had no experience in licensing and manufacturing. This created tremendous pressure, and it was made even worse because at every design meeting for the furniture, the line was growing dramatically along with our excitement.

One of the first places I called was the Capel Company in Troy, about fifty miles southeast of Lexington. Capel had been making distinctive rugs since 1917. My grandfather and father had sold them in the furniture store. I was hoping they would want to make rugs to go with my furniture line. One of my ideas was to get them to make rugs exactly like Aunt Sallie Parnell's.

Aunt Sallie wasn't my aunt; that was just what everybody called her. I had known her all my life. She was 102 years old, and had been making rugs since she was four. She was still making them on a 200-year-old cedar loom in the kitchen of her big farmhouse on Old Highway 64 northwest of Lexington near Tyro. Aunt Sallie had known both of my grandfathers. Her husband was a hunting companion of Grandfather Timberlake. I had taken my first steps on rugs she made. So had my children and grandchildren.

When the Capel people came to the studio for our first

talks, I simply showed them Aunt Sallie's rugs and said, "Make them like Aunt Sallie does."

I have a small rug that Aunt Sallie made on March 4, 1994, just days before her death at 106. It is one of my most treasured possessions.

At first, I was attempting to handle this new licensing business out of the gallery, but I could see that wasn't going to work. When Tim and I had opened the gallery late in 1977, we had hired a good friend, Frank Stoner, a former high school business teacher, to run it for us. A few years later, as the gas business continued to grow and his duties became more demanding, Tim wanted out of the gallery and left the art business to me. I couldn't turn to him for help, and although Frank and his small staff were doing what they could to assist me, they already had their hands full.

It quickly became apparent that I had to separate this business from the gallery and that I needed somebody to handle it for me.

As it happened, our daughter Kelly, her husband, Ace, and their three daughters came to spend a few days at the beach house with Kay and me early in the summer. They lived in Richmond, where Ace, a computer and mathematical whiz, worked in banking. Ace and I got to talking about work, and I could see that he was not really happy at the bank. He was talking about looking into other fields, or starting a business of his own.

"What would you think about coming to work for me?" I asked.

I explained the situation. I knew he would be uneasy about working for his father-in-law, but he was at least open to it. He, of course, knew no more about the licensing business than I did, and before he made up his mind, he wanted to research it. Two months later, he called and said that he had just one question.

"Will I be running this, or will you?"

He knew I was bad to stick my nose into things.

"You will," I assured him.

"Okay, I'm going to give my notice at the bank," he said.

Kay and I were overjoyed. We knew Ace's work ethics, knew he would do a great job—and we would have Kelly and our grandchildren closeby so we could see them more.

I incorporated the new business as The Bob Timberlake Collection, rented a house behind the gallery, set up offices in it, and in October, just six days before the furniture market was to open, Ace came to help me develop this new enterprise.

Waiting for the opening of the International Home Furnishings Market was like waiting for Christmas Eve when I was a boy, like the nervousness I felt before my first show at Hammer Galleries. I was nearly twitching with anticipation. The line that we had expected to be about twenty, or twenty-five pieces, had grown to more than a hundred. LFI was being very secretive about it. They wanted to spring it full-blown at the market. Not even the sales force knew what was coming. But those of us who had been involved with it and had seen every sample as it was made were so excited that we could hardly stand it. We knew we had something special. We were convinced that we had grabbed hold of a rainbow.

Just before the market was to open, the sales force came to the studio so that we could show them "The World of Bob Timberlake." It was their first look at what they would be selling at the market and in the months to come, and they were agog. They were bedazzled. I'd never seen such a confident and hepped-up group as left there that day.

Although we knew we had something so different and inviting that it had to get attention, there was still uncertainty. The furniture industry was in one of the most serious slumps in history, with no indications that it might pull out of it anytime soon. Having never been in the manufacturing end of the business, I had no idea what might constitute success with a new furniture line. I asked Jeff about it.

"Well," he said, "if we sell two or three million dollars worth a year, we'd be pleased."

"Wholesale or retail?" I asked.

"Wholesale," he said. That would be enough to keep the line going.

The opening day of the market was like the best Christmas ever, the Christmas you not only got everything you wanted, but things you hadn't even dreamed about. And the gifts just kept coming, a cornucopia pouring out endless wonders. It was the same the next day, and the next, as the excitement continued to grow.

I was truly besieged—and loving every minute of it.

LFI's showroom is near Thomasville, a few miles from High Point, where the market is centered. Most buyers start in High Point, then drift to the showrooms near and in Thomasville before heading to the western end of the market in Hickory. The market lasts ten days, and there truly are hundreds of acres of showrooms for the buyers to cover. They usually take their time getting from place to place.

But word quickly spread that something big and exciting was happening at LFI's showroom, and buyers and the people who write and report about the industry quickly began appearing in unprecedented numbers. At times, so many people crowded in that some had to be asked to leave because the fire code limit was being exceeded, and lines formed, waiting to get in.

LFI's decorators, under the direction of the multi-talented Don Hekhuis, had recreated my studio, inside and out, in the showroom, and they had done an incredible job. They'd even added the front porch for good measure. You might have thought it was Disney World, though, from all the people who were flocking to see it, and from their expressions of delight.

I was there every day, all day, and I loved talking to the buyers, seeing their reactions and hearing what they had to say. Over and over, people told me that they hadn't seen anything like this since the original furniture of Gustav Stickley. Stickley was a furniture designer and leader of the American Arts & Crafts movement early in the 20th century whose sturdy, practical furniture is now highly prized by collectors. In 1988, Barbara Streisand paid $363,000 for a personal sideboard made by Stickley. The other thing I kept hearing repeatedly was: "These will be the antiques of the future." That was exactly what I wanted to hear, and what I wanted my furniture to be.

We clearly were the hit of the show. The sales staff was writing orders as fast as they could, and the magazine and newspaper writers, and TV reporters all found their way to us. In the coming months *House Beautiful*, *New Home*, *Country Home*, *Metropolitan Home*, *Home and Country Living* and *Home* magazines would be just a few of the publications featuring our furniture. It even appeared in "This Old House," the Public Broadcasting System TV show.

A couple of times during the market, I stopped by to see Dad when I got home early enough at night. I sat by his bed and told him how the market was going. His face just lit up.

I also dropped by to see Fred. "You're not going to believe the response," I told him. I'd tried to get him to come to the market, but he hadn't been feeling well and he didn't care much for public gatherings, preferring his work and the familiar comforts of his shop to the crowds, glitz and clamor of the market.

New furniture lines don't go into production until orders are placed. Another six months passes before the furniture actually begins appearing in retail stores. That often creates more anxiety as both the manufacturers and retailers wait to see how it will be received by the public. I had no such anxiety. I never doubted what the reception would be, just as I never doubted how people would take to my work when I first started painting. I don't know how, I just *knew* that people would love it.

And I was right. The reception was phenomenal.

LFI had seven plants turning out the furniture at first, but eventually had to go to seventeen. Sales the first year were more than $30 million wholesale. By the second year, they had grown to nearly $50 million. Industry analysts called the figures "staggering" and soon were proclaiming "The World of Bob Timberlake" the most successful furniture line in history.

Sales of even highly successful furniture lines usually begin tapering off after five or six years. But I wasn't going to let that happen, and it was not the case with ours. We have continued to bring out new pieces based on new themes, and sales have continued to grow. In 1999, they were about $100 million wholesale annually, and we intend to see that they keep growing.

When Fred Craver's first royalty check came due, I asked Jeff Young if I could take it to him, and he agreed.

"I've got something for you," I told Fred, and handed him an envelope. "Go ahead, open it."

The check was for $18,000. He'd never expected anything like that. I only wish I'd taken a camera and gotten a picture of his face at that moment.

Not long after that, ill health forced Fred to quit going to his shop every day. The last thing he made was a miniature chest—of walnut, of course. I was determined to get him to the next furniture market, and I did. Actually, I had to conspire with his daughter, Patsy Stamey, who used a ruse to get him there. When he realized that she was taking him to the showroom, he reluctantly, but graciously, came on in.

I had told people that he might be coming, but I didn't know when. I was on an upstairs balcony when I looked down and saw Fred and Patsy coming in the front door. He was eighty-two then, very frail, and looking uncertain.

The place was jammed with people, and I noticed that a few recognized him and began whispering to others. Word just swept through the place that Fred Craver was there. Suddenly a few people began applauding, then others joined in. People came from other parts of the building to see what was going on, and they joined in, too, the applause swelling and swelling. Bravos were called, and I may have yelled one or two myself. Then everybody just swarmed around this wonderful man, shaking his hand, congratulating him, telling him how beautiful his furniture was. Watching it was one of the great moments of my life, and I was only thankful that he lived to see it.

When I finally made my way to Fred, he gave me a little smile that said, "You did this to me." But I could tell that he had been deeply touched by this reception, and that it probably had been one of the great moments of his life as well.

Later, I took him to see the furniture that had been made from his designs. When I saw him reach out to touch a piece, feeling the grain and the finish, I knew he realized that we had made it as he would have.

"I didn't know it would look so good," he told me.

We shall not cease from exploration.

And the end of all our exploring

Will be to arrive where we started

And know the place for the first time.

    —T.S. Eliot

Chapter 18

I knew that my new studio not only would be a center for creativity, but that something big would come from it, and when it immediately brought about the furniture and accessories, my expectation had been fulfilled. Unexpectedly, though, it took me away from what I had envisioned as its primary purpose.

I completed only a single painting in 1990, the year the furniture came out. That was "The Pilot," of North Carolina's distinctive stand-alone mountain, north of Winston-Salem. In January, 1991, I finished a study of a Raggedy Ann doll that I had begun years earlier for the Christmas stamp. I called it "Homecoming," but it was in effect a leaving. I didn't finish another painting for nearly six years, although I occasionally made a stab at starting one.

I was in a creative fervor all the same, just not with my paints and brushes. It was a fervor as great, though, as I had known when I first began painting. I was working with designers almost every day. We were designing furniture, bedding, upholstery fabrics, wall hangings, throws, china, lamps, rugs, pottery, clocks, mirrors, and lots of other things, basing many of them on my paintings as well as on the "stuff" I had accumulated. Sometimes I would have three or four meetings with designers in a single day, and we would come up with dozens, even scores of designs. Ideas just tumbled out of me. It truly was a stimulating period.

Within two years, we had more than 1,000 products, not counting the furniture, and that number soon would double, then grow beyond that. The furniture and accessories were being sold in more than 2,500 stores, including major department stores such as Neiman-Marcus, Macy's, Rich's, Dillards, Dayton-Hudson, Penney's, Confederated and others, and a Japanese company had opened a World of Bob Timberlake store on Madison Avenue at 53rd Street in Manhattan, not far from Hammer Galleries.

The Timberlake Collection quickly became a business too big for a rental house, and we began construction of a large office and warehouse building on East Center Street Extension, on the southeastern edge of the city limits. Our staff was growing as rapidly as our sales, and once again I turned to family for help.

My son Dan got a degree at my alma mater, the University of North Carolina, in 1985, then started law school at Wake Forest University in Winston-Salem, where his sister had studied. When he entered law school, I presented him with the original law license of his great-grandfather, Emery Elisha Raper, which had been issued a century earlier on March 3, 1885.

After getting his own license, Dan joined a law firm in Winston-Salem and soon became a partner. But he dreamed of coming home and continuing the family tradition of law in Lexington, and he did just that in the fall of 1991. He and a fellow lawyer, Jimmy Snyder, formed a partnership with real estate developer Robin Team to buy and restore the old Lexington Drug Company building, adjacent to the old courthouse where Dan's great-grandfather Raper had died. The drug company building had housed the offices of our family doctor, Dan Redwine, who had delivered Dan and for whom he was named. But before Dan could get his local practice established, I began trying to get him to come to work with Dad. Our business involved so many legal issues that we really needed a lawyer on staff.

Soon after I talked Dan into coming onboard, I learned that an old friend, Dave Hastings, was back in North Carolina. Dave had grown up in the tobacco country near Walkertown north of Winston-Salem and was a student at Catawba College in Salisbury when, like me, he'd undergone an Andrew Wyeth epiphany. He had picked up a book of Wyeth's paintings and had been moved to tears by their stark beauty and sense of loneliness. Later, he wrote to Wyeth to tell him of his feelings, and, like me, received a warm response.

Dave attended my first show at the Gallery of Contemporary Art in Winston-Salem, and not long afterward bought one of my paintings, his first original, the beginning of what would become an extensive collection of American art.

I kept up with Dave after he transferred to the University of North Carolina, where he studied radio and TV. Even after he moved to Portland, Oregon, where he got a master's degree in theology, I still saw him once a year when he came home for visits. Instead of preaching, Dave became a painters' agent and consultant to art museums.

In 1993, I realized that our company needed somebody to fill the role that Hugh Morton Jr. once had played in my life, and I immediately thought of Dave with his many abilities. I discovered that he not only was home for a visit but wanting to live again in North Carolina. It took only lunch at Whitley's and an afternoon at the studio to convince him that he should come to work for us.

Dave now lives in the former guest cabin next to the studio and serves as my assistant, the person in charge of telling me where I'm supposed to be and what I'm supposed to be doing. We are bound by our love of the paintings of Andrew Wyeth, and we have made some memorable trips to Chadds Ford to see new exhibits, buy new paintings, and to visit with Andy and Betsy. On our last visit, Betsy popped popcorn. Then Andy remembered that somebody had given him a whole pound of Beluga caviar. He brought it out and put it on the coffee table, and we spent the rest of the evening in front of the fireplace eating popcorn and caviar.

In 1992, LFI brought out a second Timberlake line of furniture based on the simple and beautiful designs of the early Moravian craftsmen in Old Salem, and that was followed two years later with another line dedicated to Keep America Beautiful, which shared in the profits. The Keep America Beautiful line received the Green Award given for products using conservation-compatible materials. With both, we developed new lines of accessories, and sales continued to climb.

For the Keep America Beautiful line, we wanted to use wood only from companies heeding strict environmental standards, and we needed to make certain of that for ourselves.

On one occasion, Masco sent the corporate jet to fly me, Jeff Young, who by then had become President of Lexington Furniture Industries, and Willis Hedrick to northern California to check out a timber company which was partly owned by the Methodist Church, my church.

I'd known Willis Hedrick all my life. He had been a rabbit hunting buddy. He's not only a fine fellow, he was the man who kept everything running at all of the LFI plants.

Jeff is sort of a white-knuckle flier, and he was a little ill at ease as we took to the air. But Willis and I were having a grand time. This was our first flight on a private jet, and we settled back in those plush seats, sampled the fruit baskets, and felt like bigshots.

We were somewhere over Kentucky when the pilot came into the cabin, squatted beside our seats and said, "Gentlemen, we've got a little problem."

Those aren't words you like to hear at 30,000 feet at 500 miles per hour. Jeff's whiteness went straight from his knuckles to his face, and I'll have to say I was a little disconcerted myself.

"One of our fuel pumps is not functioning," the pilot said, "and that shouldn't be a problem unless the others kick out. We should make it to our destination, but once we get there we won't be able to take off again without repairs. It's a small airport, and chances are we'll have trouble getting the parts and finding somebody to do the job. Our other option is to fly to company headquarters in Detroit and have the repairs done there. Of course, that'll cause a delay."

Jeff was looking as if he wanted to ask, "Can't we land in Louisville?" Instead, he said, "What do they say at headquarters?"

"Haven't contacted them yet," the pilot said, "because I wanted to see what you thought first."

"Why don't you see what they say?" Jeff told him.

This development took all the fun out of the flight, even for Willis and me. Every bump and sound now made us think that the engines were shutting down.

In a little while, the pilot returned.

"Well, I talked to headquarters," he said, "and they wanted to know who was on board. I told them Jeff Young, the president of Lexington Furniture, Bob Timberlake, the designer, and Willis Hedrick.

"They said, 'Hold on, we'll get back to you.'

"When they came back, they asked, 'How many parachutes do you have?'"

He paused, and we all looked nervously at one another.

"'Just two,' I told them," the pilot went on. "'One for me and one for the co-pilot.'"

He paused again, then grinned. "They said, 'Strap both parachutes on Willis Hedrick, and get to Detroit as fast as you can.'"

I had remained on the board of directors of the family gas company, the stock of which was owned by Tim and myself, our wives and children. Early in 1994, we began talking about the possibility of selling to a larger company. The company name had changed from Piedmont to Carolane in 1987 after we bought another company, Carolina Propane, our chief competitor, in 1985. By the end of 1994, we decided to accept an offer from Heritage Propane in Tulsa, Oklahoma, the tenth largest propane marketer in the country. Tim had decided to retire, but his son, Trip, stayed on as president.

Dad was in no condition to be involved in any of the negotiations about the company. Often, he was no longer aware, and now and then he had to be hospitalized. I don't think he would have objected to the sale. He had allowed the sale of the funeral home thirteen years earlier.

Actually, the family hadn't had anything to do with the day-to-day activities of the funeral home for some time before the sale, leaving its operation to Charles Craver, who had worked with Dad for many, many years.

A Texas conglomerate had been after us to sell the funeral home for a long time, but we took a smaller offer from Gene Vogler, an old family friend, who operated funeral homes in Winston-Salem. Dad wanted to make certain that the employees were looked after, as all of us did, and he knew Gene would do that.

When Mom died, Gene sent his staff to handle everything about the funeral and burial, trying to make things as easy as possible for Dad and the rest of the family. He did the same when Dad died on July 9th, 1996, at age ninety.

We'd had to put Dad back in the hospital three days earlier. At times, he would seem to be aware, but when he was he would forget to breathe. "Breathe, Dad, breathe," I'd tell him. I even yelled at him, "You've got to breathe!" But I don't think he really wanted to anymore. He finally just stopped.

As he had done for Mom, Howard Wilkinson returned to conduct the funeral with our current minister, Dr. J. Hurley Thomas III. On the cover of the program for Dad's service was a drawing of a dove being freed and a quote from Psalms: "And I Say, 'Oh that I had wings like a dove! I would fly away and be at rest....'"

We buried Dad next to Mom and alongside his mother and father at City Cemetery.

For many years it had been obvious that we had outgrown our gallery in downtown Lexington and needed a new one. We had only 2,500 square feet and didn't even have room to display all of our prints. Every print we produced had to be carried up and down stairs twice, down to sign, up to sell or ship. We were squeezed in next to the Y and didn't have enough parking space.

The coming of the furniture and accessories made a new gallery imperative, and soon after Dan came to work for us, I began lobbying for it. Ace, Dan, gallery manager Frank Stoner, myself and others had long, detailed discussions that went on month after month. I kept hearing that the time wasn't right, that we couldn't afford it, that it wouldn't pay for itself.

I love the movie *Field of Dreams* in which Kevin Costner

plays an Iowa farmer, who, with visions of Shoeless Joe Jackson in his mind, builds a baseball park in his corn patch because a voice keeps telling him, "If you build it, he will come." I was now hearing a similar message, "Build it and they will come." I finally grew adamant about it. I knew that if we built it, people would come, just as I had known that people would accept my paintings when I first started, and that they would buy the furniture when it came out.

One day, Dan got a little frustrated with me and my hard head. "Well, Dad," he said, "where do you want to put the dadgum thing?"

Another difficult question.

A lot of people thought it should stay downtown. Our gallery brought a lot of visitors to Lexington, and I even had a couple of local people tell me that if I put a new gallery elsewhere, they'd never pass through the doors. I spent a lot of time worrying about that, looking at buildings and sites and studying possibilities, but it finally became apparent that there was no place downtown that would be appropriate for what I had in mind.

Where to put it then?

It had to be accessible to many people passing by, and that made a site near I-85, south of town, vital. But there were only a few exits, and one was already so congested that it was out of the question, even though we owned property there. Another was too far outside of town.

That narrowed the selection to one, Exit 94, old U.S. Highway 64. Only a quarter of a mile north of the exit, East Center Street merged with Old 64, also called Raleigh Road, creating a V that was a perfect site. This tract of nearly three acres had a ramshackle old building on it that had been a grocery store and a gym, among other things. It was only a quarter of a mile from the city limits and practically adjacent to our corporate offices and warehouse. I'd tried to buy it in the past, but the owner didn't want to sell.

"That's the only place for it," I told Dan, "but we can't get it."

"Let me see what I can do," he said.

The next thing I knew, he came to me with news. "Okay, we've got the property. We can go ahead."

I still don't know how he got it. I know better than to question a good thing.

We announced the new gallery in the spring of 1995, and in September, Dan went before the city council, got the tract annexed and zoned for business. That same year, we changed the name from Heritage Gallery to Bob Timberlake Gallery, and merged it as a separate entity, along with the Bob Timberlake Collection, into Bob Timberlake Inc.

We began construction of the new gallery in October, 1995, and it was a total Davidson County project. It was designed with a contemporary rustic look by local architect Norman Zimmerman, working from my specifications, and built by Sink Construction Company, run by Danny Sink of Reeds, both of whom Dan talked into coming out of retirement for this project. The roof, which rose fifty-five feet and was supported by huge white-oak beams was put into place by my friend Renè Swing and his brothers, who built my studio. Local landscaper Ray Turner also came out of retirement to design the grounds, and local metalcrafter Robin Eanes made the nine-and-a-half-foot-long copper quill-feather weathervane, mounted on a globe of iron and glass, our new logo, that soared above the windowed cupola atop the roof, sixty feet above the ground.

I wanted this new gallery to be many things. First, of course, it was to be a place to show some of my original paintings and all of my prints, as well as a place to exhibit the works of other North Carolina artists and crafts people. I also wanted it to be a showroom for my furniture and accessories. Most dealers had relatively few items on display at any given time. Nowhere could the public see all of it in one place. This was to be that place. I didn't care where people bought it. I just wanted them to be able to see all of it.

I also wanted the gallery to be a very personal museum, a walk through my life, if you will, a place where I could show my "stuff" and pay tribute to people such as Fred Craver, Aunt Sallie Parnell, Iron Eyes Cody, and others who had played such important roles in my life. Finally, I wanted it to be a welcome center for Lexington, Thomasville, and Davidson County, a place where events could be held to celebrate home and heritage.

This new gallery, which contains 15,000 square feet of floor space, took nearly twenty-one months to complete and cost more than I want to think about. But it turned out just as I had dreamed it would.

Over the entrance I put a very personal quotation in Latin: *ILLE TERRARVM MIHI PRAETER OMNES ANGVLVS RIDET*. Visitors can read the translation over the door on the other side of the wall: "This corner of the world smiles for me beyond all others." Nothing could be truer.

At the center of the gallery is a massive flue built of our specially designed, handmade brick that rises through the high, open ceiling. It contains three stone fireplaces. Suspended before the main fireplace is my twin-sailed, mahogany and brass racing canoe, one of many canoes from my collection displayed at the gallery.

On the first floor, visitors can see a replica of Fred Craver's workshop that includes some of his work benches, tools, hand-scribbled notes, and his old pot-bellied stove, all made available by his family. Next to the workshop is a room where some of my original paintings can be seen, along with the Pennsylvania-Dutch chest I built long ago in high school, and where visitors can relax on a huge sofa and take a video-taped tour of my studio only a few miles away.

On a back wall of the first floor are large shadow boxes. In one is the bow that Iron Eyes Cody presented to me, along with some of his big collection of movie paraphernalia, including a jacket he made to wear in the movie *Grey Eagle*, buckskin pants worn by Clark Gable in *Across the Wide Missouri*, and a head-dress from *Westward Ho the Wagons*, in which Iron Eyes appeared with John Wayne. Some of my collections of Native American pottery, tools and other items are in other boxes, as are other personal treasures from my Scouting days and mementos from the four U.S. postage stamps I designed.

Furniture and accessories are displayed on the first floor, along with many other items from my collections.

A grand oak stairway leads to the second floor, where my prints can be found, along with more furniture, rugs and other items. Here, too, a customer can arrange for somebody from our interior decorating division, headed by Sharon Beasley, to design a room, a whole house, or a hotel. Framing is also available here. Frank Trotman, who owned a frame shop in Winston-Salem, opened a satellite branch in our gallery when it first opened in 1977, and that relationship has continued through my friend Stephen Triplett, the current owner of Trotman's, which has a great reputation in the Southeast. It was Frank Trotman, incidentally, who first suggested that I frame my paintings with the irregular, deckled edges of the handmade paper showing, which has become a sort of trademark for my originals.

We held a preview of the gallery on Tuesday, June 17, 1997, to which we invited family, friends, colleagues, public officials, the press and other guests. This literally was a dream come true for me, and I'd never been so emotional in public as I was when I tried to thank all the people who had helped me to reach this point, an impossible task for such a situation. I almost couldn't get out the words as I dedicated this magnificent structure to the memory of Mom and Dad, and to Kay's father, Clyde Musgrave, who died of injuries from a dust-bin explosion at Dixie Furniture just seven years after Kay and I were married, and to her mother, Lucille, who died of a stroke in 1989. My friend, Betty Ray McCain, North Carolina's Secretary for Cultural Resources and Development, spoke, as did other public officials.

It was our minister from First Methodist Church, Hurley Thomas, who best described my feelings about the gallery. It would lead us, he said, to see the beauty of home.

"It stands as a means to reveal our community's heart and soul. It communicates something of God's beauty, something about heritage, something about love and family....It helps pass a legacy to another generation."

We opened the doors to the public the next morning at 10, and just as I had known, "they" came. I spent the whole day there greeting visitors, and in the first three hours alone, I talked to people from fifteen states. After that I lost track.

We soon began construction of an annex with a coffee shop and display space for my new men's apparel lines, along with a beautiful, walled terrace and garden where visitors may relax by the fountain and coi pool, and where special outdoor events can be held.

In 1998, the gallery won the North Carolina Department of Travel and Tourism's Nesbit Award, and two years after its opening, it was averaging about 1,500 visitors a week. It has become a top North Carolina tourist attraction, just as I knew it would. *Build it*, the voice told me, *and they will come*.

That was a voice I would keep hearing as our company entered its next phase. When our furniture and accessories became entrenched after such a short time on the market, the logical next step seemed obvious: homes in which to put all of these products.

We already had licensed the Hearthstone Company of Dandridge, Tennessee, to develop a line of log homes with designs inspired by the studio and guest cabin, the finest new log houses available, built with massive, natural-shaped, hewed and dove-tailed logs.

Other possibilities presented themselves as developers came to us asking that we furnish or decorate show homes for them, or join them in building a golf course around the theme of my paintings, or in creating a Bob Timberlake housing development. Clearly this was another field that we needed to examine, and one that excited me. After all, I had spent a good part of my boyhood drawing houses and house plans and had designed and built vacation houses before I started painting.

We did not want to move in haste, though. We wanted to think this out carefully. If we decided to go in this direction, we wanted to be certain that what we did was in keeping with what we already were doing. We also wanted it to be completely different from anything anybody else was doing—or ever had done.

The more we talked about it, the more energized we became, and the more possibilities we saw. If we went into building houses, the one thing we wanted to be certain of was that we could control design and quality from top to bottom, beginning to end. Heretofore, this had been practically impossible in the building industry. But the more we talked about it, the more I began to see that it might be feasible after all.

First, we needed an architect. Then we had to line up manufacturers who could create every element that goes into a house to meet our designs and specifications. After that, we had to find and license builders and landscapers who could meet and guarantee our strict standards.

Only those who have set out on the grand adventure of building a new house have any idea of the countless decisions that must be made—more than 200 in a single bedroom, I'm told—plus the endless frustrations and frictions that are encountered. I actually know people whose marriages broke up over building a house.

We wanted to eliminate most of those decisions and all of the frustrations and frictions. I could see us saving marriages. We wanted people to be able to come to us, make a few crucial choices, and at a set date move into their new home, landscaped to look as if it had been there for years, and furnished right down to the china in the cabinets and the prints on the walls, if they so desired. And we wanted them to be assured that they had quality that would last a lifetime and beyond.

This was totally new territory, and we had no idea whether all of this could be brought together, but we decided to try. We began by hiring Jeremy Huggins. Jeremy has an accent a little different from most of us in Davidson County. He came to Wake Forest University from England and became an architect. Dan met him there when both were students. He thought Jeremy would be just the person to head up this project and he certainly turned out to be.

Soon after Jeremy started, he, Ace and Dan flew to Atlanta to meet with Stephen Fuller, one of the country's most widely hailed and award-winning residential architects. They returned filled with enthusiasm, and when I met Stephen I understood why. We saw eye-to-eye. He was ideal for what we had in mind, a terrifically talented man.

I told him that I wanted to build homes that borrowed from the wonderful old farm houses I knew in Davidson County. I wanted to use the same natural materials, wood, stone, handmade brick from the abundant red clay, materials right from the earth. I wanted a contemporary structure that looked as if it belonged to the land, as if it had been there 100 years. I wanted the sturdiness, the beauty, the comfort and the love that the people who built and lived in those old houses had put into them with their own hands.

I knew that we had made a perfect union when I saw Stephen's designs. They not only caught the feeling I wanted, they were in complete harmony with our furniture and accessories. We called the architectural style Piedmont. We produced twenty-four different designs for four types of houses, the Vacation Home, the Cluster Home, the Manor Home, and the Estate Home, ranging in size from 1,500 square feet to more than 4,700. Interiors were patterned on the seasons, and the homebuyer could choose room by room whether its themes and colors were to be winter, spring, summer or fall.

With our designs in hand, we began to line up manufacturers to produce our signature building materials: stone, handmade brick, shingles, shakes, weatherboarding, windows, floors, doors, shutters, paints, molding, mantels, plumbing and lighting fixtures, cabinets, wallcoverings, ceramic tile, hardware, all of the highest possible quality. We also licensed a retailer to carry all of the building products so they also would be available to people who wanted to use them in remodeling, or adding a room to an existing home.

Before we began licensing builders and developers, we had to make certain that all of this would work, and we knew only one way of doing that: by actually building a house.

We bought an old tobacco farm, thirty acres, in the northeastern corner of Davidson County, less than five minutes from High Point. There Williard-Stewart Inc. constructed the first Bob Timberlake Home, the largest of the four types, the Estate Home, with four bedrooms, a library, a media room, a keeping room, even a secret room with an entrance hidden behind a bookcase.

We finished it just before the opening of the International Furniture Market, and I couldn't have been more pleased. It was exactly what I had envisioned. We used it as a showplace during the market, and over and over people told me that once they got inside they felt so comfortable, so much at home, that they just wanted to plop down, prop up their feet and never leave.

We got tremendous press coverage for the house, and after the market, we opened it to the public for an admission fee of $7 for adults, with all the money going to Habitat for Humanity to build homes for the less fortunate. In the two months that we kept the house open until Christmas, thousands came to see it, not only from North Carolina, but from many other states, and the reaction was incredible.

We used the house again as the showroom to introduce our new Arts and Crafts furniture line, which turned out to be the most successful introduction of any new line in Lexington Furniture's history, then we sold the house. We had intended to build more houses on the site, but the buyer wanted all the land.

Since that first house, we have licensed builders in many parts of the country, and other Timberlake Homes have been built in Cary, Raleigh, Charlotte, Williamsburg, Atlanta and other cities. The Lake Toxaway Company, which operates a 5,000-acre resort in the mountains of western North Carolina, began developing a whole neighborhood of Bob Timberlake Homes in its Meadow Ridge community in the summer of 1999.

This is just a beginning, of course, for Bob Timberlake Homes is only in its infancy. Its potential gives me chills when I think about it. It truly is unlimited. *Build it*, I keep hearing, *and they will come.*

When we were just beginning the Bob Timberlake Collection, I told Ace and the others who were working with us then, "If this ever stops being fun, you're not going to see much of me." I would just go back to painting, which never ceases to be fun.

In all the years of working with the furniture, the accessories, the homes, and everything that all of that entailed, I never reached the point where it stopped being fun. Every day seemed to bring something new and thrilling.

After a while, though, I did begin to miss painting. Yet I couldn't find time for it. Kay, my children and friends kept urging me to go back to it. I suspect they were concerned that the long hours of work created too much stress, and they knew that painting always relaxed me.

Finally, in 1996, I promised that I would make time to paint again. Truth be known, I was a little fearful. I had been away from it a long time. What if I had lost my touch? Fortunately, that proved not to be the case. If anything, I had improved. My style had mellowed and matured, and I'm certain all of the design work had something to do with that. I could see the difference, and I liked it.

My plan had been to do at least one painting a month in 1996, but that proved not to be the case. Kay and I were building a new house at High Rock Lake—a new project—and that took a lot of my time. I actually produced only one major painting and finished a few studies I had begun years earlier. I improved on that in 1997, mainly after we moved into the new house that summer.

I began to get cranked up again in 1998, though. Early that year, shortly after a snowstorm, I went with my friends Roy Ackland and David Weatherly, who had worked with me on a couple of videos, to call on Ray and Rosa Hicks at Beech Mountain. Roy and David had been telling me for a long time that I needed to meet them. Boy, were they right.

Ray is another of those amazing but genuine characters. He is six-foot-seven, all bones, dressed in baggy overalls and an old denim jacket, a national treasure, the greatest Appalachian storyteller of our time, acclaimed by the Smithsonian Institute. He and Rosa had been married fifty years at the time, and they had spent their lives together in the same two-story, rusty-roofed mountain farm house that Ray's family had lived in when they first met. Their only modern convenience was electricity. They had no plumbing, no telephone. As soon as I saw their house, I knew I had to paint it.

We visited in their sitting room, which was where they slept in separate beds covered with handmade quilts. That was where the legless woodstove rested on rocks and where Ray told tales from the time we sat down until we left, except for when he was playing his mouth harp so that he and tiny Rosa, with her long ponytail, could sing a mountain ballad.

That visit renewed the excitement I had felt when I first began painting and was drifting around Davidson County, meeting fascinating people and recording the scenes of their lives. It brought home to me that all of the amazing developments of recent years in my own life had grown from this, a reconnection that until this moment I hadn't realized how much I needed.

I finished my painting of Ray's House that summer and we used it for our time-limited print that fall, a print which in part is used to raise money for charity each year. When we issued the print, we brought Ray down to perform at the gallery and turned out quite a crowd. He'd been telling tales for forty-five minutes before Rosa told him to put in his teeth so people could understand what he was saying.

In 1997, when Hammer Galleries discovered that I was painting again, we agreed to another show. My years away from painting had created an even greater demand for my originals. The dearth of new paintings caused resell prices for earlier works to jump dramatically, some to the $45,000 to $50,000 range. The new show, my first in thirteen years, the Millennium Exhibition, was set to open December 7, 1999, and continue until January 11, 2000. For it, I needed twenty-five to thirty new paintings, possibly more. No more dawdling. I had to get to work.

I'm pleased to report that I have painted happily, steadily, and productively through the first half of 1999, and I continue to do so. I always work better under pressure.

One thing I can honestly say is that I have never envied another human being. I am as happy with my life as it is possible for a person to be, and I have felt the same at every stage of my life.

I also know this to be true. Everything that I have, and all that I am, I owe to others. My life is a fabric woven by all the wonderful people I have known and loved, foremost among them Kay, my better three fourths, I call her.

In September, 1990, just before the furniture made its debut, a tribute dinner was held for me at the Lexington Civic Center to raise money for one cause or another. Loonis McGlohon played some of the music he had written from my paintings, and Charles Kuralt spoke.

At one point, as Charlie was laying it on pretty thick about all that I had done, he was interrupted by a familiar and distinctive voice from off stage, "Hold on, wait a minute...."

Charlie hadn't been warned about this, and he actually turned around, thinking somebody was coming on stage. The voice was recorded, and everybody recognized it immediately. It was my friend Perry Como, who wasn't able to be there. This tribute, he wanted people to know, was being paid to the wrong person. Kay, he said, was the one who deserved it. He went on to talk a little about my love for her, then, at my request, he sang "The Wind Beneath My Wings." Kay was genuinely surprised, and it was a great moment for me, because it was so true.

When we first married, I told Kay that all I really wanted from life was to spend it with her and to die in her arms, and that hasn't changed.

She has given me so much. Our terrific children and grandchildren, just for starters.

Kelly became a teacher of the learning disabled. Both happily and sadly for us, she, Ace, and their daughters, our beloved grandchildren—Carter, the athletic one; Kate, who loves to perform and tell stories; and Anne Claiborne, probably the next painter in the family—moved back to Richmond in the summer of 1999 after Ace got a great opportunity to become chief financial officer of one of the finest private schools in Virginia, the school he attended as a child. Ed, our Morehead scholar, became a pediatrician and works with handicapped children. He, his wife, Lisa, a gifted teacher who shares his concern for children, son Rob, our golfer and future astronaut, who's working on his Eagle Scout award, and daughter Abby-Liz, lover of horses and all animals, a ribbon-winning rider, live across the road from my studio. Dan remains our company's legal counsel and my adviser; he runs our family business interests. He and Rhonda live in Winston-Salem, with their son Dek, who inherited the family's outdoor genes and at seven already has his own bird dog, has shot his first quail and has caught a seven-and-a-half-pound trout fly fishing; and daughter Evanne, she of the blonde curls and bright blue eyes.

So many of the people who molded my life are gone now. Mom and Dad, my grandmothers, great aunts and uncles, many of my teachers. Dr. Dan Redwine. My childhood friends Bob Grubb, Punkin Wallace, Johnny Wilson. My high school friend Fat Cat Jack Copley. Lonnie Smalley, who helped me build my car. My hunting buddy Gene Whitley. Many from my early years of painting. Stuffer Myers. Dan and Gilley Melton. The Petreas. Mrs. Leonard. Mrs. Dorsett. And even more who helped in my career. Dr. Margaret Handy. The flamboyant Joe King. Victor Hammer. Armand Hammer, dead at age ninety-two in 1990, ironically of cancer, the disease he'd worked to defeat. Mutt Burton. Hugh Morton Jr. Iron Eyes Cody. Charles Kuralt, dead on the Fourth of July, 1997, from lupus, only sixty-two years old. Aunt Sallie Parnell. Fred Craver.

The list is far too long. But each still lives in my heart, and, I like to think, in the work that I have done.

Even Dan and Gilley Melton's house, which I painted so many times, is gone now, burned by vandals after their deaths. But every time I look at my painting "Gilley's Cows," and see those three old, green metal lawn chairs sitting on their front porch, I don't see chairs. I see Dan, Gilley, and Wanda sitting there, just as they used to on warm evenings after supper.

I have no intention of changing my life. I plan to go right on painting, designing, building, doing all the things I've always done. I greet every day with eagerness and enthusiasm, and I can't wait to see what's going to happen next.

I know that our business is going to continue to grow, even as I take more time to paint. We have a new CEO at the Timberlake Corporation, my longtime friend, Dave Johnston, who came to us from one of the South's biggest law firms, and he is really putting a push on our homes division. Our furniture and accessories are now sold in nearly 3,000 stores, including Harrod's in London and Australia. Some major department stores are developing World of Bob Timberlake stores within their stores. In 1997, the Bob Timberlake trademark was ranked the number nine designer name in the world, just behind Bill Blass and just ahead of Martha Stewart, and that was just as we were beginning our homes and home finishings lines.

The new furniture line, Cottage Pine, debuted at the fall market, 1999, and we have great expectations for it.

Despite what I have accomplished, with so much help from others, and all that I have done in my life, it seems to be only a beginning. I couldn't imagine retiring. I am reminded of what Andrès Segovia said at ninety-four when asked about retirement: "But I have eternity to rest."

If I lived a thousand lifetimes I still wouldn't have time to paint everything I want to paint, do all the things I want to do. I am constantly overwhelmed with new ideas. I often can't get one thing done for starting another.

I honestly don't feel any different than I did as a kid. I really think I'm just a little boy in a man's body. I have the same wonder and excitement that I did as a child. Sometimes I even dare to think I still have the same energy, although my sixty-two-year-old body, which has enjoyed a few too many oysters and trays of barbecue, frequently informs me otherwise.

I am reminded of what the great outdoorsman Gene Hill once wrote: "If I have reason for being here, it is contained in my small boy curiosity and wonder—the tunneling of a mole is as intriguing to me in its small way as an earthquake, the long, drawn notes of a goose are as mysterious to my ears as the stars are to my eyes."

As a kid I was never idle. I always was doing something, and I always hated to quit doing whatever I enjoyed. If I was playing football, or kickball, and the game broke up, I'd be out there after everybody else was gone, still kicking the ball.

As long as I have my wits about me and strength within me, I expect that's how I'll always be, just running along, kicking the ball, kicking the ball.....

One of the deep secrets of life is that all that is really worth doing is what we do for others.

—Lewis Carroll

Chapter 19

Anybody who has lived a life so blessed as mine, so filled with unexplainable and miraculous happenings, eventually must ask some difficult questions.

Dad used to say that success is the result of a little luck and a lot of hard work, and no doubt that is true. But my blessings go far beyond such simple explanation and leave me seeking answers where few are to be found.

I have spent my entire life as a member of First Methodist Church in Lexington, as did Mom and Dad and my grandparents. I am firm in my beliefs, but I do not make a show of my religion. I respect other faiths, and I never try to impose my views on others. I think religion is a personal matter and I rarely bring it up, although I don't avoid the topic if somebody else does.

I believe in God, but I make no pretense to knowing God's intentions. I do not know whether he takes an interest in individual lives, or an active involvement in human affairs. I do not understand why some lives are blessed while others, equally good, seem cursed. I certainly claim no special personal relationship with God, and I would be undeserving if that were possible.

Still...I know these things:

I have never felt alone. And when the path that I should take becomes clear to me, I never doubt that I will succeed by following it. When I have not been able to find that path, or have become impatient while seeking it, one way or another it has been shown to me, and I am certain that it always leads me in the direction I was supposed to go.

I can't escape the feeling that I always have been led by the hand. I am not so presumptuous—or self-deluded—as to claim that it is God who is leading me. But I know that a force other than myself walks with me. Maybe it is simply my faith.

Sometimes I feel as if I am three entirely different people.

Bob Number One is just this ordinary guy from Lexington, North Carolina. He's not any different from anybody else. He goes around doing the everyday things that all of us have to do. He's the visible front man, a desirer, a dreamer, a doer, but he's limited.

Bob Number Two does the incredible things that Bob Number One couldn't imagine doing. He's the artist, the technician, the one who's always exploding with ideas. He sees poor Bob Number One standing up before a crowd to speak with no preparation and no notion of what he's going to say and causes wondrous words to pour from his mouth, seemingly spontaneously. Bob Number One is stunned when this happens, just as he is when his hand finishes a painting that Bob Number Two actually conceived and executed. What is remarkable is that Bob Number Two doesn't understand how he does these things either. He doesn't even think about it. He just does it. To him, it's as natural as breathing.

Bob Number Three is detached. He lurks in the background, always there. Without him the other two Bobs couldn't function. He's the overseer, the reassurer, the handholder, the ever-positive guiding force: the true Creator.

I have no doubt that this spiritual force that is Bob Number Three has played the major role in my life. Consider the evidence just from my career, which never ceases to amaze me when I look back at it.

Normally, I rarely even leafed through the *Life* magazines that came to the house when I was younger. Why did I pick up the one that contained Andrew Wyeth's paintings? And why did I feel such a connection to somebody I'd never known, and to work I'd never seen before?

And how did I paint those leaves that I picked up in the yard that night soon afterward? I'd never shown that kind of ability before. It seemed truly magical.

And why did Mom notice a little article about an exhibition of paintings by Andrew Wyeth in Pennsylvania and suggest to Kay that we go?

If she hadn't read that item and we hadn't gone to that first exhibit at the Brandywine Museum, would my life have ensued as it has? Clearly not.

When we got to the museum, if I hadn't been so emotionally overwhelmed and felt the need for fresh air, I wouldn't have gone out into the parking lot and started chatting with the duPonts' chauffeur. And if I hadn't done that at exactly the moment I did, I wouldn't have met Dr. Margaret Handy.

And, of course, if I hadn't met Dr. Handy, I never would have known Andrew Wyeth, and I might never have been encouraged to start painting professionally.

Once I decided to paint full-time, would I have succeeded if Dad hadn't written to the art critic for the *New York Times*, and if the *Times* critic hadn't sent the transparencies of my paintings to a friend at an art gallery, causing Dad and me to plan a trip to New York? And what if Joe King hadn't suggested that I stop by Hammer Galleries first?

The failure of any one of those events to fall into place would have prevented everything that followed.

Think of the precision of timing that was required when Dad and I got to New York. If he hadn't suggested that I keep the cab and go on to the gallery when we got to the hotel, I would have missed Victor Hammer. He only came in that day to pick up his topcoat and stayed no more than ten or fifteen minutes. How did I just happen to arrive during that brief span? What are the odds of that?

If I hadn't encountered Victor Hammer when I did, would I have found the success that I later enjoyed? It seems unlikely. First of all, I wouldn't have met Armand Hammer, that dear, extraordinary man, and he wouldn't have taken me under wing and promoted me as he did.

All of these unlikely happenings, it appears to me, are coincidences beyond coincidence, and I can't help but see a pattern to them and a greater power at work. But what is that power? Why was it working for me? And why did these astounding coincidences keep right on occurring?

Why was Hugh Morton Jr. moved to call me and to come into my life when he did? Would my career have developed the same without him? I doubt it. Surely I would not have met Charles Kuralt, and we would not have produced our book together and I would have missed that cherished friendship, and the events it brought about.

And what if I had bought Riverwood when I tried to get it? I wanted it with all my heart, but my heart was not working in my own best interest, and I was not allowed to have it. If I had been able to buy it, I would not have built the new studio, my center of creative energy, my magnificent retreat. And if I had not built the new studio, the furniture would

300

not have come about. And without the furniture, none of the rest would have followed. The new gallery, the public expression of my very being, never would have been built. All of those things, I'm convinced, happened exactly as they were supposed to, as if foreordained.

I'm convinced as well that this unseen hand that has guided my life also has intervened to protect me. I offer as evidence one particular incident that I can't ignore. It occurred just after Christmas, 1995.

I was quail hunting with J.B. Lopp and another friend at the Wildcat Hunt Club near Denton in the southern part of Davidson County. Both J.B. and my other friend are good, cautious hunters. All of us had been hunting since we were children. Between us, we had nearly 150 years of experience. But we got separated.

Our dog pointed a bird. I could see the dog, but I wasn't sure where my friends were. I couldn't spot J.B., but I saw my other friend in the tree line about thirty yards away, much nearer the dog than was I. I thought he saw me as well, but I was soon to learn otherwise.

He called that the dog had a bird.

"Go ahead and take him," I yelled back. "I can't get down there because of the briars."

The bird suddenly burst from the tangled growth and swung toward me. My friend instinctively brought up his gun and leveled it right at my face. I could see down both barrels. I knew it was just reflex, that he was aware that I was there and would not fire. Indeed he lowered his gun, just as I expected.

I shot the bird; the dog ran to retrieve it, and a few minutes later, I met up again with J.B. and my other friend.

"I just had the strangest thing happen," my friend told

me. "I drew on that bird you killed and pulled the trigger, but the shell didn't go off."

He showed us the shell with the indentation where the firing pin had hit it right in the center.

"These are brand new shells and that has never happened to me before," he said. "Y'all ever had a shell fail to fire?"

Both of us said we hadn't, and I did my best to hide the shock on my face, because I knew then that my friend hadn't seen me when he'd pulled the trigger, and if the shell had fired we'd likely be facing a very different situation at this moment. I surely would have been blinded, if not killed, by the birdshot.

I didn't tell my friend that he had been aiming toward me. I knew it would bother him, probably even end the hunt. But I did tell J.B. a little later, and we both were in wonder that of the many thousands of shells the three of us had fired in our lives, none had failed—until one had been pointed directly at my head.

Tell me that was mere happenstance.

I stand in absolute awe of all these amazing events in my life—and all the many others. Clearly, luck and coincidence cannot explain them, and although imagination, determination, and hard work surely play major roles in my success, in themselves they are far from being enough to have brought me so bountiful a portion. No power within me could have caused so much to fall in my favor.

I know it makes no more sense to question good fortune than it does to ask, "Why me?," when catastrophe befalls. Yet I can't help but wonder why my life has been so charmed when I have done so little to deserve it. Do I have something to accomplish that I don't yet know about, can't even conceive? Only time can answer that.

For now, all I know to do is to respond to my many blessings as I always have: by sharing what I can. Somehow that seems too little, for I could never share enough to repay all that has been given to me. It seems even less because sharing always has been such a pleasure to me, an instinct over which I have little control.

For as long as I can remember, anytime that I saw something beautiful or interesting, it was not enough simply to enjoy it for myself. As just a little kid, I wanted to run and get Mom, or Tim, or Dad, to delight in it with me. To this day, if I see a good movie, or read a good book, or have a particularly good meal in a restaurant, I can't take full pleasure from it until I have told somebody about it, recommended it, shared it in some way.

Painting, of course, was a natural outgrowth of this need to share, as was everything that my paintings brought about, the furniture, the home accessories and now homes themselves. The return from all of that has allowed me to share in other ways—through the foundations that Kay and I established to aid different charities, through a program we started to promote art in public schools, through my work with my church, the Boy Scouts, the Cystic Fibrosis Foundation, the American Lung Association, Keep America Beautiful, Duke Children's Hospital, the Duke Comprehensive Cancer Center, Brenner Children's Hospital, High Point University, the University of North Carolina, and other institutions and groups. But age and experience have taught me that I never will be able to share enough.

What is evident to me is that home is at the heart of everything I have to share, as it always has been at the heart of my life. At the heart of home, of course, is family. And at the heart of family is love. Home, family and love have made my life meaningful and worthwhile and are the core of everything I believe and do.

Many extraordinary things have happened in my life, but my accomplishments aren't extraordinary at all. I simply saw what was there for all to see—the everyday things of home—and I found ways to offer them to the world, first and foremost through my paintings. I've never been surprised that the world hungered for them.

If my story has a moral, it is that in the unending search for human happiness, life's genuine treasures aren't to be found in some far-off, exotic realm, but in all that is around us, right at home.

DATE DUE

| Brodart Co. | Cat. # 55 137 001 | Printed in USA |